HOKULE'A: *The Way to Tahiti*

HOKULE'A
The Way to Tahiti

BEN R. FINNEY

Illustrations by Richard Rhodes

Photographs by Francis Wandell and Ben R. Finney

DODD, MEAD & COMPANY

NEW YORK

Copyright © 1979 by Ben R. Finney

1 2 3 4 5 6 7 8 9 10

Library of Congress Cataloging in Publication Data
Finney, Ben R
   Hokule'a: the way to Tahiti.

   Includes index.
   1. Hokule'a (Canoe) 2. Voyages and travels—
1951–   3. Pacific Ocean. I. Title.
G477.F48   910'.45   79–9410
ISBN 0–396–07719–6

Designed by Sidney Feinberg

Copy 1.

This book is dedicated to all who helped
make the voyage of *Hokule‘a* possible.

Preface

The following pages recount a story that I have found most difficult to tell. It is at once a tale of a long and demanding experimental voyage, and of a troubled attempt at cultural revival that threatened to scuttle that voyage. In order to tell it fully I must therefore re-create certain painful incidents, and revive passionate words spoken in the heat of confrontation, which some might prefer were buried and forgotten.

Much of the trouble came from groups and individuals who, proclaiming that they were acting in the name of the Hawaiian people, challenged the plans for the voyage and attempted to turn the canoe *Hokule'a* to their own ends. While many Hawaiians have repudiated what was said and done, what happened on shore before we left, and on the high seas, must be told for the reader to understand the voyage and also to comprehend the social conditions of modern Hawaii from which those protests arose. However inappropriate to the task of sailing to Tahiti those protests were, from another perspective they were the cries of anguish of a people who in two centuries of foreign contact and domination have been transformed from an independent nation to a dependent minority. I have thus tried to document the protests as faithfully as I can, relying where possible on tape recordings, as well as on notes and recollections, to re-create the words as spoken and the circumstances in which they were uttered. Furthermore, I have tried to place what was said and done within the context of modern Hawaii to show how problems and tensions resulting from the subjugation of the Hawaiian people contributed to the trials which all of us, Hawaiians and non-Hawaiians alike, went through to sail *Hokuleʻa* over the legendary voyaging route linking Hawaii and Tahiti.

BEN R. FINNEY

Contents

PART THREE

PART I

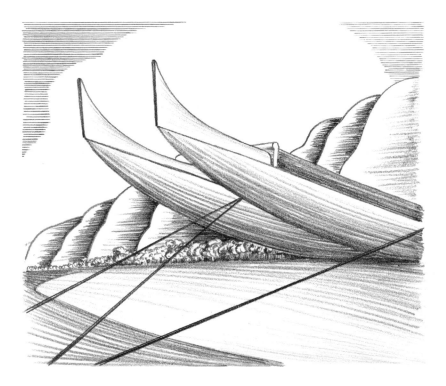

1
The Launching

"*E Hoʻomakaukau!*"

The first preparatory command: "Make ready!"

Those chosen to be the first to take the canoe out to sea tighten their grip on the curving sterns of the twin hulls. Those manning the hauling lines dig their feet into the sand and lean back, testing the weight of the massive double-canoe resting on the rise of the beach above them.

"*E alulike!*"

The master chanter shouts out the second and final preparatory command: "Pull together!"

Everyone—crew, haulers and spectators—waits tensely for the hauling chant to begin.

"Ki au au, ki au au
Huki au au, huki . . ."

There is no need to finish the chant, for the canoe literally flies down the beach and into the water, all 60 feet and 6 tons of her. The stunned crowd remains mute for a moment, then lets out a spontaneous cheer.

The crew, followed by the master and his attendants, mount the now floating canoe and take their places. Twenty-four paddles plunge into the water as one. As the canoe starts moving out to sea, the chant to the spirits who will hereafter look after the vessel begins.

Once well out from shore, the steersman gives the order to turn around and head back. As the white sand beach crowned by green-clad mountains swings into view, a basket woven from coconut leaves is thrown off the stern. It contains the bones of a black pig and of a special variety of fish and the remains of other chosen foods from a consecrated meal consumed by the crew during the launching ceremony. All aboard are warned not to look back before reaching shore lest the canoe be forever cursed.

As the canoe approaches the beach, a strange sound rolls ahead of it, a mixture of full Polynesian voices and what seems to be at first the beating of huge drums. The ritual leaders are chanting; the crew is punctuating each line by rapping their paddles sharply against the hollow hulls.

When the canoe touches the sand, the master chanter alone comes ashore. Turning, he asks of those still on board, *"Pehea ka waʻa, pono anei?"*

The ritual interrogation: "How is the canoe, is it right?"

" *'Ae, e maikaʻi loa ka waʻa Hokuleʻa!*" comes back the confident reply: "Yes, the canoe *Hokuleʻa* is indeed good!"

The canoe is now fully blessed and ready for service. The women can join their men, even climb aboard the previously taboo craft, and the dancing and feasting can begin.

Ben Finney, Herb Kane, and Kenneth Emory with master chanter Kaʻupena Wong at launching

This scene might well have taken place on some isolated Hawaiian shore many centuries ago. But the year was 1975, the site was a beach park a half-hour's drive along a crowded freeway from busy Honolulu, and the canoe was a modern reconstruction of an ancient voyaging craft. The following year, in 1976, we planned to sail her from Hawaii to Tahiti and back along a curved course that would take us over almost 6,000 nautical miles* of blue water, navigating without charts, compass or other instruments. Our object was to retrace the legendary voyages that once linked those far-flung islands and, in so doing, demonstrate to skeptics that the ancient Polynesians could have intentionally sailed across vast stretches of open ocean at a time when most

---

* Or, almost 6,900 statute miles, a distance greater than that between New York and Cairo. Distances quoted in this book are in nautical miles. One hundred nautical miles equals 115 statute miles.

other seafaring peoples were still hugging continental shores.

But the voyage was designed to be more than an experiment. It was the voyaging canoe—a deep-sea sailing craft made of two long, narrow hulls joined by crossbeams lashed in place with coconut fiber line—that enabled the ancient Polynesians to explore and settle their vast oceanic world. We hoped that our effort to reconstruct a voyaging canoe, and then sail it over a traditional route celebrated in chant and legend, would also serve the cause of Polynesian cultural revival—would make Hawaiians, and other Polynesians whose cultural identity has become blurred in modern times, know and better appreciate the great maritime achievements of their Stone Age ancestors. Hence the attention to cultural detail in the carefully researched and rehearsed re-creation of the long-extinct Hawaiian canoe launching ritual. Little did we know that, within the context of modern Hawaii, to join cultural revival with experimental voyaging was to create an explosive mixture, and that even so seemingly innocent an effort as trying to launch the canoe in a culturally appropriate way had tapped into a reservoir of jealousy and long-repressed resentments that would threaten to keep us from ever sailing to Tahiti.

Many of us worked together to plan the project, and then to build and to launch the canoe. Still more were to join in for the voyage itself. For each of us, this troubled combination of cultural revival and experimental voyaging would have its own significance, and its own starting point. For me, the tale begins with the study of ancient Polynesian migrations, and the modern controversies over how they were accomplished.

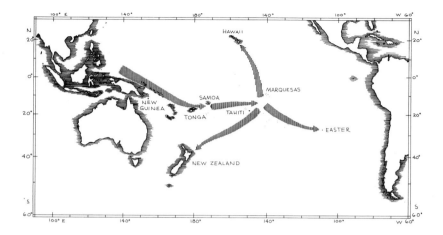

2
Polynesian Voyaging

Five thousand or more years ago, small groups of seafarers left the protected waters of the Indonesian archipelago off the southeast tip of Asia and pointed their canoes toward the ocean expanses to the east. In the many generations of wandering that followed, this migration swept across the Pacific almost to the shores of the Americas. Hardly an island was missed; colonies were implanted on practically every island that broke the surface of this greatest of oceans.

Among these seafarers one group stands out above all others: the Polynesians. They went the farthest; they discovered and settled more islands. Fragments of long-broken pots, chips of volcanic glass once used as cutting tools and the evidence of related languages mark their trail along the islands north of New Guinea and through those immediately east of this great island to the mid-Pacific archipelagoes of Tonga and Samoa. These fertile but previously uninhabited islands, which radiocarbon dating indicates were reached by 1100 B.C., provided a resting place for these wanderers. There in the centuries that followed they developed that distinctively Polynesian language and culture that their descendants were to spread over a vast ocean realm.

After a millennium-long pause in the mid-Pacific, the Polynesians resumed their voyaging, pointing their canoes once more to the east. Within a few centuries of the time of Christ they had crossed 2,000 miles of open ocean to settle in the Marquesas Islands of the eastern Pacific. But they did not rest there. They kept sailing, searching for new lands. Tahiti and the other relatively close islands were settled early. Well before this new millennium was over, Polynesian voyagers had reached the distant islands of Hawaii in the north, tiny Easter Island off the South American coast to the southeast, and the massive islands of New Zealand to the southwest.

These last three settlements form the points of the Polynesian triangle, a huge section of the world that, if projected onto the other side of the globe, would include most of Europe and Asia. Another thousand years later, when Europeans developed their own seafaring skills and ventured out into the Pacific, they were astonished to find as they "discovered" island after island within this oceanic expanse that already living on each one was a thriving community of the same tall and robust race. Upon recognizing the extent of this oceanic realm, European geographers named it Polynesia, using the Greek words meaning "many islands." Their inhabitants thus came to be known as Polynesians. Rendering this term as the "People of the Many Islands" captures some of the wonder felt by early European explorers when they realized that Stone Age voyagers sailing in slim canoes and navigating without instruments had preceded them into the Pacific and had settled virtually every volcanic island and coral atoll in a vast oceanic world.

Hawaii was the most remote of the Polynesian settlements, lying well north of the equator almost as far from other Polynesian centers as from the shores of Asia and North America. Yet these voyagers did reach there. When Captain James Cook chanced upon Hawaii in 1778, he found over a quarter million Polynesians living on the eight main islands of the group. Their ancestors had arrived around A.D. 500 say the archaeologists who have excavated

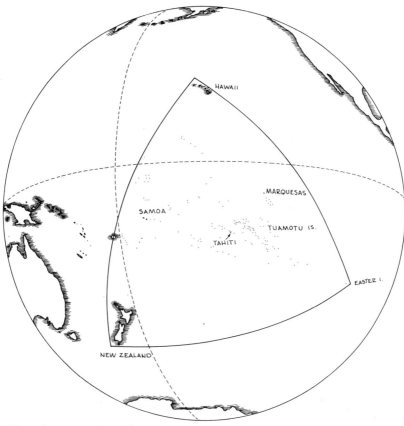

The Polynesian Triangle

the coastal settlements of the first Hawaiians. Fishhooks made from bone and shell, stone adze blades and other artifacts found in the lowest layers of these ancient settlements show that these early settlers came from Polynesian islands below the equator— the main candidates being the Marquesas, 1,800 miles to the southeast, and Tahiti, over 2,300 miles to the south-southeast.

Hawaiian traditions are hazy as to exactly which island or islands the first Hawaiians came from. However, a number of chants and legends tell of the later arrival of Tahitian seafarers and celebrate the exploits of a series of chiefs who sailed back and forth between the two centers in the 12th and 13th centuries, as dated by genealogies contained in the traditions. That is why we built our double-canoe *Hokule'a**—to retrace those legendary two-way voyages.

We also had a cause to pursue, as well as an adventure. Late 19th-century and early 20th-century compilers and interpreters of the Tahiti-Hawaii tales and other Polynesian migratory epics had gone too far in constructing romantic visions of great fleets of giant canoes manned by heroic navigators who "explored the Pacific as a European would a lake." By the 1950s their exaggerated notions of Polynesian voyaging capabilities were coming under heavy criticism. But, as so often happens in such controversies, the skeptics went too far. They dismissed the legends as fabrications; declared Polynesian canoes to be unseaworthy for long, planned voyages; and decreed that it was impossible to navigate more than a few hundred miles of open ocean without a compass, sextant and other navigational aids equally unknown to the ancient Polynesians. By sailing from Hawaii to Tahiti and back, and navigating the whole distance without instruments, we wanted to demonstrate how wrong those skeptics were.

Thor Heyerdahl of *Kon-Tiki* fame became the most widely known critic of Polynesian voyaging. After his 1947 raft trip from South America to the Tuamotu islands of Polynesia, he published *American Indians in the Pacific*, a massive book in which he argued that Polynesia was settled from the east not the west; that the first Polynesians arrived by raft from South America and by dugout canoe from North America. Basic to his theory was a logic that downgraded Polynesian canoes and seamanship. Primitive man, Heyerdahl reasoned, could sail only with the wind and current, never against them. The prevailing trade winds and equatorial currents of the Pacific flow from east to west—from

---

* Hoh-koo-lay-'ah. The inverted comma (') stands for the glottal stop, a consonant that occurs frequently before vowels in Hawaiian and other Polynesian languages. English speakers can naturally make the glottal stop: say the letters of radio station WEEI rapidly and you will find that you automatically stop the flow of air in your throat by momentarily closing your glottus before pronouncing each vowel, and thus really say W'E'E'I. A glottal stop occurs in *Hawai'i*, but following convention it is not shown in this and other geographical names, except where rendered phonetically, as for example: Hah-waee-'ee.

North and South America toward Asia, not vice versa. Thus Polynesian seafarers, whom he judged to be primitive, could never have sailed their canoes from west to east, from Indonesia to Polynesia. To Heyerdahl, the capacity to sail across the ocean against wind and current was a later, European development. The first settlers of Polynesia must therefore have come from the Americas, drifting before the current and the trade winds.

Within the scientific community hardly anyone believed Heyerdahl's theory. I found that out when, after finishing a tour of duty in the Navy, I began graduate studies in anthropology at the University of Hawaii. The language of the Polynesians, their artifacts (including the essential voyaging canoe) and other basic elements of Polynesian culture came from Southeast Asia, not the Americas.

Another new theory, one that held that Polynesia was settled by "accident," was gaining wide acceptance in academic circles. The author of this theory, a retired New Zealand civil servant named Andrew Sharp, proposed that the many islands of Polynesia had been colonized through a long series of accidents: primarily by a succession of canoe loads of islanders who were drifting helplessly after losing their way because of a storm or because of navigational error, and who by chance fetched up on uninhabited shores; plus a few canoe loads of exiles who, after being driven from their homeland by war or famine, let the winds and currents push them about in hopes that they would happen upon some new island. Sharp's theory was orthodox in that it stuck to the accepted view that settlement had proceeded from west to east, but its major appeal came from his skillful debunking of the exaggerated vision of an heroic age of Polynesian voyaging, and his dismissal of Polynesian canoes and navigation methods as inadequate for the task of planned voyages of exploration and colonization assigned to them by the romantic interpreters of Polynesian legend. To those scholars who had always found the idea of navigating without instruments over thousands of miles of open ocean in little canoes unbelievable, Sharp's accidental theory was most believable.

In large part the appeal of Sharp's theory reflected a basic fact: most scholars are landlubbers to whom the ocean, and especially the idea of sailing across it in anything less than the most modern craft navigated by the latest methods, is alien. They could not accept the possibility that Polynesians could have developed an ocean-voyaging technology independent from that which evolved in Europe (with borrowings from the Chinese and the Arabs). Nor could they grasp that the Polynesians might have had a uniquely ocean-oriented world view—that to Polynesians the world was an ocean, an ocean over which one sailed to reach islands that must, according to Polynesian logic, be there. The notion that Polynesians would deliberately sail out against wind and current to settle unknown and uncharted islands was absurd to them, for they failed to realize that voyaging experience accumulated over so many generations of movement from Southeast Asia, past New Guinea and through the other Melanesian Islands told the Polynesians that by continuing to sail to the east, to windward, they would find more new islands, uninhabited ones inviting settlement.

Sharp was as European-centered in his thinking as was Heyerdahl. Europeans could sail across the Pacific and navigate accurately from one island to another because of their superior technology. They had large and sturdy ships with deep keels and sophisticated sails; and they had the compass, sextant, chronometer and all the other instruments and aids that enabled them to calculate their exact position and chart an accurate course. The Polynesians had none of these. To Sharp, their canoes were fragile craft, made of bits of wood sewn and lashed together with sennit braided from coconut fiber instead of being securely fastened with metal nails and screws. Because the canoes had a low freeboard, they were in constant danger of swamping; because they lacked deep keels, centerboards or a modern sail rig, they could not sail to windward. Above all, Sharp maintained that without instruments Polynesian navigators could never have been able to fix their position at sea or steer an accurate course. Therefore planned voyaging over long distances was out of the question.

Sharp had to admit, of course, that long, one-way voyages had occurred. He claimed that once a drifting canoe had chanced on

Hawaii, Easter Island or any of the other far-flung islands of Polynesia, a return to the homeland was impossible. His mental rubicon was 300 miles; beyond that distance there could be no two-way voyaging. Once Hawaii had been settled, the people were totally cut off from the rest of Polynesia but for the chance arrival of other accidental migrants. Thus the legendary travels of Moʻikeha, Laʻa, Kila, Paʻao and all the other heroes of Hawaiian legend who sailed back and forth between Tahiti and Hawaii were to him figments of the imagination of Hawaiian storytellers.

All this seemed absurd to me and to some of my more ocean-oriented professors. How could anyone believe that Polynesia was settled by accident? It is over 7,000 miles from Indonesia to the far reaches of Polynesia. Canoes could not drift all that distance against the direction of the prevailing trade winds and currents. And the idea that once Polynesians sailed beyond 300 miles they were lost on the great ocean was incredible. Yet Sharp had many followers, and the debate between camps was a lively and at times bitter one that was to fill the pages of many a scholarly journal and book. The disagreement was not going anywhere, for the needed information on the sailing ability of Polynesian canoes and on the accuracy of the Polynesian navigation system just was not there. The early European explorers had failed to document exactly how well Polynesian canoes sailed or how accurate were the Polynesian navigators, and it was too late to get firsthand information. The voyaging canoes had long since disappeared from Polynesian waters. In their stead were trading schooners, freighters and passenger liners.

Why not reconstruct a voyaging canoe and sail it without instruments over the legendary voyaging route between Tahiti and Hawaii? That would break the stalemate. A successful voyage would demolish Sharp's claim that Polynesians could never have intentionally sailed back and forth between distant islands. That was the plan I hatched one afternoon after my classes at the University—while flying before the trades in a racing catamaran, a modern descendant of the ancient voyaging canoe.

However, as a young graduate student I did not have the means to launch such an ambitious undertaking. Besides, it was not advisable to go around talking about canoe trips to Tahiti if I wanted to obtain a Ph.D. and become a professional anthropologist. So the plan remained a secret dream while I continued my studies and worked on more standard anthropological problems—until 1965. By then I had earned a Ph.D. at Harvard,

Outrigger canoe and double-canoe

landed a job teaching at the University of California in Santa Barbara, and with my wife (who was also teaching anthropology there) had saved enough to start building a double-canoe.

We chose to build a double-canoe rather than an outrigger canoe. Both are solutions to the problem of making long, narrow canoe hulls stable enough to venture out to sea and to carry sail, one by joining two hulls with crossbeams, the other by rigging an outrigger float to a single hull. Although the ancestral Polynesians sailed both types, it was above all the greater stability and carrying capacity of the double-canoe that enabled them to move far out into the Pacific—to cross first hundreds and then thousands of miles of open ocean, carrying heavy loads of colonists, food and water, plus the domesticated plants and animals needed to implant successful colonies on the increasingly distant but resource-poor oceanic islands ahead.

It took nearly a year for a group of students and myself to build a double-canoe 40 feet in length and weighing nearly 1½ tons. Ideally, we would have reconstructed the type of voyaging canoe that sailed between Tahiti and Hawaii in the 12th century. But it would not have been easy to duplicate a craft that had not been seen for eight centuries. Instead, we built a replica of a known canoe type: an 18th-century Hawaiian interisland sailing canoe, a craft that could be duplicated in wood and fiberglass without tremendous difficulty by following drawings made by early explorers and using a mold taken off an old Hawaiian canoe hull. Our idea was to try out the canoe in a series of trials to obtain basic information on sailing performance, then to sail it, or a larger canoe built from the lessons learned, from Hawaii to Tahiti and return.

In Hawaii the canoe was christened *Nalehia* (Nah-lay-hee-ah), Hawaiian for "The Skilled Ones," after the graceful way her twin hulls glided over the swells. Earlier, in Santa Barbara, yachtsmen had not been so complimentary about those hulls. During construction one had declared flatly, "Her hulls are too shallow and rounded. She'll make too much leeway to sail to windward." He had a good point. Yachts have deep keels or centerboards that project down into the water to resist the sideways push of the wind and keep them moving to windward with a minimum of leeway. *Nalehia* had neither keel nor centerboards, only her shallow, rounded hulls. Yet these proved to offer enough resistance to leeway to enable the canoe to sail to windward.

We found that out the first time we hoisted sail off Santa Barbara, and then spent several months sailing in Hawaiian waters testing her windward ability. The trick was to keep the canoe moving fast and never to force her too close into the wind. In a 15-knot trade wind, that meant sailing at about 4½ knots, making good a course of around 75 degrees off the wind (calculated by measuring the heading to the true wind and adding the leeway angle). If we tried to point the canoe higher into the wind, she would start skidding sideways at an alarming rate and her forward speed would fall way off.

Although *Nalehia*'s windward performance was nothing to be

proud of in yachting circles, it was enough to show how wrong
Andrew Sharp and other critics had been about Polynesian
canoes. Even this modest windward ability would have enabled
the ancient Polynesians to have planned and carried out their
long voyages. A case in point involved the legendary route between Hawaii and Tahiti. Using what we had learned from sailing
Nalehia, together with figures for the direction and strength of
winds and currents prevailing over the route, I calculated that
canoe voyagers could have successfully sailed back and forth
between these centers.

The leg from Tahiti to Hawaii looked to be the easiest. Tahiti
lies almost 500 miles east—to windward—of a line drawn due
south from the middle of the Hawaiian archipelago. That means
a canoe could be sailed across the trades and accompanying
currents and, even after being set to the west, would fetch up
somewhere in the Hawaiian chain. The return to Tahiti was the
challenge. You would have to fight those same easterly winds and
currents to make up the 500 miles of easting in order to reach the
meridian of Tahiti. Yachtsmen with their more weatherly craft do
not relish butting into the wind and current to make it to Tahiti.
With a shallow-hulled canoe the voyage would be much harder—

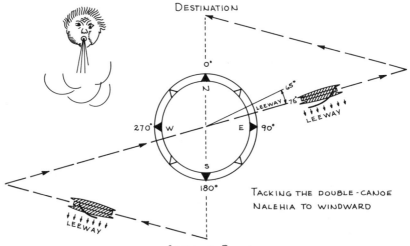

DESTINATION

STARTING POINT

TACKING THE DOUBLE-CANOE
NALEHIA TO WINDWARD

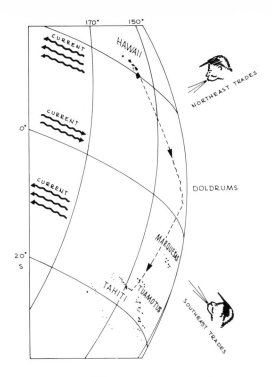

*Projected course
to Tahiti*

yet just possible, at least according to armchair calculations that I worked out for a birthday party.

Kenneth Emory, the archaeologist who had taught me Polynesian prehistory at the University of Hawaii, and who had spent a lifetime studying Tahitian and Hawaiian culture, was about to turn seventy. I was asked to contribute a chapter to a book on Polynesian culture that was to be published in his honor and presented to him on his birthday, and was only too happy to oblige by challenging Sharp's theory of accidental voyaging with an analysis of how ancient voyagers could have sailed their canoes between Tahiti and Hawaii.

My essay was more than an academic treatise. It was also a theory to be tested by actually trying to sail a canoe over the thousands of miles of blue water that lay between these islands.

3
Star of Joy

"Here comes the wind!" The full force of the trades hit the crab-claw–shaped sail. *Nalehia* shot through the narrow channel in the reef past the surf breaking on either side and out into the open sea. Three of us were now in the canoe experiment business. I was handling the sail. Herb Kane, a tall, heavyset Hawaiian, and slim, athletic Tommy Holmes were steering. They were all smiles; this was their first sail in a double-canoe.

"Porpoises! Porpoises ahead!"

We were sailing just offshore suburban Honolulu in waters where porpoises are seldom seen anymore. Herb Kane (Kah-nay, a Hawaiian word meaning "man"; also the name of an important god) was unusually excited by the sighting. Later he explained that his father had once told him, "If you see porpoises right after you launch a newly built canoe, they are messengers from the sea god Kanaloa signifying that he accepts the vessel into his domain."

Nalehia had just been relaunched. It was early 1974, almost eight years since she last sailed. While building the canoe I had injured my back. Three operations, a long period of recuperation and the problems of getting reestablished in Hawaii had kept me on dry land till now. Several months before the relaunching, Herb Kane, Tommy Holmes and I had formed the Polynesian Voyaging Society as a research corporation to fund the construction of a large canoe for the Tahiti voyage. *Nalehia* was to be our training vessel, and also a lure to attract funds. We intended to sail her around to show potential contributors that we were serious about our plans and that we already knew something about double-canoes.

I had returned to Honolulu three years earlier to take up a teaching post at the University of Hawaii, and to get back to the canoe project. The latter had not been easy. *Nalehia* had been left at an oceanarium near Honolulu with the agreement that they would use her as a display in their Hawaiian village in return for research support later. Unfortunately, by the time I had recovered from my third back operation and returned to Hawaii the oceanarium had fallen into financial difficulties. In addition to reneging on the promised support, the new management went so far as to demand storage charges for keeping *Nalehia* on public display! That, plus the time needed to develop courses and finish some more orthodox research in order to secure tenure, made me shelve the project for a while. After rescuing *Nalehia* from the oceanarium, I loaned her to a Hawaiian group interested in using the canoe to teach young Hawaiians about their marine heritage and settled down to more mundane tasks.

During this period I began to get many inquiries about Polynesian canoes and about sailing to Tahiti, especially from Hawaiians. There was much more interest in the project now than there had been when *Nalehia* was sailing in the mid-1960s. This growing interest was part of a new development. When I had been a student in Hawaii during the late 1950s, interest in Hawaiian culture was minimal. It was a thing of the past and better left that way seemed to be the common attitude on the part of Hawaiians, then a dispirited minority comprising less than one-fifth of Hawaii's multiracial population, dominated by Americans of Caucasian and Asian ancestry. By the time I returned to teach at the University in 1970 this attitude was fading. Young Hawaiians who had grown up speaking only English were trying to learn Hawaiian and were studying old forms of chanting, dancing and other practices of the ancient culture. I found this development exciting and tried to help through my teaching, and by working with other faculty to establish a Hawaiian studies program. It therefore was a natural step to think about organizing the canoe project so that it could be part of this nascent cultural revival. Earlier I had seen how *Nalehia* had a positive impact on those Hawaiians who sailed her, how it made them think a little more about who they were and how their ancestors had settled the islands. Now with this growing Hawaiian consciousness, it seemed time to take Hawaiian participation in the project a step further by getting Hawaiians fully involved in retracing their ancestral migrations. The project would then have a dual significance, both for scientific research and for cultural revival.

That is why I responded so readily to Herb Kane's appeal in early 1973. He and Tommy Holmes had been talking about building a large voyaging canoe and then sailing it to Tahiti and back with a crew made up largely of Hawaiians, Tahitians and other Polynesians. "Sounds good to me," I replied to Kane, and the three of us were soon deep into planning the venture.

Lean, deeply tanned Tommy Holmes was in his mid-twenties. In Hawaii both he and I were classed as *haole* (haow-lay),* a Hawaiian term applied to whites. But we were of different varieties. Tommy was a local *haole* born into a prominent Honolulu family. I was an immigrant "coast *haole*" from California. Yet we were alike in that we shared a common passion for the Polynesian water sports of surfing and paddling outrigger racing canoes.

---

* In this case the two vowels form a diphthong and are not separated by a glottal stop.

Herb Kane was a little older than I, in his mid-forties. He was Hawaiian, or more accurately part-Hawaiian; his mother was of Danish immigrant stock while his father was half-Chinese. Tall, heavyset, with a broad, handsome face, Kane nonetheless looked fairly Hawaiian. To be only one-quarter Hawaiian is not at all unusual in the Hawaiian community; over the past two centuries Hawaiians have freely intermarried. What made Kane an unusual Hawaiian was his background. Although born in Hawaii, he had been raised in his mother's home state of Wisconsin, had gone to art school in Chicago and then had engaged in a successful career as a commercial artist working with leading advertising agencies of that city. As a result Kane seemed more Midwestern than Hawaiian, closer in speech and manner to a Chicago businessman than, for example, to my Hawaiian friends who had sailed *Nalehia*.

Yet Kane had abandoned the Chicago advertising world and now wanted to get back to his Hawaiian roots. Building a voyaging canoe was part of that quest. During his last years in Chicago before returning to Hawaii in 1972, Kane had been dreaming about canoes all the time he was drawing the Jolly Green Giant and other advertising motifs. He was then working on a portfolio of detailed line drawings and vivid paintings of Polynesian canoes. For him, the step from drawing voyaging canoes to building and sailing one would be both the fulfillment of his dreams and an affirmation of his identity as a Hawaiian.

Although the three of us were of like mind about the experimental research and cultural revival objectives of the project, we initially disagreed on the size of the canoe to be built. Knowing how expensive and difficult it was to build a double-canoe, I proposed that we construct one no more than 45 feet long, or even consider fitting out *Nalehia* for extended voyaging. Kane and Tommy would have none of that. They wanted to build a massive double-canoe 60 feet in length. It was two against one; and anyway theirs was an exciting idea. So a 60-footer it was to be.

"A thousand dollars a foot." That was the bare-bones estimate boatbuilders gave us for building such a canoe. We planned to fabricate it out of plywood, following modern catamaran construction techniques. The old voyaging canoes were not simple dugouts. Although a single log might form the base of a hull, the rest of the hull would be built up with planks painstakingly shaped to fit exactly edge to edge and then sewn together with sennit. To try to revive that lost art in order to build a big voyaging canoe the likes of which had not been seen for hundreds of years would have been to invite disaster. So we had to pass up the opportunity to test the strength and durability of ancient materials and, as in the case of *Nalehia*, concentrate on re-creating the shape and weight of an ancient canoe in order to duplicate its sailing performance. Our goal was a performance-accurate replica, not a construction-accurate one.

But $60,000 was a lot of money!

There were no donors waiting to give us $60,000 or anywhere near it. Our solution: form a membership corporation and solicit funds from individuals, businesses and foundations. And so the Polynesian Voyaging Society was born. A corporation requires officers and a board of directors. Kane, both because he was Hawaiian and was experienced in business, seemed the natural choice to head the Voyaging Society. But he insisted I take the job; he became vice-president and Tommy became secretary of the corporation. For members of the board of directors we rounded up a few scientists, experienced sailors and as many Hawaiian community leaders as we could interest in helping us develop Hawaiian participation in the project.

Fund raising was not easy. However, we had a lot going for us: Kane's artistic and promotional skills; Tommy's family connections in Honolulu society and business circles; and a solid research base with *Nalehia*. In a hectic six months we raised enough cash to start construction—thanks to contributions from hundreds of newly recruited Voyaging Society members and other donors; a down payment on story rights from the National Geographic Society; a grant from the Hawaii Bicentennial Commission, which accepted our venture as an official U.S. Bicentennial project; a generous donation from Penelope Gerbode-Hopper of San Francisco; and a handsome advance from the publisher of this book.

How do you reconstruct the design of a voyaging canoe of

eight centuries ago when there are no ancient plans, no remains of sunken canoes, not even rock engravings to follow? Yachtsmen acquainted with Pacific canoes urged us to adopt features like the lateen sail and the deep-V hull for maximum windward efficiency. But that would have ruined the whole idea of testing the performance of the ancient type of Polynesian canoe, for these are features of recent outrigger canoe types of Micronesia (the group of islands north of New Guinea and well to the west of Polynesia), not of ancient Polynesian double-canoes. Instead we followed a conservative method of design reconstruction based on principles of geographical distribution. We studied the drawings of Polynesian canoe types from all the islands and archipelagoes, looking for design features occurring commonly throughout Polynesia and rejecting those appearing in just one island group or region. Localized features, we reasoned, would represent recent introductions or developments whereas widespread features would reflect the design of the original voyaging canoes.

This design strategy led us to choose hulls with a semi-V cross-section (wedge-shaped at the bottom with wide bulging sides) and sails shaped like an inverted triangle even though we knew that Micronesian deep-V hulls and lateen sails might give better performance. Yet we were confident that these Polynesian design features would serve us well. The inverted triangular sail would drive the canoe to windward; we knew that from the *Nalehia* trials with the Hawaiian crab-claw version of that sail type. And upon study it looked as if the semi-V hull shape might be ideal for a voyaging craft that had to carry heavy loads over long distances. The wedge-shaped bottom would help the canoe track to windward; the bulging cross-section would provide the needed carrying capacity.

Herb Kane took over the design job. First he created an artistic rendering of the canoe sailing over the blue ocean that really launched the project, providing a visual image people could grasp more readily than words. We used it on posters, T-shirts and other promotional materials to attract members and contributions. Then Kane drew a series of detailed drawings of the canoe. Rudy Choy, a pioneering catamaran designer and a member of

the Voyaging Society's board of directors, and his partners
precisely calculated and drew out the lines of the twin hulls.

Warren Seamens, one of Rudy's partners, then got us started
laying up the hulls, the most critical construction phase. Even
minor errors at that point would have led to crooked hulls and
poor sailing performance. The hulls were built something like the
way the wooden fuselage of a model airplane is made. Over a
skeleton made of plywood frames and long wood stringers, three

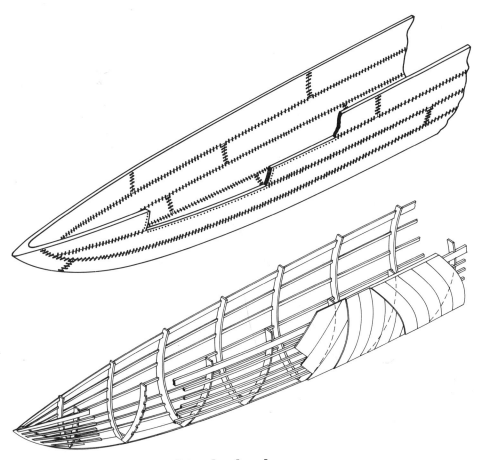

Canoe construction: traditional and modern

layers of narrow strips of very thin plywood were laminated, each layer applied diagonally in the opposite direction to the previous one in order to add strength. This time-consuming process gave us two extremely strong hulls which, once interior fixtures were added and a protective layer of fiberglass was applied, took on the weight of the hulls of a traditionally built craft.

Next came the equally labor-intensive and expensive tasks of fabricating the tall prowpieces and even taller sternpieces. Then long oak strips were laminated to make ten massive crossbeams (in olden days these would have been made from tree limbs or trunks grown or selected for just the right shape). Finally the decking, masts, booms, steering paddles and other components were fashioned.

Volunteers were of some help, but no one could afford to drop his job to work full time on the canoe. To keep the work on schedule, we had to employ several boatbuilders. Their wages, plus the high costs of materials (even though much was sold to us at discount prices), soon depleted our treasury and we had to intensify fund raising. The formula we hit upon was to "sell" the crossbeams and paddles, including the big steering paddles and the long steering sweeps. Purchasers of crossbeams had the right to name them; the paddles would actually go to the buyers once the canoe returned to Hawaii. This campaign quickly took off; soon we had enough to finish the canoe and also to finance the testing and training period to follow launching.

That was late in 1974; launching was scheduled for early 1975. The rest of that year was to be spent testing the canoe, learning how to sail it efficiently, and then selecting and training a crew. Departure for Tahiti was to be in early 1976 to help celebrate the Bicentennial year.

We were enjoying marvelous public goodwill and acceptance in Hawaii. We had hit upon a theme to which both Hawaiians and non-Hawaiian residents could respond. Maybe some people in Hawaii thought we were crazy and would never make the voyage. If so, they kept quiet about it. Not so critics from overseas. Followers of the accidental voyaging theory of Andrew

Sharp, who died just after we began the project, were predictably outraged.* In addition, a number of experienced sailors around the world expressed their pessimism about our chances of actually sailing to Tahiti and back. One was a fellow experimental voyager, Vital Alsar, a Spanish adventurer who had twice sailed a *Kon-Tiki*–type balsa raft from South America to Australia. He came to Honolulu, inspected our partially completed canoe and pronounced that we had only one chance in forty of completing the round trip.

Yet the three of us had every confidence of success. The name we finally chose for the canoe reflected that feeling. *Hokuleʻa* is the Hawaiian word for Arcturus, the bright star that passes directly overhead Hawaii. Fragmentary Hawaiian traditions indicate that returning navigators used *Hokuleʻa* as a homing beacon for Hawaii. *Hoku* (Hoh-koo) means star, *leʻa* (lay-ʻah) means joy; hence *Hokuleʻa* is the "Star of Joy," a fitting name for a navigation star pointing the way homeward and, we thought, a perfect name for our canoe.

---

* Following publication in 1967 of my essay on the feasibility of long-range voyaging between Hawaii and Tahiti, Andrew Sharp denounced my work in an article published in an anthropology journal, and followed that with a letter warning me that my professional career was "in grave jeopardy if you go on sticking to your views of Polynesian migration and experimental voyaging."

4
Spaceship of the Ancestors

After the launching in March 1975, the job of testing *Hokule'a* began. The launching site on the north shore of Oahu Island across the mountains from Honolulu was an ideal base: a beach park facing the northeast trade winds. From there we could beat out to sea, spend the day tacking back and forth in the open ocean, then sail back with the trades to a safe anchorage within the reef.

Those first sea trials were exhilarating. It was a joy to discover how seakindly the canoe was: smooth and stable even when sailing against wind and wave.

No sailor looks forward to sailing to windward against steep seas. I first had a taste of that kind of sailing in 1953 crewing back to California after a summer's surfing at Waikiki, aboard a yacht that was anything but seakindly. She was a broad-beamed ketch

called the *Marmaduke*: we rechristened her "Mamaduck" from
the way she waddled about when close-hauled against the northeast trades and bucking into the head seas built up by those
steady winds. Under the exact same conditions, pushing out
against the trades from our base on the north shore of Oahu,
Hokule'a sailed serenely over the steep swells with only a gentle
loping motion. It was the combination of the fine lines of the two
narrow hulls and their semirounded cross-section that gave the
canoe her smooth riding qualities. *Hokule'a* was a tribute to her
designers and builders, but more so to the ancient canoe masters.
It was they who over the centuries had developed the hull form
that Herb Kane and Rudy Choy had striven to copy.

Although elated by the canoe's seakindliness, some things
about sailing *Hokule'a* did not make us so happy. The hulls took
on a lot of water and had to be bailed frequently. Steering was
anything but easy; we left a trail of splintered steering paddles
broken while trying to force the canoe to go where we wanted.
The long, curving booms lashed to the afteredge of the sails kept
cracking because they were too flimsy. And the sails themselves
were a problem. Instead of tall, narrow ones like *Nalehia*'s, Herb
Kane had come up with a much stubbier design. His broad, baggy
sails were fine for running before the wind, but they did not take
the good airfoil shape needed to drive the canoe efficiently to
windward.

During those first weeks of sea trials we worked to remedy
these and other defects. Canvas covers modeled on the woven
mat covers used on the old Hawaiian canoes were fitted over the
open sections of the hulls to keep out the spray and boarding
seas, and sturdier paddles and booms were made. However,
instead of staying put to revamp the inefficient sail rig, or to
develop a good system for bailing out the water that still seeped
into the hulls past the covers and through the lashing holes, or to
take care of other design and construction problems, we got
involved in a flamboyant cruise around the Hawaiian chain.

In contrast to other experimental voyaging projects, we had
planned to spend a good year testing and refining the canoe and
training the crew before setting sail. Had we followed precedent,
we would have loaded up *Hokule'a* right after the launching and

immediately sailed for Tahiti. That strategy had worked magnificently for Heyerdahl; the long drift from South America to Polynesia was *Kon-Tiki's* maiden voyage. But Heyerdahl's venture, like most other experimental voyages, was a one-way trip in which the main challenge was to stay afloat sailing and drifting before the wind and current until land was reached. Ahead of us was a tough two-way voyage with one leg to windward; we could not count on following winds and seas or on buoyant balsa wood logs to forgive any shortcomings in craft or seamanship. And, as part of the attempt to navigate Polynesian style, we had to know *Hokule'a* well enough to be able to plot accurately her speed and course without resort to instruments. That is why we had allowed for a good year of sea trials and training before the voyage, and why we had planned on recruiting an experienced captain, preferably an old catamaran hand, to command the canoe.

Both these ideas came to be modified as the project developed. No expert catamaran sailor stepped forth. It would be almost a year and a half between the launching and the projected return from Tahiti; who had the time and dedication for such a long haul? Besides, Herb Kane became interested in assuming the captaincy, at least during the training period. Although Kane's experience was mostly limited to sailing catamarans on Lake Michigan, as chief designer of the canoe he was confident that he knew more about *Hokule'a* than anyone else.

During those first weeks of sailing Kane proved to be an inspired leader, although it was not long before his enthusiasm developed into a messianic vision. *Hokule'a's* sacred mission, Kane began to preach, was to uplift the Hawaiian people, to be *the* catalyst for the Hawaiian renaissance. A culture is nothing without its artifacts, he reasoned. The restoration of the voyaging canoe, once the central artifact of Polynesian culture, would reawaken in young Hawaiians an ethnic pride worn down by the Americanization of Hawaii and all the developments that have transformed Hawaiians into an underprivileged group.* Follow-

---

* A survey recently conducted by a Hawaiian organization indicates that Hawaiians have the lowest life expectancy of all ethnic groups in Hawaii; that their median family income is almost $2,000 below the State average; and that they find their way into prisons and other correctional facilities at twice the State rate.

ing the logic of ethnic movements underway on the American mainland, his idea was that this reawakened pride would lead Hawaiians to adapt better to modern life.

To develop *Hokule‘a*'s mission, it was necessary, Kane urged, that we sail the canoe around all the Hawaiian islands now, before the voyage to Tahiti. The vital task of testing *Hokule‘a*

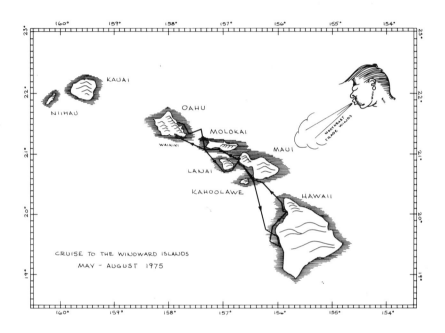

and getting her ready for the voyage would not be forgotten, he promised. The cruise would realistically test the canoe under a variety of conditions, including the wild winds and high waves that surge through the channels separating one island from another. In addition, an interisland cruise would give us a chance to recruit some good crewmen from the outer islands. So, all too hastily, two months after launching, *Hokule‘a* sailed for Maui (Mow-ee), the first island on the tour.

I awoke with a start. The incessant swishing, gurgling rush of water past the hulls was now muted; the canoe was no longer hurrying through the sea. Anxiously I squirmed out of my sleeping bag and through the low opening of the hut onto the deck between the two hulls. The sea was calm, with only a hint of a cool breeze. We were in the lee of a high island, barely moving through the wind shadow cast by the steep peaks now beginning to stand out in the dawn sky. It all seemed so familiar, as if I had sailed into this place many times before. Yes, of course; it was just like approaching Tahiti aboard a copra schooner coming in from the outer islands of French Polynesia. The cool dawn air, the quiet seas and the looming mountains looked and felt the same.

But I was not back in Tahitian waters. The island was Maui, not Tahiti. We had just made the crossing from Oahu.

"*Aloha!*"

No answer. The only person on the beach was a startled tourist who, once the bows touched the sand, asked who we were and where we came from. We were hours ahead of schedule; our Maui friends were still asleep, or planning our welcome over breakfast.

What a welcome it was, even if late. A hovering helicopter loosed a cascade of plumeria blossoms over the beach and the canoe moored just offshore. Then came formal Hawaiian prayers and a kava circle modeled, curiously, on protocol borrowed from the Samoan Islands of western Polynesia. As we sat cross-legged on the beach forming a large circle, each of our names was called in turn and we were served a coconut cup full of a ritual Polynesian beverage. After that came a feast, and an afternoon divided between catching up on sleep, dipping in the surf and just lazing around listening to Hawaiian music played by our Maui hosts.

I had to fly back to Honolulu that evening to return to my classes at the University, although I did get back to Maui on the following weekends to take part in some of the day sails Kane organized for the Maui people. It was on one of these excursions that Kane abruptly announced, "Ben, there's no room for you on the Hawaii crossing. We want to give as many Maui boys as possible a chance to sail *Hokule'a* over."

I should not have been so surprised. Kane's control over the canoe had been growing over the last two months, and Tommy followed his lead as a loyal lieutenant. They had been assuring me that they could handle the canoe, implying that I should be content to mind Voyaging Society business back in Honolulu. Still, I had been looking forward to the sail across the rough channel to Hawaii Island, the biggest and anciently most important island of the group; it was a shock to be so boldly maneuvered off the crew.

Instead of objecting, I rationalized to myself, "Hawaii is Kane's home island, and this cruise is his baby. It's become a very Hawaiian thing, so let him carry it through." Before we left Oahu, Kane had gathered the crew together and solemnly told them that the tour around the islands would be *more* important than the voyage to Tahiti, for it would take the canoe to the Hawaiian people. In a magazine article he had written how *Hokuleʻa* would speak to young Hawaiians, telling them, "I am the spaceship of your ancestors," the kind of craft that carried them across the Pacific, an achievement Kane pridefully likened to today's feat of sending men to the moon. Better, I thought, to back off and let him get this pilgrimage worked out of his system. When the canoe got back to Oahu, maybe we could return to the task of preparing for the Tahiti trip.

Two months later, when the canoe finally did return, it was clear that we were not going to have an easy time getting the project back on track. Reversing priorities, putting *Hokuleʻa*'s cultural mission ahead of the long experimental voyage, had unwittingly opened the Hawaiian equivalent of Pandora's box. We had sailed into the uncharted waters of an awakening Hawaiian consciousness and were being buffeted by strange winds and currents.

Launch a magnificent double-canoe amidst much publicity and fanfare proclaiming it to be a faithful reconstruction of an ancient voyaging canoe; campaign it around the islands advertising it to Hawaiians as their ancestral spaceship; then encourage them to step aboard and make of it whatever they wish. That became our self-made recipe for trouble.

First *kahunas* started giving us trouble. A *kahuna* (kah-hoo-nah) is a Hawaiian "priest," an indigenous religious practitioner who claims spiritual powers handed down from the ancient days before the coming of Christianity. *Kahunas* are a divided lot, each jealous of his own particular specialty, be it healing, blessing buildings, or—although few would openly admit it—practicing sorcery. Our launching ceremony had been an affront to every *kahuna* who felt that he should have been the one chosen to lead the ritual.

Had one of these men been a genuine canoe *kahuna* we would have gladly engaged him, not only for the ritual but for the building of the canoe as well, for a canoe *kahuna* of old was more than a ritual expert. He was a master craftsman who directed the whole operation of canoe building, from the selection and shaping of the timbers to the ritual launching. For the launching of *Hokule'a* we had engaged a master chanter, a Hawaiian scholar who because of the way he applied spiritual devotion and technical expertise to his chanting would have been considered a *kahuna* in the old days. But a number of those who now proclaim themselves to be *kahunas* rejected him and our carefully researched and conducted ceremony. To them, the canoe was "dirty," ritually impure, and would never make it to Tahiti.

We had tapped into the darker side of Hawaiian character, the obverse of *aloha*, the warm friendliness and compassion for which Hawaiians are justly famed. Soon many Hawaiians, not just our *kahuna* critics, were "making maggots," to use the literal translation of the Hawaiian verb that means figuratively to foretell misfortune. I cannot remember how many people went out of their way to tell me how, on the night after the launching, a fireball came swooping down from the mountains, and then out over the lagoon to hover above the anchored canoe. The fireball was an evil spirit, they said, a sign that something terrible would happen. That was typical. Other signs that reportedly appeared around the canoe were also interpreted as harbingers of disaster— never good fortune.

It was not long before a number of Hawaiians working on the project began to complain about strange illnesses that they believed to be spiritually caused. Some even dropped out of the project because, they said, it was "too dangerous." Others, notably several of the regular crewmen, took to wearing armbands, anklets and headbands made from the shiny green leaves of the ti plant (*Cordyline*), a ritually important plant reputed to have protective powers. The effect was striking, particularly when they were aboard a similarly decorated *Hokuleʻa*. One day when I flew out to visit the canoe at an outer island anchorage, I found her festooned with ti leaves, looking more like a floating Christmas tree than a voyaging canoe. *Hokuleʻa's mana* (mah-nah), that spiritual force essential to all Polynesian enterprises, must be protected, I was told.

Some of our crew members had fallen prey to those *kahunas* who wished to exert their will upon the project. One held a series of meetings with crew members and other Hawaiians involved in the project at which he fingered the cracked booms, broken paddles and other things that had gone wrong with the canoe as signs of deep spiritual problems. These problems, he ominously warned the suggestible crewmen, would have to be corrected— or else *Hokuleʻa* would sink and drown them. The *kahuna* even seized upon a newspaper story about how a shark had bitten off the end of a steering paddle to proclaim that the shark spirit was showing his wrath. He had no idea that the story had been made up by a crewman for the benefit of a credulous reporter.

At first I ignored all this talk, hoping it would pass. But it did not, forcing me to have second thoughts. The fears were real, and disruptive. We had blundered deep into an aspect of Hawaiian culture that had survived the coming of Christianity and all the other changes wrought over the last two centuries. Accounts of ancient Hawaii are filled with references to evil spirits, to sorcerers and to victims being "prayed to death." Early chroniclers had been surprised that the strong Hawaiians, so active on land and sea, could be so susceptible to malevolent threats and fears of the unknown.

One man deeply affected was Kimo Hugho, a handsome young part-Hawaiian fireman whom Herb Kane had personally selected to be crew chief on the interisland cruise and the nucleus for the Hawaiian crew members on the Tahiti voyage. Kimo (Kee-mo,

Hawaiian for Jim) was strong and athletic; he lifted weights, paddled racing canoes, surfed and had been a member of the Honolulu fire department's elite rescue unit. Yet the optimistic and self-confident image he had projected during those first exhilarating sails right after launching faded as the interisland cruise progressed. Kimo still cut a striking figure; the ti-leaf headbands and other charms he wore made him look all the more dramatic. But new lines on his face betrayed his worries. He feared the possibility of accidents at sea. He himself seemed accident prone; once he had been bloodied and knocked cold by the flailing handle of a steering paddle torn from his grip by a passing wave. And he had begun asking cautiously about the possibility of inscribing prayers within the canoe hulls and of taking other measures for spiritual protection.

It might have been possible to have extricated the project from the spiritualistic depths into which it was sliding had the situation not been complicated by a vigorous *"Hokuleʻa* for Hawaiians only" movement.

The growing feeling that only Hawaiians should sail aboard *Hokuleʻa* was probably inevitable, although all the propaganda about the canoe being the ancestral spaceship hastened and intensified its appearance. It must have been confusing for a Hawaiian from one of the outer islands to behold what he thought was a Hawaiian canoe, only to discover that *haoles* as well as Hawaiians ran the project and that a multiracial crew would sail to Tahiti. I saw that confusion on Hawaiian faces when, at outer island anchorages, I stepped aboard the canoe and was introduced as the president and cofounder of the Voyaging Society. But I did not then personally experience the kind of vocal opposition to my presence on the canoe that had greeted Tommy Holmes and a few other *haoles* when they sailed aboard *Hokuleʻa* from Maui back to Molokai, the last island on the cruise itinerary before returning to Oahu.

Molokai (Moh-loh-ka-ʻi) is the most economically depressed of the islands; the recent closing of the pineapple plantations that had been the island's main source of employment had led to unemployment rates of 30 to 40 percent. There were a lot of angry

Kimo and Buffalo

young Hawaiians around, some of whom were just then starting a militant movement for the return of alienated Hawaiian lands. When *Hokule'a* pulled into the harbor on Molokai, the movement's leaders were waiting. They were incensed when they spied Tommy and two *haole* benefactors from Maui amongst the Hawaiian crew. "What are those *haoles* doing on the canoe? Isn't *Hokule'a* a Hawaiian canoe?" they asked pointedly.

The project was now in real trouble, and I was in a quandary. Being the *haole* president of an increasingly Hawaiian movement was making me feel as out of place as I would be if heading the University's ethnic studies department or its women's studies program. Worse, it impaired my ability to act. To suggest that it was a mistake to go around trumpeting *Hokule'a* and her cultural mission before we completed the voyage to Tahiti and back was to be unpatriotic, to be un-Hawaiian. And what could be done when prominent Hawaiian members of the Voyaging Society's governing board called for more, not less, spiritual emphasis, and declared that they had "the greatest respect" for the *kahuna* who had been particularly vicious in his criticism of the canoe and those of us who were organizing the project?

A Hawaiian president might have been in a better position to get the project back on track; at least he would not have had to bear the stigma of being an "uptight *haole*." Yet Herb Kane had insisted that I take the job precisely because he believed that a *haole* president would be better able to withstand pressures from within the fractionated Hawaiian community than a Hawaiian president. I doubt, however, if he foresaw the difficulties we would encounter.

I did think long and hard about stepping down and assuming a purely advisory role. I might have done so had those advocating "*Hokule'a* for Hawaiians" been sailors, and had they been interested in the goals of the project. But those making trouble were not experienced seamen by any stretch of the imagination. They were a collection of *kahunas* and would-be spiritualists, Hawaiian rights activists and just plain opportunists who wanted to use the canoe to glorify themselves or their particular cause.

Because he was commanding the canoe, Herb Kane bore the brunt of public criticism about a *haole* presence on *Hokule'a* and about the canoe's scientific mission. At this time no attacks were openly directed at me. However, a number of Hawaiian acquaintances did go out of their way to advise me that the word was out that I should not sail to Tahiti on *Hokule'a*. They said that they had not been delegated to warn me; they had just heard talk that it would be unwise for me to attempt the voyage.

How naïve it had been to think that scientific research and cultural revival could be easily combined in today's Hawaii. Angry young Hawaiians feel that things *haole* must be rejected; *haoles* and *haole* culture are their oppressors. Their ethnic sensitivity, so unlike the apparent resignation with which their fathers and grandfathers had accepted the loss of Hawaiian sovereignty, their lands and much of the old culture, is beginning to mirror that of the blacks, Chicanos, Indians and other American minority groups. How could they accept the fact that the canoe project— something they defined as Hawaiian—had a research base?

Scientific research is part of that *haole* world and must be rejected, especially if it aims to tell them more about their own past. Their way to find out about that past is to ask the elders, not look in books, dig in the ground or perform experiments.

5
Hanalei Bay

Although several of us wanted to end the interisland cruise once the canoe returned to Oahu and get on with needed modifications, Herb Kane insisted that we sail on to Kauai (Kow-ah-'eeh) and back to complete the circuit of the islands. The channel between Oahu and Kauai, 65 miles, is the widest between any of the populated islands of the Hawaiian chain, and it can be rough. It defeated Kamehameha (Kah-may-ha-may-ha), the warrior chief from Hawaii Island who early in the European era conquered all the islands along the chain as far west as Oahu and then set out for Kauai. A storm struck his warrior-laden canoes in midchannel. Many were lost, the rest fled back to Oahu. But we were to be lucky, on the way over at least.

The weather was perfect: a clear, warm night with gentle trades, rolling swells and current all flowing in the right direction, boosting us westward toward Kauai. We left the western coast of

Oahu at dusk, using a compass to set a course toward the north shore of Kauai. As the sunset faded into blackness, we tried covering the compass and steering by stars low in the horizon that bore in the direction of Kauai. Soon, however, the loom of the Kauai lighthouse became the inescapable guide to the islands ahead.

Although the wind was light we made a good 6 to 7 knots on a broad reach, with the wind coming over the stern quarter of the starboard hull. The canoe gave only the gentlest hint of a roll in the following seas. I have never enjoyed a smoother ride in the normally rough Hawaiian channel waters.

New to the canoe was a three-man film team hired by the National Geographic Society to make a film of our project for a series to be shown on nationwide public television. Our tie with the National Geographic Society had come early in the project. Largely because Herb Kane had illustrated an article on Polynesian canoes for their magazine, he had been able to obtain welcome funds from the Society in exchange for story rights. Just recently he had concluded an agreement with them to make a documentary film of the project. Although some aid to help pay for an escort vessel was involved in the contract, we received no payment for the film rights. We preferred it that way so that they would not try to tell us what to do. By not accepting pay, we reasoned, we would be free from possible interference by film makers trying to direct the project for the benefit of their dramatic interests.

That was another bit of naïveté. I should have foreseen what was to be in store for us by the way our reception was staged that morning at Hanalei Bay. The wide semicircle of blue water, the coral sand beaches and the backdrop of abrupt green mountains makes Hanalei (Hah-na-lay) a cinematographer's delight. *South Pacific* and a number of other South Seas epics had been filmed there. Now Hanalei was hosting a new crop of cameramen and sound men headed by a film producer who, we were later to learn, was more suited to directing one of those fantasies than documenting our venture.

The passage across the channel was faster than expected. As

the mountains along the north shore of Kauai took form in the dawn light, the tall, pale film producer anxiously asked, "Will the Hanalei people know we're going to get there ahead of schedule?"

His anxiety was relieved when, as we neared the headland protecting Hanalei Bay, several outrigger racing canoes were paddled out to greet us and escort the canoe into the bay. Then the conch shells sounded, trumpeting our entrance as we rounded the reef. Cameras, on the canoe and on shore, were grinding away now, shifting between us, the outrigger canoes and the scenic surroundings. Once well inside the bay we lost the wind and had to start paddling in order to reach the anchorage. Our reward, when the anchor was set, awaited us in small canoes and boats that had pulled up alongside. To the delight of the film team, troupes of laughing girls—some local Hawaiians, others *haoles*, hippies recruited from nearby communes by their look—clambered aboard, garlanded us with fragrant flower leis and embraced us Polynesian style.

It was not long after going ashore that a load of beer arrived. Guitars were then produced, and our crewmen and their newly found hippie friends were soon enjoying a midmorning party. A number of the crew were talented musicians, and all could sing Hawaiian songs well. The film producer was all over the place, directing his cameramen to take this or that shot, and making sure the sound man was properly placed to capture the music. Our welcome was indeed warm. Inescapably, however, it was also a media event, the first of many to come.

"Have they been taking any long sails north to test windward ability?" I asked Tommy Holmes over the telephone after the canoe had been on Kauai a few weeks. "No, they're just going out on short day sails," was his disgusted reply.

The canoe was to be on Kauai all of September. Departure for Tahiti was set for April 1, just seven months ahead. We could not afford to waste a precious month. There was still much to be done in the way of testing, making changes in the sail rig and other features, and completing additional preparations for the voyage.

The only virtue of having the canoe at Kauai was that Hanalei Bay, like our launching site, faced into the trades and was therefore an ideal site for taking long slants against the wind. To see exactly how much easting the canoe could make, all we had to do was to sail out on a starboard tack, holding her as close to north as possible for twelve hours or so; then go over to the port tack, head southeast till she fetched up on the Kauai coast, or in the channel somewhere between Kauai and Oahu. The miles made directly eastward would then give us a good indication of how well the canoe would make easting on the actual voyage. We even had an offer from an experienced yachtsman anchored at Hanalei to pace us with his yacht. He had sailed his boat to Tahiti and back several times, so we could compare *Hokule'a's* performance with his to get a realistic measure of our chances of making enough easting to reach Tahiti.

But those opportunities were lost. Tommy Holmes and others reported that *Hokule'a* would occasionally go out at midday, sail around for a few hours, then be back in the bay before dark. Except for Kane, Kimo Hugho (who had left his job as a fireman to stay on the canoe) and sometimes one or two others from Oahu, the crew would be made up of Kauai youths who knew little or nothing about sailing, and who certainly did not want to go out for a hard twenty-four hours of sailing dead against the trades.

The third weekend the canoe was on Kauai I flew over to see what was happening. The atmosphere was bad. The Kauai people were not interested in going sailing, and some of the Oahu crewmen who also had flown over were already drunk at midmorning. There would be no sailing that weekend, so I flew right back to Honolulu.

By now the estrangement between Herb Kane and myself had grown to the point that he seldom even bothered to call me to consult about the canoe; I had to seek him out to find what was happening. He was now treating the canoe almost as if it were totally his. Many others also felt shunted aside. Even Tommy Holmes, who had been working so closely with Kane, and Kimo

Hugho, Kane's personal choice as crew chief, had become estranged.

Tommy sought me out a week before the canoe was scheduled to return from Kauai. Usually Tommy takes an ultracasual approach to everything, passing over problems with a smile and a laugh. But now he was deadly earnest.

"Look," he began excitedly, "we're having trouble, we're having trouble with Herb Kane. We can't take it anymore!"

When Tommy calmed down I got him to talk about specifics. He roundly criticized Kane for lack of sailing experience and seamanship skills, for a domineering personality and for the way Kane put showing off the canoe before any real testing and training.

"Is this just your feelings, or do others feel this way too?"

"Kimo Hugho is behind me, and so are lots of others. We all feel this way. There's no way we can go on."

Kimo and another man who had regularly been sailing on the canoe also came to me at this time. They were all against Kane continuing to captain the canoe, and they all cited the same incident in his command to buttress their case. It took place on Oahu one Saturday morning a month earlier when the canoe was anchored in a little cove at the foot of Diamond Head. I was there that day. A big surf had come up overnight. Sets of powerful waves were pounding the reef and sweeping diagonally across the narrow channel leading into the cove. To everyone's consternation, Kane was trying to organize a day sail that morning.

The canoe could have made it out the pass, for the wind was blowing directly from the shore out to sea. The trick would have been to wait just inside the pass for a lull between sets, then unfurl the sails and boom through the pass before the next set of waves came. Coming back in was the problem: the canoe would have to beat back directly against the trades. Even if there were time, we could not tack the canoe in because the pass was too narrow to allow *Hokule'a* to swing from one tack to another. Nor could we safely depend on our outboard motor—it had a nasty habit of sputtering to a stop at crucial moments.

As Kane stalked up and down the beach trying to drum up support to go sailing that morning, an awful vision of us trying to get back through to the pass flashed in my mind. The sails are furled, the high-revving outboard motor is pushing us toward the pass. Just at the entrance the motor quits. As we attempt to restart it, the swells start to hump up on the horizon. Soon a powerful set of curling waves is upon us, washing the canoe broadside onto the reef where, like a catamaran that ran aground there a year earlier, she is ground into kindling on the sharp coral heads.

"No, I want to go. We can go. The canoe can take it. She's been in surf like this before," was Kane's angry reply to those who counseled against going out. Kane was affronted by the idea that *Hokule'a* could not handle the surf and would not survive an encounter with the reef. He reacted as if he had been told that he himself was inadequate.

A long-time acquaintance of Kane had earlier warned, "Herb will never survive the canoe. It will become too much for him. The canoe will become part of himself, bigger than life, and he will become bigger than life." Kane's identification with the canoe had been growing as the interisland tour progressed. He had lately begun accepting full credit for starting the project and designing the canoe; he did not bother to correct commentators at public gatherings, or reporters, who referred to *Hokule'a* as "Herb Kane's canoe." Now he was being told that "his canoe" could not make it safely through the surf-filled pass, and he was incensed.

Reason finally prevailed. The canoe remained safely at anchor, and we started on some routine maintenance tasks.

Within a few hours the beach was jammed with spectators to see the finish of a canoe race. Outrigger racing canoes starting from the other side of the island were due to come through the pass to a finish line in the cove opposite our anchorage. Modern Hawaiians may not be sailors but they are great surfers, and the waves sweeping across the pass excited them. Many a canoe race has been won at the last minute when a lagging canoe caught a wave and passed the leaders to be first across the line. That prospect was on everyone's mind, as was the danger of surfing through the pass. A false move or a misjudged wave could send a canoe crashing onto the reef.

One by one the long, narrow racing canoes started coming in. Most made it through the pass between sets; a few successfully caught medium-size waves and surfed in. Then, just as a big set was building up on the horizon, two canoes showed up off the pass. They were side by side; neither had a clear lead. Without hesitation both teams kept paddling as the waves began to hump up. Their parallel courses put them right before the first big wave of the set, in perfect position for a long surf slide to the finish line. The growing wave picked up the canoes and started sliding them forward at an accelerating pace. But the wave was too big. As it peaked it passed under the stern of the canoe lagging slightly behind the other, leaving the steersman helpless, his paddle stranded in midair. The canoe spun out of control, skewing to the right and ramming the other. Both capsized and were quickly pushed onto the reef. Miraculously the erring canoe washed over the reef without serious damage; the other was smashed to bits. As we silently watched the crying crew swim what pieces of their shattered canoe they could find across the finish line, we could not help but think that might have been *Hokule'a*'s fate had we gone sailing.

The question of the management of *Hokule'a*, and especially the issue of who should command her for the Tahiti trip, had to be faced. I set up a meeting for the following week.

First the canoe had to be sailed back to Oahu. Departure was set for that Friday night. Kane was optimistic; he felt they would reach Oahu sometime during the weekend. I did not share his optimism. *Hokule'a* had not yet been tested on a long windward passage, and the problems with the hulls taking on water and the inefficient sails remained uncorrected. This crossing would be her severest trial, for the canoe would have to be tacked against the wind, swells and current to reach Oahu. Still, I thought she could make it—after three or four days of hard sailing. Hanalei is 95 miles from Oahu, but the long, shallow tacks that the canoe would be forced to take would add up to a sailing distance of several hundred miles. Maybe late Monday or sometime Tuesday they might show up.

Sunday morning, thirty-six hours after departure, I was working in the office I had built below my house, which sits high on a ridge overlooking the ocean. The sea below was flecked with whitecaps, and fresh winds were buffeting the house. That was fairly normal trade wind weather, nothing to be concerned about. Yet I had already received several anxious telephone calls from relatives of crewmen. There had not been a single radio transmission from the canoe, and she had not been spotted. Probably she is tacking way up north, I thought, out of sight of land. And that damned radio must be out again. Then the phone rang once more.

6
"A Very Fortunate Accident"

"Ben, have you heard?" began the excited caller. "*Hokule'a* is sinking! I've been listening to a Kauai radio station. They just flashed the news. The canoe is sinking off Kauai!"

I did not want to believe her. How could *Hokule'a* be sinking? Wooden canoes do not sink. They swamp when the hulls fill with water, or they capsize. In either case they remain afloat, awash in the sea, and do not go down like yachts weighted with metal ballast and a heavy engine. After my caller hung up I dialed the station. Their first report was incorrect, but the news was still bad. *Hokule'a* was swamped 10 miles off the southeast coast of Kauai, and the Coast Guard was on the way.

I raced upstairs, blurted out the awful news to my wife and immediately left for the airport. Luckily I was able to board a Kauai flight right away. Before taking my seat I asked the pilot to keep a lookout for the canoe. He seemed curiously unmoved by

47

the disaster and probably wondered why I was so excited about a canoe swamping. Excited was not the right word for my state. My heart was pounding, my hands were cold and I had a nauseous feeling that we might lose *Hokuleʻa* or, worse, some of the crew.

Just as the plane started descending toward Kauai I spotted something in the sea far below. It looked like a canoe, or some

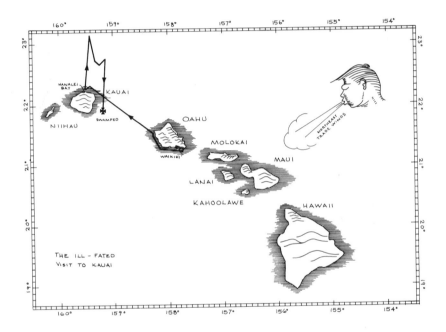

kind of craft, lying broadside in the sea with white crests churning all around it. But we were too high to be sure. Whatever it was, I was glad it was afloat.

Once out of the plane I made my way to a nearby harbor. There I learned what had happened. Only one hull of the canoe was swamped. She had run into trouble in the channel around dawn, the radio was out and they had no flares. Tommy Holmes, afraid that the canoe would drift past Kauai and out of interisland shipping lanes, had taken a surfboard and started paddling for shore to raise the alarm.

A few hours after he paddled off, the disheartened crew

spotted a vessel moving fast toward them. The canoe had swamped slightly north of the route between Oahu and Kauai used by a newly inaugurated hydrofoil service, and they had fortunately drifted right into the path of the only hydrofoil scheduled that day. Ironically, the craft was the *Kamehameha*, named after the warrior chief whose invading canoes had once swamped in the same channel. The hydrofoil captain radioed the Coast Guard, stopped to pick up the National Geographic film team and some young and frightened crew members, and resumed her course for Kauai. On the way Tommy was spotted, still paddling for shore, and was picked up. He could have made it, he said, although Tommy did admit to being so exhausted that he kept falling asleep as he struggled to keep paddling.

Hokuleʻa was a sad sight a few hours later when we spotted her being towed toward the harbor. The starboard hull was down, completely submerged except for the tips of the prow and stern-pieces, while the port hull was thrust up and canted over to one side. The deckhouse was gone, and the crew left on board was clinging to the rail along the port hull. Then, just at the harbor entrance, cross-swells caught the canoe and dumped water into the port hull, which then also began to settle. By the time she had been maneuvered alongside the pier, the canoe was totally swamped. Both hulls were completely filled with water and the raised deck was awash.

Using high-speed pumps supplied by the Coast Guard, and with the aid of stout hausers and the pulling power of a heavy truck, we were able to lever up first one hull and then the other, pumping the water out of each in turn. There would have been no way we could have gotten the canoe floating again at sea unless we had pumps, airbags and probably an assisting vessel. According to old Hawaiian accounts, double-canoes swamped far from shore were usually lost forever. Unlike outrigger canoes, big double-canoes are virtually impossible to bail out, particularly in heavy seas. Even if only one hull is flooded, the buoyancy of the other hull keeps the flooded one depressed at or below the water level, or so near to it that waves push water in faster than it can be bailed out.

By nightfall the canoe was floating quietly in the water, and what gear had not been lost was spread out over the dock. Never had the chances of sailing to Tahiti seemed so remote as at that moment of stocktaking. It was not only the near loss of *Hokule'a* that was depressing. The canoe had swamped 10 miles east of Kauai; in thirty-six hours of tacking for Oahu she had made only 18 miles of easting! At that painfully slow rate of windward sailing we would have to stay at sea for months to make enough easting to reach Tahiti. Among other things, changes would have to be made in the manifestly inefficient sail rig before we could even think about attempting the voyage.

The attitudes of Herb Kane and his chief lieutenants, Tommy Holmes and Kimo Hugho, made the already dismal situation even worse. Kane wanted to fix up the canoe immediately; he minimized the damages and said only minor repairs were needed before she could sail again. Tommy and Kimo did not agree; nor did they want to sail under Kane again. They were openly bitter in their denunciation of Kane's leadership, and Kane in turn raised the question of their negligence since they were on watch at the time the swamping occurred. To have an open blowup over the swamping would have shattered the project and probably destroyed chances for making the necessary changes in the canoe and in the way it was operated. So at the Voyaging Society Board of Directors meeting the following week, against much opposition, I quashed all discussion of the swamping and instituted a formal board of inquiry with the mandate to investigate thoroughly the causes of the swamping and to make recommendations for necessary changes in the canoe and its management.

After several weeks of interviews and deliberations, the board, chaired by Rudy Choy, the Korean-American catamaran designer who had worked out the lines of *Hokule'a*'s hulls, presented its report to a somber group of Voyaging Society directors.

The immediate cause of the swamping was readily apparent. When sailed hard on the wind the canoe heeled over so that the leeward hull was partially depressed. Waves funneling between the hulls washed against and occasionally over the leeward hull, especially the stern section, which rides more deeply in the water than the bow when the canoe is trimmed for windward sailing. Neither the caulking where the crossbeam lashing lines enter the hulls nor the canvas covers over the gunwales kept the water out completely. A light decking within the hulls below the gunwales covering a series of supposedly watertight compartments did not help; water worked through the seams and under the unsecured hatch covers.

We had run into this problem of the hulls taking on water on the first channel crossing to Maui when the canoe had come very close to swamping, but nothing had been done about it during the intervening months when the canoe was on tour. The sea had not been especially rough on this last attempted crossing; it was a metal bracket for the outboard motor (which was required to get in and out of harbors) that turned a dangerous condition into a near disaster. Usually the bracket was retracted after leaving port. This time for some reason it was left down. Located between the hulls adjacent to the stern section of the starboard hull, the bracket kept hitting the tops of the swells and deflecting them against the starboard hull, which at the time of the swamping was the leeward, depressed hull. Due to lack of rigorous inspection and bailing procedures, coupled with the dissension between Kane and his lieutenants (who at the time of the swamping were apparently more concerned with talking Kane into aborting the trip and turning back to Kauai than keeping tabs on the water level), the stern section flooded completely. Then the light plywood decking gave way. Water surged forward, quickly filling compartment after compartment through the negligently unsecured hatches until the whole hull was swamped.

But these were only the immediately apparent causes of the disaster.

"It is our inescapable conclusion," Rudy Choy gravely pronounced, "that *Hokule'a* swamped due to lack of seamanship, an absence of knowledgeable command at sea and the omission of acceptable standards and procedures for all oceangoing vessels. The euphoric aura present during the launching and most so-called training trips whether day sailing or interisland jaunts, the remarkable success of *Hokule'a* despite major warning signs that serious command and organizational deficiencies in fact existed, and the lack of serious problems due to favorable weather conditions and good luck all contributed to laxity and poor seamanship which led inevitably to the swamping."

Following seafaring tradition, the report declared that Herb Kane, as captain, was responsible for the swamping. Blame also was assigned to his officers, Tommy, Kimo and the navigator, for their inattention to duty. Final responsibility was placed on the Voyaging Society directors. We all agreed. The directors, and especially myself as president, had been remiss in allowing conditions to develop that led to the swamping. But the report did not dwell on who was to blame. At my urging, Rudy had made the report a forward-looking document. The swamping was described as "a very fortunate accident" that laid bare our deficiencies and gave us a second chance to correct them before the trip to Tahiti.

Rudy, warming to his role as technical advisor, then went on to outline the report's recommendations. These included construction of truly watertight compartments with hatches that could be easily and completely secured, provision of bilge pumps and other safety equipment, selection of an experienced captain and rigorous selection and training of a crew for the voyage.

The report was accepted unanimously. Enough time had elapsed since the swamping for people to cool down and gain a better perspective of what had occurred. The worst of the crisis was over; we could now get back to work. Rudy Choy assumed the chairmanship of a newly constituted canoe committee that was to oversee the modifications and selection of captain and crew. Tommy and I worked out arrangements for barging the canoe back to Honolulu Harbor and berthing her at the University's oceanographic facility. Thanks to some timely donations, including another handsome gift from Penelope Gerbode-Hopper, our benefactor from California, we were able to hire boatbuilders, purchase materials and get started on the modifications.

The construction of truly watertight compartments was the most crucial modification from the point of view of safety. The flimsy compartments that had been hurriedly installed in *Hokule'a*'s hulls to meet the launching date had been an unhappy mating of *haole* boatbuilding with Polynesian canoe design. We could have ripped out the ineffective decking to open up the hulls so that they could be easily inspected and bailed out. But that would have left us particularly vulnerable to swamping in a gale or a hurricane. Many a Polynesian canoe must have been lost at sea in stormy weather, and we were not willing to risk lives against the odds; our primary object was to test sailing performance and navigational accuracy, not survivability. We therefore had no qualms about installing a watertight decking and compartment system in the hulls.

We were not alone in thinking that this modification was essential. The Coast Guard was looking over our shoulder. They have the right by law to prevent any vessel they declare unseaworthy from leaving port. The swamping had raised the question of *Hokule'a*'s seaworthiness. The Coast Guard had another recent canoe disaster in mind: just before *Hokule'a* swamped, another experimental double-canoe built hurriedly in California to compete with us had managed to sail downwind from San Diego to the Marquesas Islands, although not without trouble. En route several crossbeams failed and the escorting yacht had to tow the canoe for several days. After a short stay in the Marquesas, during which most of the crew deserted, the hastily repaired canoe left for Hawaii, just at the beginning of the winter storm season. North of the equator they ran into a storm. The weak crossbeams snapped, then both hulls turned inward and swamped. Luckily the escort boat picked up all survivors. The incident got much publicity in Hawaii and made the Coast Guard scrutinize our canoe even more closely.

7
Kawika

We needed a captain for *Hokule'a*, someone with extensive catamaran sailing experience. Rudy Choy had the experience but declined to be considered, as did Kane, Holmes and I. Who then could we get for this all-important job?

There was one additional qualification in back of everyone's mind: the captain should be Polynesian, preferably Hawaiian. This narrowed the field considerably, but one name stuck in my mind: Kawika. Kawika (Kah-vee-kah) is really his nickname, the Hawaiian way of saying David, which is not his name at all. Because his real name is a tongue twister—Elia Kapahulehua (El-ee-ah Kah-pah-hoo-lay-hoo-ah)—most people called him just Kawika.

Kawika, a heavyset man of medium height, with a pleasant face and manner, was then in his mid-forties. He is about as Hawaiian as anyone can be today. As far back as he can trace on both sides of his family there are none but Hawaiian ancestors.

(Above) Hokule'a *approaching Maui from Honolulu*

(Below) Sam Kalalau, Rodo, Mau and Lewis

(Above) Lyman doing fancy knotwork

(Below) Tommy and a tuna

(Above) Buffalo steering

(Below) Arrival at Mataiva

Kawika

Mau

(Above) Kealanahele and Kaʻai before the temple altar

(Below) Hokuleʻa *full and bye*

He is also one of those rare Hawaiians who knows Hawaiian, a language he speaks both fluently and beautifully. He learned his mother tongue on the small island of Niihau (Nee-'ee-how), off the southwest coast of Kauai. Niihau is Hawaii's forbidden island; none but Hawaiians may live there, and Hawaiian is the language of the home and school. So Kawika had the rare opportunity of growing up in a totally Hawaiian setting, enjoying a rural Hawaiian lifestyle greatly different from that of the vast majority of Hawaiians who live in Honolulu and other urban and suburban settings.

Kawika began sailing catamarans in 1949 when, after moving to Honolulu, he started crewing on Rudy Choy's beach catamaran at Waikiki Beach. Although on Niihau sailing canoes had long since disappeared, and Kawika's sailing experience there was confined to boyhood projects of making rafts and using his mother's sheets for sails, he quickly took to catamaran sailing. Within a few years he was the captain of a large catamaran used for sunset dinner cruises off Waikiki. These cruises are as much musical as nautical outings; to be able to sing and to play a ukulele and a guitar is almost as much of a job requirement as sailing ability. Here Kawika also excelled, so much so that he and his crew caught the attention of film promoter Mike Todd and his wife Elizabeth Taylor, and ended up playing as "The Catamaran Boys" in a Hawaiian restaurant in New York.

From New York he went to Los Angeles, where he landed a job with Western Airlines and started sailing again with Rudy Choy, who had also moved to California to start a catamaran design and construction firm. This time Kawika was racing catamarans, not catering to tourists, although his Hawaiian ex-perience served him well. He was soon in demand as a steersman and sail handler, and managed to sail in four straight Transpac catamaran races from California to Hawaii, including two in which he was a watch captain on the *Seasmoke*, a fast Choy catamaran that finished first in both races.

Kawika eventually returned to Hawaii to work evenings as a captain for Rudy Choy's newly inaugurated catamaran cruises and days as an air cargo agent for Western Airlines. I first heard of him in connection with his day job. He helped us air freight some plywood and other materials in from the coast; then he tore up the bill! Later I had him captain *Nalehia* on a sail along the coast and give her a formal Hawaiian blessing. But I had not seen him since the day of the launching, when he had served on the crew that took *Hokule'a* for her ritual sea outing.

It took me some time to realize fully why Kawika, and some other Hawaiians interested in *Hokule'a* who were also expert sailors, never came out on those first sea trials after the launching or on the interisland trips during the cruise. "Watermen" had taken over the canoe, driving away the sailors.

"Waterman" is a term used in Hawaii for an expert surfer and canoe paddler; to be called a "top waterman" is to receive a great compliment. But it says nothing about sailing ability. Typically, watermen are not sailors, certainly not experienced blue-water sailors. As one cynical Hawaiian later told me, they are really "shallow-water men."

From early on in the project watermen had got a grip upon the canoe that never could fully be shaken. I was partially at fault. I thought it would be a fine thing to get young Hawaiian canoe paddlers involved in sailing *Hokule'a*; paddlers had done a good job of handling *Nalehia* during the 1966 trials. But while I soon became disenchanted with having only surfers and paddlers crew *Hokule'a*, Kane and his lieutenants kept pushing the idea that watermen were the ideal crew members. Why? Because, so their theory went, *Hokule'a* was totally different from any other sailing craft, even a catamaran. Watermen, with their unique experience paddling canoes and surfing giant waves, would be much more adapted to sailing a voyaging canoe than anyone practiced only in sailing modern craft.

With that theory in vogue it is little wonder that men who were expert sailors but who supposedly lacked watermen credentials were either pushed to one side or just plain put off by the absurdity of the situation. After the launching Kawika asked to go out sailing on the canoe; after a couple of rebuffs he got the message and gave up.

Now that the running of the canoe had been reorganized, it was time to try to bring Kawika back into the project—as our captain, if possible. I went to Kawika and raised the question. Yes, he would be interested. Then I went to the Voyaging Society directors. They were excited by the prospect, particularly the Hawaiian members who were gratified that the search for an expert captain had ended with the nomination of a Hawaiian.

There was one obstacle to bringing Kawika on board as captain. We needed a full-time captain, someone who could start working as soon after Christmas as possible and stick with the project till the canoe returned in July. Yet Kawika had to hold down two jobs to make ends meet in expensive Honolulu. There was no way he could take seven months off without pay, especially since his wife was occupied with the care of their handicapped child and could not work.

The solution, which took a great deal of arranging, was to get half of Kawika's salary paid out of an educational grant—on the basis that he would be teaching both crewmen and, in a series of public lectures, the general public about canoe sailing and proper Hawaiian sailing terminology. The other half of his salary was paid by his employer, Western Airlines, as their contribution to Hawaii's celebration of the Bicentennial.

Even before Western Airlines released Kawika to start work on the canoe, I had to turn to him for help. Talk of the canoe being cursed was growing. The day after the swamping a front-page story, headlined KAHUNA PREDICTED TROUBLES, CHARGES TABOOS VIOLATED, gave a great deal of publicity to a leading *kahuna* critic who had captured a following among Hawaiian members of our group. Then, to make matters worse, word spread that Kimo Hugho had been warned that should *haoles* sail on *Hokule'a*, the canoe would sink and he, Kimo, would die.

When I approached Kawika during his lunch hour at Western Airlines about this talk of curses and threats, he was not at all surprised. Kawika, who hardly betrays any emotion when he speaks, looked more sad than disgusted when he replied, "I've been hearing about so many people who are jealous of the canoe and who are mad about how you folks are running it. You, Kimo, *Hokule'a*—all of you have a heavy weight. I've already been feeling that we should have the canoe blessed again to stop all these bad feelings. I want to ask *Kahu* to help us."

Kahu (Kah-hoo) is Hawaiian for reverend; Kawika had in mind Reverend Akaka (Ah-kah-kah), Hawaii's leading *kahu* or Protestant clergyman, who at times is called upon to bless construction sites plagued by mysterious accidents and other projects that have run into problems rumored to be caused by the violation of ancient taboos or the curses of some *kahuna*. Kawika wanted Akaka to perform a special Hawaiian Christian ritual to cut out all the evil things of the past and give the canoe and those directing it a clean slate for the voyage to come. Kawika could have suggested that we engage a *kahuna* to turn the curses heaped upon us back to those who had uttered them, a practice which, according to Polynesian belief, can kill those who initiated the curses. But Kawika is a conciliatory man; he preferred the Christian way of trying to bring detractors over to our side.

On December 15 Kawika brought Reverend Akaka to the canoe for the ritual. Kawika, Kimo, Tommy, Herb Kane and I, plus a number of others prominent in the project, stood with Akaka on *Hokule'a*'s stripped-down deck. Akaka first lauded the project and spoke of its importance to the people of Hawaii. Then he acknowledged that tensions existed both within and without the project. His answer to them was a long series of prayers, followed by a plea for brotherly love to prevail.

"This project and this craft," he said, "is like a musical instrument whose purpose it is to make sweet harmony. Every one of you is a string, an important string in the instrument. Every string is different, but every string is important. How do you get sweet music when you have many different strings? The only way is if you have one tuner, and that tuner is God. And the tune from God to everyone I take from the Bible. *He aloha kekahi i kekahi*, love one another. Love one another, because when you love one another you help each other."

Kawika was especially buoyed by Akaka's words. In answer to my query as to whether or not those critics who were not present would heed Akaka's advice, Kawika said, "We don't have to worry about these people anymore. They will get the message."

8
Mau

Despite the appointment of Kawika, and Reverend Akaka's blessing, the ranks of the dubious were growing. Here we were trying to fix up the canoe after its swamping during our only significant windward trial, yet we still were sticking to our claim that early next year we would sail the canoe to Tahiti and back—and navigate it without instruments.

Since the inception of the project we had been working with David Lewis, a New Zealand physician and yachtsman who is the foremost authority on Polynesian navigation. I had first heard of Lewis in 1965 when I was building *Nalehia* and he was sailing his catamaran from Tahiti to New Zealand, navigating it Polynesian-style without instruments. A few years later we were colleagues at the Australian National University, where he had managed to win a most unusual fellowship that allowed him to sail about the Pacific in search of islanders who might still know the old ways of navigating.

To his delight, Lewis did find one traditional Polynesian navigator, a man in his seventies who still sailed his own canoe from island to island without instruments. But the navigator was not from Polynesia proper, where dislocating economic changes and the development of modern transport systems had led to the disappearance of interisland sailing canoes and the old ways of navigating. He was from a Polynesian outlier, a small atoll located in Melanesia well to the west of the great ocean triangle. In this quiet backwater of the Pacific, both ocean-sailing canoes and noninstrument navigation had survived—although just barely—in the person of the aged navigator.

After Lewis returned to Australia he received a letter from his friend with the curious message, "Now I am alive, but you will meet me one day or not?" Later that year Lewis learned what was behind the message. One day the old navigator had bade formal farewell of his fellow islanders and then set sail in his canoe, purposefully never to return again. "An era of Polynesian voyaging has closed with his passing," was how Lewis eulogized this last of the Polynesian navigators.

When we recruited Lewis to organize the navigation part of the voyage, he told of his friend's suicide at sea and said that he saw no possibility of finding another Polynesian navigator for the voyage. A Micronesian, yes. On a few isolated atolls of Micronesia, located in the western Pacific north of New Guinea, there still survives a vigorous system of ocean voyaging involving deep-sea outrigger canoes and a noninstrument system of navigation much like that which Polynesians once employed. In 1968 Lewis had sailed to Puluwat (Poo-loo-wat) atoll and recruited a traditional Micronesian navigator to guide his yacht to the Marianas Islands, some 500 miles to the north, and back. Although no one had made the trip since the turn of the century, when German colonial administrators had forbidden distant voyaging, the sailing directions, the winds, currents and the stars to follow had all been preserved in oral traditions. The round trip was completed without incident. It was a magnificent demonstration of the worth of noninstrument navigation, but it also piqued the navigators from the adjacent atoll of Satawal (Sah-tah-wall).

Navigators in Micronesia are especially prideful. Theirs is a skill gained through years of rigorous training in small outrigger canoes under the night skies, and there are few who ever become known as master navigators. Great rivalry exists between navigators from the same island, more so among navigators from different islands. The Satawal men could not allow their rivals from Puluwat to get the upper hand. So several of them took a sailing canoe and, using the old style of navigation, duplicated the trip to the Marianas and back. Then a group from Puluwat did the trip by canoe.

I had learned about this revival of long-distance voyaging through correspondence with Mike McCoy, a Peace Corps volunteer stationed on Satawal who wrote an article on the subject for a book I was editing on Pacific Island navigation and voyaging. Mike had married the niece of a famous Satawal navigator, an intriguing man whom I had met several years previous. When we started working on the project the Satawal navigator was our immediate choice, for he combined two essential virtues: skill in noninstrument navigation and an ability to work across cultural boundaries rare among his navigator colleagues.

Pius Piailug (Pee-us Pee-eye-luke) was his official name, although everyone in Hawaii soon fell to calling him Mau, his more easily pronounceable nickname. The plan was to bring Mau to Hawaii twice, once when we were just finishing the canoe and trying to figure out how to sail it, and then a year later for the voyage itself. The first trip was no less essential than the second. Mau was then in his early forties. He had been sailing canoes since he was a small child, he was an expert canoe builder and he had a reputation for coolness under dangerous conditions that had allowed him to survive several hurricanes at sea. We needed the help of a man like that to learn how best to sail *Hokule'a*, and he in turn needed to familiarize himself with the canoe, with us and the navigation task before him. What a task it was! Navigate a strange canoe over a route five or six times longer than any crossing he had ever made that took him into strange waters and unfamiliar Southern Hemisphere skies.

A few months before the launching, as I was arranging for

Mau's first trip, Herb Kane caught me by surprise. He did not want Mau to come to Hawaii until just before the actual voyage. "We Hawaiians want to do it ourselves. We want to learn to handle *Hokuleʻa* on our own. Then let Mau come to Hawaii later to help us learn how to navigate," was how Kane phrased his argument.

I was flabbergasted that Kane's desire to Hawaiianize the project would go so far so soon. I knew that the boatbuilders then rushing to finish the canoe, including a few young Hawaiians, wanted Mau to come out and help them with vital tasks, and that some other Hawaiians interested in trying out for the crew were intrigued that an island canoe master—not a yachtsman or a modern catamaran sailor—would be their teacher. I persisted till I had won Kane's begrudging acceptance.

We obtained a special grant from Micronesia to pay for Mau's air fare and his stay in Hawaii so that his visit would not burden our treasury. After the inevitable delays of trying to get someone from an isolated Micronesian atoll to Hawaii, Mau arrived coincidentally on the day of the launching. Although he did not participate in the ritual, within a week he had assumed a key role in the project. It was he who had the knack of setting the sails at the best possible angle, and it was he who could show us tried-and-true lashing techniques and how to work wood the island way with an adze as opposed to the saws, planes and chisels we had been using.

For example, when the first set of laminated booms for the sails proved too flimsy and snapped under the stress of the wind and our inexpert sail handling, Mau was the only person who really knew how to make more serviceable replacements. He took a crew of young Hawaiians into the hills and selected long, slender tree limbs with just the right curve. Then, under a shady tree by the water's edge, he used his adze like a virtuoso, shaping the limbs to just the right dimensions and making lengthy, perfectly fitting scarf joints so that three of the limbs could be joined together to make a single long boom. Then, using some specially made coconut sennit he had brought with him from his island, Mau lashed the pieces together to form a set of strong yet light booms.

Mau's beachside worksite soon became a popular gathering place for crew candidates and others who wanted to watch this canoe master at work. His round, compact physique, his skin burned dark brown from years of sailing under the tropical sun, made him stand out among the spectators, even the Hawaiians. They were mostly much taller and heavier than Mau and, because of racial admixture or a more indoor lifestyle, were much paler. Mau worked with a quiet intensity, although he had a ready smile and a seemingly humble demeanor that charmed everyone.

He soon won a cult following among some of the young Hawaiian crewmen, including Kimo Hugho, who seemed especially fascinated with this man from another island—really another age—who had so much to teach modern Hawaiians. By the time Mau had to leave, just a few weeks before the departure for Maui inaugurating the interisland cruise, I felt confident that some key Hawaiians admired Mau and appreciated the chance to work with him. Mau's opinion of the Hawaiians as sailors was not very reassuring, however. He was worried about the lack of sailing skill and deep-sea experience of some of those who had been sailing aboard *Hokule'a*. They were, in a word, watermen. Few had sailed before, and none had made any extensive ocean crossings.

Today's Hawaiians are world renowned for their surfing, but few of them ever sail. In Hawaii yachting is mostly a *haole* pastime, too expensive for most Hawaiians and not popular among those few Hawaiians who can afford to purchase yachts. If Hawaiians do go to sea, they typically go just offshore in an outboard skiff to spend the day fishing for their table. It was not always this way. As late as the middle of the last century Hawaiians were recognized as being expert deep-water sailors— so expert that New England sea captains would sail out to the Pacific with a minimum number of hands, and then head straight for Hawaii where they would hire on Hawaiians to serve for the duration of their long whaling and trading cruises. These sea captains found that Hawaiians were natural seamen, that they could do things such as swim in the open ocean and surf a boat to shore that American sailors could not, and that they could eat almost anything, endure hardships easily, and were intensely loyal. But that was over 100 years ago, and much has happened since to alienate Hawaiians from the sailing life.

Mau realized the dilemma of the young Hawaiian crew candidates: wanting to learn how to sail, to recapture some of the glory of their seafaring ancestors, yet woefully lacking in seamanship and discipline. Although he had misgivings, when he left for home he was still game and assured us that he would be back to navigate *Hokule'a* on her long voyage.

There was one major obstacle to bringing Mau back. Hawaii is a mecca for Micronesians and other Pacific Islanders who come to study or just to look around and end up staying for good—to the frustration of immigration officials. The latter had given Mau a hard time upon his arrival in Honolulu for his first stay. It did not matter that ours was a Bicentennial project, that we were not paying Mau a wage, and that he was a volunteer. They accused him of coming to Hawaii to get work, and in so doing of trying to take a job away from an American citizen. Although they finally did heed my pleas and gave Mau a temporary visitor's permit, they warned me that he would not be treated so leniently if he tried to come back to Hawaii.

The way out of this problem involved the East-West Center, a federal institution that brings Asians, Pacific Islanders and Americans to Hawaii for cultural and technical exchange programs. Since 1971 I had held a joint appointment between the Center and the University, and I decided now was the time to try to get their aid for the canoe project. My idea was to bring Mau to Hawaii on a Center fellowship; that would give him air fare, a monthly stipend, and more importantly a special visa that would enable him to stay in Hawaii. At first I did not get far with the Center bureaucracy, even though I argued that this would be a rare chance to reverse the usual direction of technical exchange programs in which technical aid flows from the United States to Pacific Island countries. In this case a Pacific Islander would be the technical expert, and the Americans would be the recipients of the foreign aid.

Then, after several months of negotiations, I finally succeeded in arranging for a most unusual exchange program involving a fellowship for Mau—and also fellowships for David Lewis, a Tahitian sailor as yet to be selected, and (with the aid of extra funds from our California backer) Herb Kane and Kimo Hugho, so that New Zealand, Tahiti and Hawaii were represented along with Micronesia. Two men, heads of separate institutes within the Center, were primarily responsible for approving the program: a Filipino economist and a British educator. Unlike the continentally bred American officials of the Center whom I had initially and unsuccessfully petitioned, both these men were islanders and thus naturally sensitized to the importance of ocean voyaging.

Christmas morning 1975. Only three months remained till departure, and still no Mau Piailug. He needed to start working with David Lewis, who had already arrived. Lewis's job was to familiarize Mau with the route to and from Tahiti and with the winds, currents and stars along the way. We also needed Mau to help us relash the canoe, make new booms and take care of many other jobs that needed his unique skills. It had taken time to process Mau's fellowship and his travel papers, and then to get him from his island to the district headquarters, from where he could start the plane journey to Hawaii. The last we had heard he was there, waiting for space on the first airplane. But that was two weeks ago, and we had received no message since.

Then the phone rang while I was reading the newspaper comics to my elder son. Unlike that other morning call three months earlier, this one carried a happy message. The Micronesian college student on the other end of the line had Mau in tow; they had just flown in from Micronesia.

9

Grumbling and Dissension

The appointment of Kawika and the arrival of Mau gave the project a great boost. We looked forward to the Bicentennial year of 1976, the year of the voyage, with great anticipation. Yet, once work resumed on the canoe after the holidays, our troubles returned, grew and then multiplied.

It was not too many weeks before an exasperated Kawika was saying, "Too much *namunamu*! Too much *hukihuki*!" Both are pithy Hawaiian terms formed by duplicating shorter, more innocent words. *Namu* (nah-moo) alone just means to mutter; said twice it means to grumble openly. *Huki* (hoo-kee) means to pull; duplicating it as "pull-pull" graphically describes the act of causing dissension. Earlier I had been warned by Hawaiians that grumbling and "pull-pull" were ills characteristic of Hawaiian organizations. I was at first dubious; my social science training had taught me to be wary of such stereotypes. However, by now I was willing to accept that there might be some folk wisdom in this and other negative sayings Hawaiians have about the difficulty they experience working together. Grumbling and dissension were growing within the ranks of the Voyaging Society, although much was fueled by outside pressures.

The most innocuous of these came in the form of unsolicited advice about all the things we were doing wrong, including how we were breaking a number of canoe taboos.

"You cannot have anything yellow or black on the canoe. Those are taboo colors."

"No women. It was taboo in the old days for women to sail on double-canoes."

"You cannot take bananas on the trip. If you do you will not catch any fish."

How those who claimed that black and yellow colors, and women, were taboo on double-canoes could reconcile their pronouncements with the fact that canoes were traditionally stained black and yellow, and that at least one double-canoe that reached Hawaii must have had women aboard, was a mystery. Only the taboo on bananas seemed to have an actual basis. Modern Hawaiian fishermen do believe that they will catch no fish if they carry bananas on their boats. The only trouble with following that taboo was that it would entail throwing out the hundreds of pounds of dried bananas that volunteers had already prepared as a primary staple on the voyage! Many people did take these taboos seriously, and it required some hard talking to save the bananas, keep the women from being banned from the canoe, and rescue all the yellow life rings and yellow suits of foul weather gear that had already been purchased.

Other talk was not so easy to dismiss. Warnings that *haoles* should not sail on *Hokule'a* continued to circulate. A few crewmen took to bragging, "When we get out to sea we're going to throw the *haoles* overboard." They may have been joking—partly—but Kimo was not when he started once again to complain about threats. This time he said someone was talking about blowing up the canoe. At Kimo's request I lodged a complaint with the police, who assigned an experienced old Hawaiian detective to investigate. After I explained to him about all the *kahunas* who had been giving us trouble, and more recent evidence that a number of petty hoodlums were trying to exert their will on the project, the detective chuckled and started telling me about all the times he had been threatened by *kahunas* and local criminals. But he did promise to look into the matter. Some weeks later he informed me that there was no immediate danger.

"Don't worry," he said, "all that talk is just Hawaiian psychological warfare. They're always doing that." His words were not totally comforting, even though he assured me that he had tracked down some of the people involved and warned them to stay away from the canoe.

Our arch critic from the ranks of the *kahunas* got into the act again at this time. Kawika, true to his conciliatory nature, wanted to get this man to stop all his talk against the canoe and to start supporting the project. He went out to see the old *kahuna* in his rural retreat.

"We want you to stop talking against us. We want you to help us, to work with us to get *Hokule'a* ready for the trip to Tahiti," was Kawika's entreaty for cooperation.

"You are wrong," replied the *kahuna*. "I am not against the canoe. I want to see it go to Tahiti. But the canoe is dirty. Much has to be done to make it clean. I have to pray for weeks. Then there must be a big feast. Forty black pigs are needed. . . ."

A buoyant Kawika came back from this meeting pleased with the idea that the *kahuna* would stop cursing the canoe and start helping us. "How much?" I asked Kawika, for I knew from former followers of this *kahuna* that he charged rather healthy fees for his spiritual interventions. Kawika had no idea, so I suggested that we could go as high as $500—if his prayers could be taped. That way the payment could be called a consulting fee on ancient Hawaiian religious practices, and we could get the funds from an educational grant.

The following week Kawika went out to see the *kahuna* again. When he returned he was not at all cheery.

"You know what that guy told me?" Kawika said, forcing a

laugh. "He went on and on about how he was already praying for us, about how when he was finished the canoe and everything would be all right, and about the forty black pigs and all the food needed for the feast. Then he said it would only cost us $150,000!"

The whole affair might have been funny but for the trouble this man's fulminations had already caused and, from all indications, would continue to cause. Kawika's announcement at the canoe about the *kahuna's* extortionate demands was greeted with glum silence, and more than a few crew candidates looked annoyed. It was as if they thought the story had been manufactured to discredit someone they believed in.

The project was sick. Harping critics, muttering *kahunas* and devious threateners had all contributed to the malaise, but they fed on basic ills imbedded within our organization.

First and foremost was the split between Hawaiians and *haoles*, a debilitating division that had a way of making simple matters tortuously complicated. Most of all it greatly weakened my ability to act decisively on matters dealing with Hawaiians, and it poisoned the possibility of a rational crew selection.

That task should have been easy. The main people going had already been picked: Kawika as captain; a part-Hawaiian professional seaman named David Lyman as Kawika's first mate; Mau Piailug as navigator and David Lewis as his assistant; a veteran Tahitian sailor named Rodo Williams to be our pilot in his home waters; Kimo Hugho, Herb Kane, Tommy Holmes and myself. All we really needed were a few extra hands.

But crew selection had been the least rational part of the project and the one most embroiled with the pressures to Hawaiianize the project. In those first enthusiastic days of planning, we had made the mistake of proclaiming that the canoe would sail with twenty-four men and women (plus pigs, dogs and chickens) to simulate the crowded conditions of an ancient migratory voyage. Then came Kane's campaign around the islands advertising for Hawaiian watermen to crew the canoe for the voyage. All this resulted in a large pool of expectant Hawaiian candidates, many of whom had their champions among members of the Voyaging Society's governing board. By now Kane was largely out of the picture, but he had left a legacy of personal choices we felt bound to honor. Then Kimo maneuvered so that he took charge of selecting the remaining Hawaiian crewmen. After much deliberation he drew up a lengthy list composed mostly of his favorites. Tommy, who was supposed to assist Kimo in crew selection, had reservations about many on the list, but in the end he rubber-stamped it without making any cuts.

My greatest error at the beginning of the project had been to delegate crew selection and to allow it to be based on waterman ability. Now I compounded that error by still hanging back and not insisting that strict criteria based on sailing skills and general character be applied to weed out unsuitable candidates. All the anti-*haole* talk had its effect, and I passed the buck to Kawika. After a series of shakedown cruises, he was to make the final selection from a too-large pool of twenty-six candidates.

Had we been able to take the candidates out as planned for a few tough shakedown cruises (we had talked of going out of sight of land for up to five days at a crack), weak candidates would have voluntarily dropped out and any other unsuitable ones could have been easily selected out. But the canoe was not yet ready, and during the successive weeks the candidates assembled at the canoe (most just on weekends, although some without jobs came every day) to sand, paint and carry out other chores rather than sail. These work sessions did weed out a few candidates who decided the trip was not worth it, but most stuck it out and began to form a cohesive group tightly identified with the canoe.

I took this as a good sign until I realized that under Kimo's tutelage the candidates were now calling themselves "the crew." And because of their previous few sails on *Hokule'a*, plus their work contributions now, they were beginning to claim that they knew more about the canoe than Kawika, myself or any of the others of us they derisively called the "leaders." Then, before Kawika and I fully realized what was happening, Kimo and Tommy worked out a deal whereby all the candidates would be able to sail on *Hokule'a*, half on the trip to Tahiti and half on the return to Hawaii. I should never have acquiesced. But, rather than face a fight, I gave in.

My influence over the project was fast eroding. It was not just Kimo and his crew favorites, or the outside pressures, that were draining me. I was also having problems with some of my fellow board members, whose servant I was according to the Voyaging Society bylaws.

"You can't build a canoe by committee," warned a veteran yachtsman at the beginning of the project. We had proved him wrong. No one of us alone could have launched *Hokule'a*; certainly not a whole project the magnitude of ours. Kane, Tommy and I had worked well together promoting the project and getting the canoe built, just as the other members of the board of directors were essential to helping raise funds and managing the fledgling project. But our strength now turned into a disadvantage as problems of divided authority came to the fore.

Since the swamping I had been working on the project from dawn till late into the night—except when I had to teach at the University or attend meetings at the East-West Center. From early in the project, authority over the various aspects of the project had been delegated to separate committees each chaired by a board member. I chaired only the research committee, and I tried to coordinate the other committees in order to keep everything on schedule. At best this meant touching base from time to time with the committee chairmen. At worst, when the work lagged, it meant that I had to prod the chairman or take over the work myself. Some of the committee heads who could not spare the time to keep the work flowing welcomed intervention. Others did not, jealously guarding their territory and resenting even the gentlest suggestion.

Then I contracted viral pneumonia, which put me in bed for almost two weeks. My absence from dockside allowed those committee chairmen and other Voyaging Society board members who had always chafed about strict control over canoe design to try their hand at "improving" *Hokule‘a*. When I finally got out of bed and down to the canoe—which by then had been hoisted up on the dock to clean, paint the hulls and relash the crossbeams—I discovered that they had directed the boatbuilder and his crewmen helpers to install deep keel fins on each hull to make the canoe sail better to windward.

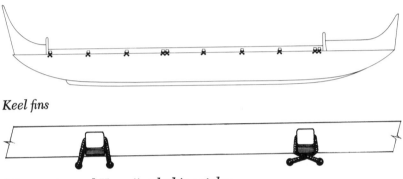

Keel fins

Micronesian and Hawaiian lashing styles

"We can't have *haole* keel fins on a Polynesian canoe."

"There are too damned many bosses around here! I quit!"

That was the gist of my conversation with the boatbuilder. I sympathized with his position, but the keel fins wrecked the experimental design and had to go. Most of the crew wanted the keel fins to stay. All the talk of leeway and the problem of making enough easting against the trades made them seize on the keel fins as a necessary addition that would allow them to reach Tahiti. The argument that ancient Polynesians did not use keel fins on their canoes failed entirely to sway them. Some even took it as an insult: "Our ancestors must have had keel fins. They weren't dumb!"

The keel fins came off, but one thing led to another. Herb Kane, who had taken a leave of absence from the project after the swamping to get back to his own work, now made a rare appearance at the canoe. When he spied the way the crew, under Mau's capable direction, was relashing the crossbeams to the hulls, Kane strenuously objected. Instead of following the Hawaiian method of crossing the lashings each time they go around the crossbeam, Mau was using the straight up-and-down Micronesian method. Kane seized upon this difference, declared the Micronesian method unsafe and demanded a meeting of the canoe committee to decide the issue. Although I had prevailed in the previous dispute over the keel fins, I lost on this detail. The majority sided with Kane.

Mau plainly thought the change was crazy, not to mention personally insulting, but he went along with it anyway. Not so the crew. Even after Kawika and I effected a compromise whereby most of Mau's lashings could remain in place, they kept going on and on about how much work they had already put into the lashings and about how much more it would take to change them. They had a point, but they tipped their hand by carrying it too far. It was now apparent that the real issue was control of the canoe. Kimo and his followers, a majority of those crewmen regularly working on the canoe, were delighted to use this lashing imbroglio and the keel fin episode as evidence of the incompetence of the project's leaders and the need for the crew to take control.

The error of having Kimo play such an important role was now all the more apparent. He might have made a good crewman, but he had neither the sailing skills nor the strength of purpose for the critical role in which he found himself. His position was unenviable; more than one malefactor had seen that he was the pressure point upon which they could lean to bend the project for their own ends. Yet Kimo was also playing his own game, publicly complaining about how the crew did all the work while the "leaders" did nothing, or just sat around giving orders.

Kimo performed very well before the cameras. Later, when some viewers saw him castigating the "leaders" in the National Geographic film, they wondered if Kimo was not a professional actor. They were partly right. Kimo plays bit parts in television films and is a man who falls into a pose easily. That, plus his weightlifter's physique and good looks, perhaps explains why Herb Kane chose him for the project. Kane, who had used Kimo as a model, must have looked at him with an artist's eye, seeing Kimo as the ideal young Hawaiian to symbolize the rebirth of Hawaiian seamanship.

Following Kane's lead, the National Geographic film team had early picked Kimo as a key figure around which to structure their film. They would show mainland audiences the rebirth of Hawaiians as Polynesian seamen through the adventures of Kimo. Their probing cameras and tape recorders were thus always there, boosting Kimo's ego, inviting him to state his case to the wider audience.

"I smell an Emmy," the National Geographic film producer Dale Bell was reported to have said one day several weeks previously. The film was to be shown nationwide on public television; his hope was that it would capture a coveted Emmy award.

I had not then realized the full import of his remark. Now I did. Herb Kane had earlier steered the film makers toward the cultural revival aspect of the project. Now when I tried to point Bell toward the central tasks of sailing and noninstrument navigation that he was neglecting, he acted bored and patronizing. He apparently saw the heart of the project to be the Hawaiian effort to make it their own. To Bell, the arguments and confrontations were the raw material for the drama of ethnic revival and conflict that he was betting would bring far more critical acclaim than any straight chronicle of the voyage.

Bell acted more like a frustrated new-wave cinema director than the producer of this documentary. Unfortunately, too, his penchant for directing went beyond loudly ordering his team around telling them where to stand and what to shoot. My anthropologist colleagues who make documentaries strive to record what *happens*, not what they would *like* to happen. Their cardinal rule is to avoid influencing events. Dale Bell evidently did not share totally in that ideal. He always seemed to be trying to get people to pose for this or that scene he had in mind.

At first his "documentary" approach had seemed fairly innocuous, as when he had me sit before the cameras tracing our route on a map or discussing a computer printout on canoe performance with a student in the University computer center, a place I had never been before. But as our problems grew, so did Bell's excitement; he appeared to relish the conflict and was not above trying to arrange confrontations in dramatic settings— as on the ruins of an ancient Hawaiian stone temple. Complaints also reached me that Bell was seeking out Hawaiian radicals for interviews during which he asked them provocative questions about Hawaiian rights and the project. In addition, it was reported that Bell had declared, "I don't care if the canoe swamps fifty miles out. I have my story."

When I moved to rein in the film team, Bell and his two bosses (one from the National Geographic and the other from WQED, the Public Broadcasting Service television station that was actually producing the film) treated me to a combination of wounded reproaches and syrupy words of assurance. Of course they would not think of interfering in the project, and so on. I was not totally assured and was tempted to tell the film team to clear out. But we were already in too deep with the National Geographic and I did not relish the thought of adding to our troubles by taking on that giant.

10
Setting to Right

An early April departure was crucial. As recorded in Hawaiian traditions, the voyaging season opened then, after the winter storms had subsided and the regular trade wind pattern was reestablished. Chances were that the doldrums would be only weakly developed in April, and that the angle of the trade winds would be most favorable then. In addition, by leaving in April we would have time to get back to Hawaii before the onset of the late summer storm season when hurricanes spawned off the Mexican coast have a nasty habit of curving west—right across our returning track.

We had planned to sail to Maui in early March and set up camp in a secluded cove from where we could take short training sails, and then wait there for the first fair winds of April to sail for Tahiti. Yet all through March *Hokule'a* remained high and dry on the wharf as the work dragged on. The realization that the ideal sailing days of April were fast approaching; the continued bickering; the sun glaring on the wharf's bare concrete surface; the flies our garbage attracted; the roar of the big jets taking off from the nearby airport; all combined to torment us, to make us loathe each new day the canoe remained on land.

The trouble, the vocal segment of the crew now openly claimed, lay with Kawika and the *haoles*. Get rid of them, let the crew take over the canoe, and all will be well, was their argument. That Kawika was pure Hawaiian, that he spoke Hawaiian fluently, and that he had grown up in a traditional Hawaiian community, counted for little. These crewmen, like so many other young part-Hawaiians growing up in Honolulu alienated from their cultural roots, felt they had to proclaim their Hawaiianness by being aggressively anti-*haole*. Kawika would not play their game; he would not side with them against the *haoles* in the project. In the eyes of his detractors, that made Kawika a "coconut," the local term for an Uncle Tom, which is explained as "brown on the outside and white inside."

The obvious solution, that of firing those crewmen who wanted to take over the canoe, would have been bitterly opposed by many Hawaiians, including all or most of those on the Society's Board of Directors. The Hawaiian board members were torn between having the project proceed as planned, and their deep sympathy for the rebellious crewmen. They had always seemed embarrassed that the project had sprung from an ethnically mixed, "elitist" group and not from the grassroots level in the Hawaiian community. They were desperate to have the Hawaiian crewmen, in their mind the heart of the project, share in its direction.

These board members had a social theory to back up their feelings. In the ancient days, they said, a canoe crew was organized along family lines with everyone sharing in the making of decisions as well as the work. No one should be ordered around by a captain or any other leader. Their catchword was 'ohana ('oh-hah-nah), the old term for extended family now used by many young Hawaiians to apply to protest groups and other aggregations of individuals who would like to believe that they are acting like the people in ancient days. We were supposed to be the 'ohana of the canoe; we were supposed to sail together as one big happy family with love and sharing as our guide.

Not only was it absurd to propose an idealized family organization where survival at sea dictates a firm command and discipline, but this modern theory of the 'ohana misconstrued the nature of ancient Hawaiian society. Relationships were anything but egalitarian in the old days. Within the extended family a senior male ruled and other roles and duties were assigned according to age and sex lines. Outside the extended family relationships were starkly hierarchical. A hereditary class of chiefs ruled over the mass of commoners with a strict hand.

It is exactly that rigid governing system composed of the powerful chiefs, their *mana* or supernatural power derived from the gods, and the strict system of taboos that regulated chiefly commoner relations and all other aspects of life, that was totally swept away in the last century, leaving a void among the Hawaiians that has yet to be filled. About all that remain are memories, some brilliant red-and-yellow feather cloaks and other chiefly insignia locked away in museums, and a recently restored palace (the only genuine royal palace in the United States say the tourist brochures) built by the last chief to rule as Hawaii's king. If anything, today's Hawaiians are archly distrustful of authority and have immense problems uniting behind leaders and common goals. While cynics among them may say, "We all want to be chiefs and none of us want to be Indians," the cultural void is genuine. That is what the advocates of the 'ohana system would like to fill with amorphous pseudo-family groups.

Part and parcel of this family system is a ritualized way of resolving conflict called *ho'oponopono* (hoh-'oh-poh-no-poh-no) which literally means "setting to right." Since we were (or should be) a family group, reasoned those board members intervening on behalf of the rebellious crewmen, our conflict should be resolved in the authentic way once used by Hawaiian families. Accordingly, they called in a pair of social workers, a Hawaiian couple I had known since my student days at the University who had made a speciality of applying the old method to troubled Hawaiian families.

After several false starts, the board members finally managed to get the majority of the crew, plus some of the non-Hawaiians in the project, together at the social workers' home. After seating us in a circle on the floor of their living room, the couple explained the *ho'oponopono* procedure and informed us that this session would be devoted only to captain-crew relations and that a subsequent session would deal with *haole*-Hawaiian relations. Then they opened the session with a long prayer to the Christian God, and to the Hawaiian gods and ancestors as well.

The key to the *ho'oponopono* procedure is to get aggrieved parties to air their "hurts" and openly complain about those they feel have wronged them, on the assumption that family divisions stem from problems between individuals which have to be solved in order to reunite the family. So complaints were called for against Kawika. The previously vocal crewmen were suddenly shy and it took some prodding to get anyone at all to speak up. A couple of young crewmen mustered up enough courage to charge that: "Kawika doesn't work alongside us." "Kawika doesn't know anything about the canoe." "Kawika is not a strong enough leader."

Although stung by the criticism, Kawika followed the rules, answering each complaint without attacking those who had criticized him. He pleaded that he was new to the canoe and that his lectures and other duties connected with his grant took much of his time, and then added that he himself felt let down by the lack of support among the crew. Neither Kawika nor the complainants looked each other in the eye, but, as instructed, stared steadily toward the center of the circle to keep them from giving each other the "stink eye."

After everyone had spoken his piece, the social workers led them through a painfully forced progression of mutual repentance, forgiveness and finally the ritual severance of antagonism.

The whole process was unreal. Despite the sincere efforts of the social workers to get all complaints out in the open, Kimo and his followers had said little, and the central charge that

Kawika was a tool of the leaders had not even been raised. Nonetheless, the next day the crew attacked their work with a rare enthusiasm. But it did not last. Within a few days they were back in the dumps and work once more dragged. The underlying issue of *haole*-Hawaiian relations had to be faced.

To start the process at the second session, the social workers asked that the crew bring out their hurts and problems with me as a person and as president of the Voyaging Society. Silence as before with Kawika. Finally, after some prodding, a couple of board members complained about my interference in their committees. I apologized, told about my concern for getting the canoe ready for the voyage, after which we came to an understanding and went through the required steps of repentance, forgiveness, and ritual severance.

Still the crew was not ready to talk about the central issue of *haole* participation. So I was asked to state my own grievances, and told about how it felt to hear that I had no business sailing on the canoe and that my work stifled Hawaiian self-expression.

"I can't ask you to quit disliking *haoles*," I added. "You have suffered too much over the last two hundred years for that to happen overnight. We can't right the wrongs of history at this *ho'oponopono*. All I ask for tonight is a truce. Let's stop our conflict for a time. We have a beautiful canoe, a beautiful project. If we work together we can get *Hokule'a* to Tahiti and back. The project is bigger than our conflict. I think we will all benefit by carrying it through together."

Again silence. Then a Hawaiian board member volunteered that, "There has been too much hurt, to our ancestors, to our history. That is why we find it so hard to talk to *haoles* about problems like this."

Finally a few crewmen spoke up. One talked about how he had wanted to slug me the day I brought the news that the canoe committee had voted down Mau's lashings. The other was more to the point. He said when he first saw the canoe upon its arrival at Hawaii Island during the interisland cruise he thought "it was all Hawaiian, that *Hokule'a* was a Hawaiian canoe and would have an all-Hawaiian crew."

"It was really great," he exclaimed. "We went sailing in our *malos* [loincloths]. It was a real experience. Later I found out there were *haoles* involved in it, that it was a scientific project, and that *haoles* were going on the canoe. It blew my mind!"

Other crewmen then joined in to say that they too had been deceived. Kimo at last spoke up to admit that he was partially to blame for not telling Hawaiians from the start about the research base of the project and about *haole* involvement.

At this point I suggested a compromise. The trip to Tahiti would be the one on which the experiments in sailing performance, navigation, and transport of plants and animals would be concentrated, and on which the *haoles* would sail. The trip back could be a Hawaiian cultural celebration, a return to the homeland with an all-Hawaiian crew.

No response. Did that mean the crew would not compromise, that they wanted the entire round trip to themselves? I could not tell. Their defensive silence closed in again.

The social workers tried to move the process along by getting others involved in the discussion, but with only marginal success. Finally, after they had ritually resolved a number of petty grievances, they stated the key question: "Are the Hawaiians ready to include *haoles* in the project, and are the *haoles* ready to include Hawaiians so that we have a *Hokule'a* team working together?"

Following a lengthy and strained discussion, the social workers finally won agreement from everyone, although Kimo and a few others held out for what seemed hours. Then they completed the session with a long ritual of severance, after which they advised us that the whole *ho'oponopono* process would not be finished until we completed a final ceremony ten days hence. Kawika and I, with all the crew and board members in attendance, were to wade into the sea just before sunset wearing leis made of a special variety of seaweed. At the exact moment the sun set we were to place the leis in the water to symbolize that our troubles were cast away forever.

By now it was already mid-April. Two weeks of good winds had already been lost and it would still be another two weeks before we could leave. The lei ceremony was set for the 22nd; departure from Honolulu for Maui was scheduled for Sunday the 25th.

By the 22nd the canoe was back in the water and was ready to sail except for loading water and provisions and some final alterations. For some reason we had many visitors that day, some tourists and local well-wishers but mostly friends of various crew members, including a rowdy bunch that occupied the dock and started drinking beer there. Then, to add to the confusion, a crowd of Hawaiian radicals arrived to try to enlist the crew and *Hokule'a* in their political protests. By the time the sun's rays were beginning to slant in from the west, the atmosphere was one of bedlam. Work on the canoe had ceased, and many of the crew had joined in the drinking.

Half an hour before sunset, Kawika and I and a number of other board members drove out to the beach where the final ceremony of reconciliation was to take place. The crew was to follow. They never came. We just stood on the beach watching the sun sink lower and lower, then drop quickly below the horizon. There would be no ceremony that day, or ever, to cast off our troubles. They remained with us, for the moment contained symbolically in the shiny wet seaweed leis coiled in a cardboard box.

11

Radicals and Patriots

The next day Kawika and I were summoned to Coast Guard headquarters. Coast Guard inspectors had been watching closely the rebuilding of *Hokule'a*. Satisfied with the new watertight compartments and safety equipment, they had certified the canoe as seaworthy. Our attendance was required at a press conference where the admiral would announce the certification and declare that as far as the Coast Guard was concerned, *Hokule'a* was ready to sail.

Before the assembled reporters and television cameras the silver-haired admiral proclaimed his confidence both in the canoe and in Kawika as the captain. But that was his public performance. Once the cameras were packed up and the reporters had left, he turned to Kawika. "Captain," he sternly said, "if you take *Hokule'a* to Kahoolawe I'll confiscate it, tow it to Honolulu and you'll never get it back!"

"Don't worry, I'm not going to Kahoolawe," replied a smiling Kawika. "Im taking her to Tahiti."

That brief exchange stemmed from the previous day's visit to the canoe by Hawaiian radicals. At about 2:30 that afternoon a caravan of cars drove up. Out tumbled a crowd of Hawaiians— several men, a number of distinguished-looking dowagers and a dozen or more teenagers. The new arrivals, our crew and their drinking friends merged briefly. Kisses and hugs were exchanged. Then the whole group converged toward *Hokule'a*, where first mate David Lyman and I were standing.

When I recognized the leader as the man who had given us trouble on Molokai Island, I realized they were a protest group who had flown over to Honolulu to attend the trial of one of their number who had been charged with trespassing on Kahoolawe, a small uninhabited island off the south coast of Maui that the Navy uses for bombing practice.

Kahoolawe (Kah-hoh-'oh-lah-vay) is extremely dry. Maui, lying upwind, robs the trade wind clouds of their rain, and the island is too low to cause much new condensation. Goats intro-duced in modern times and, since World War II, Navy bombs have combined to make the already desiccated island a barren, inhospitable place. The protest group had recently seized upon Kahoolawe as the symbol of *haole* violence to Hawaiians and their culture. To them, the bombing of this little island was the ultimate act of desecration of sacred Hawaiian soil by an alien people. To dramatize their protest, they had lately begun staging "invasions" of the island, which had resulted in arrests and the Honolulu trial they were now attending. Their leader made his way toward me.

"You're Ben Finney," he said as he offered his hand for a thumbs-up handshake favored by young Hawaiians. "The elders have something to say to you. They want to go to Kahoolawe before they die; to step on this Hawaiian soil before they shut their eyes." He went on to explain how he wanted *Hokule'a* to carry to Kahoolawe seven elders from Molokai, plus himself and some other leaders of the movement.

Ever since their invasions had started a few months back, I

had been half-expecting, half-dreading this encounter. Already there had been indirect inquiries about using the canoe as a ferryboat to land protesters on the island. But today's appeal was not really directed to me. The crew was the target. Soon a public address system appeared, as did a videotape camera to record the event. The show was on. First came an emotional plea, followed by Hawaiian songs and a graceful hula performed by one of the dowager Hawaiians in a long flowing gown. Then came a fiery appeal to Hawaiian patriotism that gripped the crew. It set the slight amount of Hawaiian blood in first mate David Lyman's blood racing, but above all it excited Kimo.

"Ben, the guys really want to do this," exclaimed Kimo, smiling for once. "Going to Kahoolawe will really make *Hokule'a* a Hawaiian canoe."

I was a minority of one. *Hokule'a* would be a boon to the Kahoolawe cause, especially when the Coast Guard seized it and national headlines proclaimed, "Hawaiian Bicentennial Canoe Seized Liberating Island." The funny thing was that this vision greatly appealed to me—but only after the voyage was completed. To get involved in invading Kahoolawe now would wreck the project; we would never sail for Tahiti.

When Kawika returned to the canoe his response was as unequivocal as it was immediate. "No!" he said with a resolve I had never seen in him before. "If we go to Kahoolawe the Coast Guard will confiscate *Hokule'a*, I'll lose my license and the project will end right there."

The next day was Saturday the 24th, the day before we were scheduled to sail for Maui. The mood at the canoe was especially ugly that morning. Those who had been so fired up about going to Kahoolawe felt disappointed. And a new problem was coming to a head: money. Some crewmen were angry that Kawika and David Lewis were being paid. To be sure, the two did have grants from outside sources, but so did Kimo Hugho, the leader of this protest. In addition, Kimo had also requested and received generous cash payments from the Voyaging Society, as had two of his followers, for working on the canoe since the swamping. But that did not make any difference to the protesters. They were sure that Kawika, Lewis and the rest of the "leaders" were profiting from the crew's labors, and they were demanding payment for wages lost while working on the canoe as well as for the time they would be sailing on *Hokule'a*.

A week earlier I had met with the crew to arrange distribution of the $3,000 set aside—as earlier promised—to help crewmen meet extraordinary expenses and especially to help the families of those few crewmen who were married. At that time many of the crew declined to ask for anything, or just requested a token amount. Not so Kimo and a number of others. They demanded anything from many hundreds to a few thousand dollars apiece. Their bickering broke up the meeting and prevented the allocation of what funds we did have.

I had then asked Tommy Holmes if he could try to solve the money problem. Tommy had been scarce around the canoe until a few weeks previous, when his job with the State Legislature had ended with the adjournment of that body. Since then I had given Tommy his share of jobs to do. One of his main assignments was the plants and animals we were to carry to Tahiti as a part-experiment, part-demonstration of how Polynesians were able to transport their domestic flora and fauna from island to island on their migrations. He had obtained all the necessary plant materials and had lined up special backbreeds of the Polynesian dog, pig and chicken from the Honolulu Zoo. Then, just after he went to work on the money problem, the Hawaii Humane Society struck. Alerted by a visitor to the canoe who had been shocked when she saw the small size of the animal cages we carried on board, the Humane Society sent me a three-page resolution demanding that we not carry animals. And they put pressure on the Zoo director to deny us those animals he had promised. Fortunately we already had the dog; the director withheld the pig and the chickens, forcing Tommy to start searching around the islands for zoologically appropriate replacements while he also worked on the payment issue.

Tommy had some help on the money from a Hawaiian board member who thought that if he surveyed the requests of each crewman, then added up the total, those demanding too much would realize the situation and automatically lower their demands.

He spent all week making the survey, then left it to Tommy to announce the total and work out the necessary adjustments in a day. When noon came around, Tommy opened the meeting by announcing that an extra thousand dollars had been obtained; a total of $4,000 was now available for distribution. But, Tommy added, the total of all requests stood at over $24,000. Some crewmen would have to scale down their demands. Then he read off the individual requests, exposing to public scrutiny those who had made inflated demands. Just then a self-styled radical Hawaiian sporting an Afro hairdo butted in. "Can't you divide the money up the Polynesian way?" he demanded. "Why do you impose things on people? Why don't you just give them the money!"

"We've been trying to," answered a crestfallen Tommy Holmes.

Until now Kimo had been in the background. He had arrived shortly before the meeting, carrying two large sheets of cardboard covered by a length of tapa cloth. The old relaxed, smiling Kimo was completely gone. With his newly grown black beard and the perpetually pained look he had acquired over the last half year, Kimo looked at once mysterious and worried as he stepped forward to challenge Tommy, his old friend.

At first Kimo protested the small amount of money available. Then he started arguing that we could not leave on Sunday and would not be ready to go for some time.

"That's not the Hawaiian way, placing a deadline to leave," he said, ignoring the fact that a late start threatened to make the trip to Tahiti more difficult and to force the canoe to return during the hurricane season. "It's the computer's deadline, right? The computer runs everything. I've got proof right here."

With that Kimo unveiled the sheets of cardboard on which he had pasted photographs of *Hokule'a* swamped in the Kauai channel and had carefully printed in large letters lists of all the things wrong with the canoe that prevented her departure. As Kimo started to speak, a camera team from a Honolulu television station joined the National Geographic group to film Kimo and his placards. Neither Kawika nor I had called the station. This was Kimo's press conference.

"We're not ready to go," was his central message. The

"computer" was forcing the crew to leave when they were not ready. According to Kimo's meandering speech, too many things still had to be finished on the canoe; seamanship, safety and medical training had to be conducted; above all, the crew's morale needed attention. "There's a lot of work that has to be done," he proclaimed. "*Hoʻoponoponos* are going to take months."

"That's my feelings and that's what's so," Kimo finally concluded. "Thank you very much. I've been accused of being a radical, but I think I know what the Hawaiian people deserve. They've been taken for granted." Then, pausing for effect like a veteran actor, he shouted out, "Two hundred years later, gang!"

That rhetorical flourish was designed to bring out the irony that our voyage would celebrate almost to the year another bicentennial in addition to the American revolution: the coming of Captain Cook in 1778 and the arrival of all the woes brought on by contact with the outside world. To Kimo, our project had become just another *haole* rip-off.

Kimo was maumauing us and all those who would be watching his performance on television—on the evening news and later in Dale Bell's film. I well knew one major effect his speech would have on viewers in Hawaii. It would scare off contributors, including those from whom we were just then soliciting funds for additional crew support. But I was not sure how the crew would react to Kimo's words. Would they all follow him and refuse to sail? Much depended on what Kawika now did.

Our captain calmly moved to reassert his command. "The canoe is ready," he said to the assembled crew. He then explained once more how the wind patterns made it imperative that we leave right away. The Articles, a formal contract that spelled out the duties and rights of the crew (not just "the crew" but all of us who sailed), was ready to be signed. Kawika announced in a matter-of-fact tone, "You can sign on as a crew member for the trip for those of you who want to go. For those of you who don't feel you're obligated—don't want to sign; fine, no problem."

Some signed immediately, others only after protesting. Still others like Kimo just walked away. They were the losers. "No problem," as Kawika had said. If they did not want to go, they did not have to sign up.

It was not going to be as easy as that. Many a time later we were to wish that those who refused to sign, or who signed under protest, had walked away from the canoe forever. But the next day, Sunday, the day of departure, they were back, including Kimo. They did not do much of anything except form angry little caucuses, which drew most of the other crew members as well. That left us "leaders," plus Society regulars and volunteers drawn from the huge crowd there to see us off, to finish loading.

At noon Kimo took the stage again and began agitating for a delay until Tuesday. Now his story was that the canoe really only needed minor alterations and that the crew (including those who had accepted the expense monies originally offered once they realized that was all that was available) only needed a few extra days to settle their affairs. Kimo had lost yesterday. If he could delay the sailing just a few days he would save face. Kawika, trying to be reasonable, wavered, said okay, then reversed himself, declaring, "No, we leave today at four."

That left practically everyone on the crew, even those who had willingly signed the Articles the day before, either angry or confused, or both. The sailing time may have been firm in Kawika's mind, but whether or not we could actually cast off was another question.

Both Kawika and I wished that we could have dismissed those crewmen who had been protesting and dragging their feet the last weeks. But Hawaiian self-respect, so battered by the events of the last two centuries, was at stake. If any Hawaiians were dismissed it would be a further blow, one that would not be allowed, at least not without a battle. The word had already been passed along that some of the Hawaiian board members would automatically "vote with the blood" if there was an attempt to dismiss any "brothers" from the crew.

Prudence dictated that we abort the voyage, maybe abandon the project altogether. But that would have brought dishonor to all involved. We had to go. Yet, given the mood prevailing as four o'clock approached, it began to look doubtful that it would be possible to cast off. Then a *kahuna* stepped forward.

Edward Kealanahele (Kay-ah-lah-nah-hel-lay) was his name. He was a gray-haired but otherwise boyish-looking Hawaiian in his late forties. Herb Kane and I had met him several years previously on his home island of Hawaii. He had offered his services to us, but we had seen no need for spiritual aid at the time. Subsequently I had come to know and trust him well, and had recently asked him to help us through our trials.

Now at the eleventh hour Kealanahele intervened, asking the crew to follow him to a corner of the wharf away from the canoe and the crowd. Most followed, except for Kimo and a few others. So did the camera crew, but Kealanahele immediately shooed them off. He knew how their cameras had a way of evoking protest and magnifying controversy.

"I want to see this canoe go," he said, his voice breaking and tears welling in his eyes. "The Hawaiian people are looking to you Hawaiian boys to make this trip. You have to go for yourselves, for your families, for your ancestors!"

Then he asked that each crewman give his opinion whether or not the canoe was ready to leave that afternoon. He knew better than to throw the question out for anyone to respond. Instead he turned to Sam Kalalau, a rugged cowboy from Maui in his early fifties.

"Papa Sam, you're the oldest here. What do you think? Is the canoe ready to go?"

Kealanahele chose wisely, for Sam Kalalau was one of the few crewmen who had not been caught up in the protests and foot dragging. In fact, that behavior had disgusted him to the point of quitting. But more than that, like both Kawika and Kealanahele, Sam was secure in his Hawaiian identity. As a *kuahiwi* or "back-country" Hawaiian, he was the direct antithesis of the urban Hawaiian watermen who were at the heart of our crew problem.

"Sure I think we gotta go," Sam readily replied. "We gotta leave this place. The longer we stay here, the more trouble we get."

That did it. The rest fell into line, agreeing that *Hokule'a* was ready to leave as planned. One or two of the crew lamely tried to support Kimo's case, but in the end they also admitted that the canoe should go.

By 4:30 most of us scheduled to sail to Tahiti were on board, along with some members of the return crew who would sail back from Tahiti to Hawaii. Kealanahele prayed for a safe passage to Maui. Then all on the canoe and on shore joined in a tearful rendition of "Hawaii Aloha," after which we cast off.

Kimo was with us, but not for long. After angrily muttering something to a couple of crewmen, he dramatically dove off the canoe and swam back to the wharf, leaving *Hokule'a* to those who wanted to sail.

At last! What a joy it was to pull out of Honolulu Harbor after being stuck there so many tedious months. Even those crewmen who an hour before had been milling around the wharf debating whether or not they should follow Kimo were relieved to go.

As the lights of Honolulu faded into the distance, one crew member turned to his friend and said in the local pidgin English dialect, "Suppose we no leave today. I no can go home. Shame."

12
Maui

Monday morning, after a smooth crossing, we pulled into Honolua Bay, a deep indentation in Maui's rocky western shore that would shelter us for the next six days while we completed final preparations to sail to Tahiti.

The first few days on Maui were peaceful—Kimo and the other dissenters were still in Honolulu. Once we had touched shore, most of the crewmen who had sailed over with us took refuge, as sailors will before a long voyage, in the bars of Lahaina, the old whaling port that is now a tourist haven. That left Kawika, Dave Lyman and me to work on the canoe, while Sam Kalalau and Rodo Williams, our Tahitian recruit, were busy getting fresh food for the voyage.

The absence of Kimo and other crewmen gave us a welcome respite. What is more, for once we found ourselves in a friendly and supportive atmosphere. Our Maui hosts, particularly the

Hawaiians among them, were outraged at Kimo's television performance. They declared their support for Kawika against all those who would delay the voyage or use the canoe to invade Kahoolawe. That gave Kawika a needed boost. When Kimo finally did show up Thursday evening, Kawika took him aside and dismissed him from the crew.

Kimo's dismissal came as a shock to his supporters, both on and off the canoe. An alarmed Dale Bell, aghast at the thought of all the thousands of feet of film he had already shot of Kimo and the difficulty he would have building up another crewman to star in his film, urged Kimo to make a stand. Yet Kimo took his dismissal without great protest. Had he made a stand, had he tried to mobilize all those who had been harassing us, we might never have been able to sail.

The truth was that Kimo did not want to go. Like many who enthusiastically sign up for a long voyage, when it came down to actually leaving, Kimo was not prepared to commit himself to the sea. After having been built up as the archetypical seaman of the Hawaiian cultural revival—first by Herb Kane and then by Dale Bell—how could Kimo admit, even to himself, that he did not want to go? Mau had seen this tension building for some time. To his eyes, that was behind all of Kimo's protesting and foot dragging, and then his denunciation of the canoe and the leaders at the dockside press conference.

Yet Kimo could not just quietly walk away from the canoe. On Friday morning, the morning after his dismissal, Kimo and his now distraught supporters formed a sullen caucus on the beach. The departure ceremony was scheduled for midday; we would sail the following day, Saturday, May 1. A fine misty rain was falling, a blessing rain according to Hawaiian belief. But the gray dampness it imparted to the normally sunny bay combined with the black mood of the crewmen to cast gloom over what should have been a happy occasion. Our *kahuna* ally Kealanahele, realizing that something had to be done, called a meeting on the beach.

It started out like a *ho'oponopono* session, with Kealanahele working toward a reconciliation, and mutual forgiveness, between

Kawika and Kimo. Kealanahele stated the "hurts" that had to be resolved before *Hokule'a* could sail: Kawika's anger over the unauthorized press conference and Kimo's public denunciations coupled with Kimo's chagrin at being so summarily fired by Kawika. But the meeting soon got out of hand as crewmen responded to the cameras and microphones of our built-in media representatives, the National Geographic Society film team, and started extolling Kimo and charging Kawika with having overstepped his authority.

"I think what Kimo did was out of love for the canoe and the whole crew," tearfully exclaimed Billy Richards, a young crewman who had supported all of Kimo's protests back in Honolulu. "Kimo has done so much for all of us. We're here because of Kimo. I'm here because of Kimo. You think we can go on the trip knowing that this happened to Kimo? The spirit is not going to be there. I think Kimo doesn't have to apologize for what he said. . . ."

Others joined in the attack, including Voyaging Society board members sympathetic to Kimo. Kawika could hardly get in a word edgewise about how Kimo had gone behind his back to complain before the television cameras. Kealanahele, struggling to regain control of the meeting, resorted to speaking to Kawika in Hawaiian. That shut up Kimo and the others, for they could not speak the language or understand much of what was being said.

"Will you forgive this boy? The decision is yours. Will it be yes or no?" implored Kealanahele of Kawika, trying to initiate the *ho'oponopono* process of mutual forgiveness by having Kawika be the first to apologize.

After a long dialogue between the two, all spoken in Hawaiian, Kawika finally said that he forgave Kimo and asked in turn that Kimo forgive him.

Kealanahele, switching back to English, then started working on Kimo, begging him to apologize so that the meeting could end and the departure ceremony could begin. But Kimo, maybe because he did not understand what Kawika had said in Hawaiian, reacted by starting in again on his grievances, even dragging in his disappointment over not going to Kahoolawe.

"Okay, hold it there! Hold it right there, Kimo!" interrupted

Kealanahele, after which he rephrased his plea for Kimo to apologize. "The decision is now. What's it going to be?"

"I will not be a member of the crew going to Tahiti," replied Kimo, assuming a statesmanlike manner and acting as though it were his decision and not the captain's to make. A sobbing crew member collapsed in despair at Kimo's feet, adding to his apparent grandeur.

"Okay. I still want you to apologize to the captain."

Kimo continued to resist, forcing Kealanahele to resort to asking that he merely shake Kawika's hand. After much urging, including pleas from his distraught father, Kimo finally clasped Kawika's hand in a thumbs-up grip. The encounter was over; the departure ceremony could begin.

From the beach we moved up to a grassy clearing. There Sam Ka'ai, a full-bearded Hawaiian who was our chief host on Maui, directed us to sit in a large circle. Then came the deep-throated sound of conches, echoing against the valley walls, announcing the opening of the ceremony. The first to speak, a tall and dignified Hawaiian minister, prayed that our mission be a success and asked for God's blessings. He spoke in a Hawaiian so eloquent that even those who could not understand a word listened attentively as his cadenced phrases spread over the narrow valley floor. Then Kealanahele, also speaking in Hawaiian, added his blessings, after which came a speech in Tahitian.

The speaker was Rodo Williams, the white-haired Tahitian mariner recruited to pilot us through Tahitian waters. He had a serious message to deliver to the crew about how they should act in Tahiti, and particularly that there should be no marijuana on the voyage. Since joining us two months earlier, Rodo had come to know our crewmen and had realized that they might well ignore the prohibition against taking marijuana and other drugs on the canoe.

Rodo, whose English is halting, chose to speak in Tahitian, with Professor Kenneth Emory translating. Seventy-eight-year-old Kenneth did a good job on the first part of Rodo's speech but stumbled over one word, a Hawaiian word, that he could not translate: *pakalolo*. Kenneth had learned his Hawaiian early in the century and had no idea that *pakalolo* (pah-kah-loh-loh) was the neo-Hawaiian term for marijuana.

Our crewmen of course did. Several snickered over the confusion. It was all a big joke to them. Recently marijuana use has become common in Hawaii, where the plants flourish in the rich, volcanic soil and humid conditions. It is even becoming a major export crop. Tons of "Maui Wowie," "Kona Gold" and other local varieties are surreptitiously grown and shipped to California and points east, where they bring premium prices because of their reputedly superior properties.

The serious tone was restored when Mau rose to speak. Coming from a culture where ritual was highly valued, Mau wanted to use this formal setting to tell the crew how they should behave at sea. Everyone waited anxiously to hear what our canoe master would say. He started speaking loud and clear in his native Satawalese. Mike McCoy, the former Peace Corps volunteer married to Mau's niece, had just flown in from Micronesia, and he translated Mau's forceful speech, phrase by phrase, into equally forceful English.

"I want to tell all of you how you must act on the ocean to survive. On the ocean we don't eat the same, or sleep the same or work the same as on land. Everything we do is different. On the ocean all the food, all the water, is under the control of the captain. When he says eat, we eat. When he says drink, we drink.

"Before we leave, throw away all the things that are worrying you. Leave all your problems on land.

"On the ocean you are under the control of the captain and the navigator of the canoe. Everything the captain says we follow. If you have a problem, come to me first and I will talk to the captain.

"When on the ocean we cannot see any islands. All we have to survive on are the things we bring with us. That is all I have to say. Remember, all of you, these things, and we will see that place we are going to."

Wise words for the sea, but the content and stern phrasing stunned the crew. They had always heard Mau when he was at a linguistic disadvantage trying to express himself in broken English.

Now, with Mike McCoy's help, Mau had been able to speak his mind freely.

Kimo's close disciples among the crew were also shattered that Mau had not said a word in support of their leader, but instead had chosen to admonish them to follow the captain and the rules of the sea. Mau was actually greatly relieved that Kimo was not going. While staying with Kimo and his parents in Honolulu, Mau had come to know our former crew chief well enough to realize long before the rest of us that Kimo was not prepared to make the voyage.

Following a ritual meal served to us by Sam Ka'ai, two wooden images were taken out to the canoe and lashed on tightly, one to the sternpiece on the port hull, the other to the sternpiece on the starboard hull. Then conches sounded to announce that the ceremony was over and that *Hokule'a* was free to sail.

As we broke up, someone in the crowd called the crew over and began passing out T-shirts emblazoned with the motto "Kahoolawe—Stop the Bombing." But that was all that happened. There was scuttlebutt that the Molokai protest group had been planning to descend in numbers on Honolua Bay to make one last appeal to have *Hokule'a* ferry them over to the disputed island of Kahoolawe. However, they had been warned off by a *kahuna*— not Kealanahele, another *kahuna* to whom they had gone for advice, not knowing they were petitioning Kawika's personal spiritual advisor. It was heartening to have *kahunas* helping us for once.

PART II

13
North

May 1—Departure for Tahiti

"Let go! Let go!" shouted Kawika. Only a thin line tied the canoe to the land. On shore Kealanahele strained to hold on. He could not hear us above the noise of the wind and the crowd. Some minutes before he had delivered us to the sea, blessing us one by one as we were shuttled out to *Hokule'a* in a small outrigger canoe. Now he seemed determined to hold us to the last.

The canoe wanted to go even though the sails were still furled, bunched up against the twin masts. An offshore breeze had sprung up in the normally calm bay as we assembled on board and was catching the sails, pulling folds loose and making them whip and pop. The anchor was up, the bows were pointing seaward; only the single stern line held the canoe. Finally, just as Kealanahele was about to be dragged into the sea, he let go. The canoe began to move out. The crowd on shore and lining the cliffs above cheered. We were underway at last, bound for Tahiti.

First we let out the big sail forward, then the smaller sail aft.

Kawika guided us out of the bay that had sheltered us since arriving from Honolulu. We skirted the waves curving around the headland. Then the full force of the trades hit us as we broke away from the lee of the cliffs. The canoe surged forward, her sails drawing her into the open ocean as we headed north.

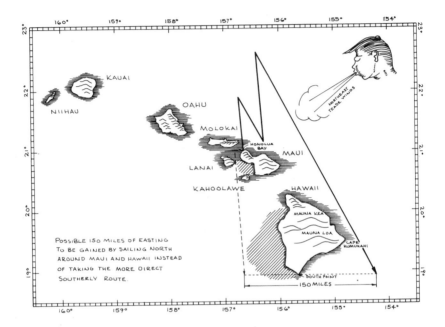

Sailing north?

A strange way to be heading for Tahiti, an island thousands of miles in the other direction! But it makes sense in terms of the central challenge of the voyage: making easting. We have to drive the canoe far enough to the east against wind and current if we are to reach the longitude of Tahiti and not end up pushed west of our target. That is why we are tacking north around Maui and Hawaii—to gain extra miles of easting before turning southward toward Tahiti.

The obvious route would have been to sail south from Maui, pass between the small islands of Kahoolawe and Lanai, and then, after sailing down the west coast of Hawaii Island, turn hard into the wind to tack southeast for Tahiti. That would have been the quickest way to quit Hawaiian waters; in a day or so of fast sailing we could have cleared South Point, the southern tip of Hawaii Island and the southernmost point in the archipelago, and have been on our way directly to Tahiti. What is more, we would have been retracing the course taken by the legendary Tahitian voyager La'a, who started his homeward journey by sailing south through the channel separating Kahoolawe and Lanai, a passage that ever since has been known as "The Way to Tahiti" (Ke-ala-i-Kahiki). But that route would have put us at a disadvantage in terms of easting.

Our way to Tahiti will take us down the windward side of Hawaii, following the route that some other early voyagers took when they sailed for Tahiti. Although this may add several days to the length of our voyage, it should pay off in terms of easting. By the time we clear South Point we should be a good 150 miles farther east of where we would have passed it had we sailed directly south from Maui.

May 2—One day out

Everyone is tired after a wet night of getting drenched by spray from the short, choppy seas. After sailing north for about nine hours, last night we came about to the port tack and headed east-southeast against the fresh northeast trades. From then till dawn we watched the lighthouse back on Molokai and the one on the northeast coast of Maui ahead of us in order to gauge how much easting we were making. To our gratification, the Molokai light gradually faded in the distance as the Maui light became brighter and brighter. By nine this morning we were getting so close to Maui that we had to go back over on the other tack and head north once again to gain enough distance from land to make it around Hawaii on the next tack to the southeast. Judging from where we were opposite the Maui coastline when we tacked, it looks like we made over twenty miles of easting in the first eighteen hours of sailing. Not bad, considering that we have been tacking against a strong coastal current. Thanks to the new sail rig installed after the swamping, the canoe is sailing far better to windward than she did on her last windward trial—the ill-fated attempt to cross the Kauai Channel.

"Bacon and eggs! Come and get it!" Kawika was joking of course. All we had this morning were selections from the Polynesian fare we are carrying: salt fish and slices of dried banana and sweet potato. These, plus a load of preserved taro, some eggs (chicken eggs in lieu of the unobtainable seabird eggs traditional voyagers carried), some fresh produce, and what fish we catch along the way, are the sole foods we are pledged—for the sake of science and the budding Hawaiian cultural renaissance—to subsist upon for the next month or so of sailing.

So far, so good with the crew. Although some are still seasick from the bouncy ride over the choppy seas, everyone is trying to work together, willingly turning to at the command to come about, or to take a turn steering or bailing. That is why it was so jarring this afternoon to discover crewman Billy Richards listening to a transistor radio—Kimo's special waterproof radio. What that radio was doing on board the canoe is a mystery. I thought we had made it clear back in Honolulu that transistor radios were taboo—because they would undermine the navigation experiment. In skilled hands a transistor radio can be used to take bearings on broadcasting stations and thus is a handy navigational aid. However, I do not think the erring crewman realized that. "I was just listening to music," Billy explained when ordered to stow the radio for the duration of the voyage.

May 3—Two days out

This morning, after tacking north for a day, we came about on the port tack to head southeast for Tahiti. No land is in sight, but we know that the huge island of Hawaii lies to the south. The hope is that if the wind keeps coming from the east-northeast, and if the current we are pushing against is not too strong, this tack will take us past the eastern cape of the island in a day or so.

Hokule'a is heavy, as heavy as she will ever be. She is weighed down by a full crew, a collection of Polynesian plants, a dog and a pig and two chickens, enough food and water for thirty days on full rations, plus all manner of gear. She now wades through the head seas instead of lightly cutting across them as she did on her last practice run out of Honolulu, sailing empty and with a clear deck. Weight cuts down the good riding qualities of double-canoes, and slows them also. Still, sailing close to the wind, *Hokule'a* is making about 5 knots.

The deck—a long, narrow platform made of wooden planks interspersed with bamboo poles and lashed to the crossbeams between the hulls—is crowded, particularly the forward two-thirds. Large burlap sacks stuffed with coconuts, taro roots, sweet potatoes and sugarcane take up much of the space. At any one time half a dozen men from the off watch will be resting or napping among the sacks, coils of line and other items on deck. But no one sunbathes, for it is too cold and wet. We are all wearing full foul weather gear—rubberized pants and jackets—for protection against the cool wind and spray that showers the canoe as we plow through the head seas.

The afterdeck is less crowded with cargo. There the men on duty are to be found. While one person steers, the others lean against the side rails of the deck, talking idly or just staring out to sea.

There are seventeen of us on board: Kawika, our captain; Dave Lyman, our first mate; Mau, the navigator; Rodo Williams, our Tahitian pilot; David Lewis, Tommy Holmes and myself as crewmen with special duties to document various aspects of the experiment; eight general crewmen, including cowboy Sam Kalalau; and two National Geographic Society representatives, one to take still photographs for the magazine, the other to film our adventure for the television special.

Conspicuously absent from the canoe is Herb Kane. Wounded by the suggestion that he not join us until we reach Tahiti (in order to give Kawika a free hand to establish his command on the way there), Kane declared that he would not sail at all. However, in a sense he is with us. In its overall conception the canoe is in large part his legacy, and Sam Kalalau is carrying with him another example of Kane's artistry: an advance copy of the richly illustrated book on the original Polynesian discovery of Hawaii that Kane was able to finish after withdrawing from Voyaging Society affairs following the swamping.

May 4—Three days out

"Four o'clock. You're on, Ben." Tommy's overly cheery voice announces that it is time for me to surrender our common air mattress and sleeping bag and stand the watch from 4 to 8 A.M. I sleepily get out of the damply warm sleeping bag and make my way aft, stepping carefully along the slippery deck and over bags of tubers and sleeping forms. It is cold and wet. We might be in the tropics, but the 15-knot trade wind blowing across the deck plus the nearly constant spray from the head seas makes it downright cold, especially at night when there is no warming sun. I still feel chilly, even wearing a jogging suit under my foul weather gear.

Those old Polynesians must have been tough. Rain capes made

of leaves plus blankets of bark cloth and matting were all they had to protect themselves against the elements. Some think that the blocky Polynesian physique, so amply endowed with muscle and fat, must have helped them withstand exposure to the wind and sea on long voyages. Probably, although I suspect that living the life of sea rovers also made them tougher in body and mind so that the discomfort we city dwellers feel was ignored or maybe not even noticed.

Take Mau, for example. Before leaving Honolulu I gave him a jogging suit with the thought that he would like to have something warm to wear under his rubberized gear. But Mau carefully packed the jogging suit with the rest of the clothes he left behind in Honolulu. And so far he only occasionally dons his foul weather gear. Mostly he wears only a pair of shorts and a T-shirt—even when the rest of us are bundled up. Thank God we did not try to go all the way in this experiment and ban the sweaters, jogging suits and all the other gear so essential to our comfort.

I am on Kawika's watch. He has divided us into two groups of six men to alternate watch duties, one under his command, the other under first mate Dave Lyman. On a yacht these groups would be known as the starboard and port watches. But, as part of his effort to teach us Hawaiian, Kawika uses the Hawaiian terms for the watches: *akea* ('ah-kay-ah) for starboard and *ama* (ah-mah) for port. These terms go way back into Polynesian prehistory, when the outrigger canoe was primary. *Ama* basically refers to the float of an outrigger canoe, which is always rigged on the left, or port, side of the hull. *'Akea* refers to the hull, which is always on the starboard, or right, side of the float.

Mau belongs to neither watch; he sets his own schedule according to navigational requirements. At their request the photographer and the cameraman have been excused from watch duties.

The night watches are four hours long, the day ones six hours, which results in a constantly shifting schedule that keeps us from having to stand watch the same time day after day, night after night. For example, this morning we went off duty at 8 A.M., and will go on again from 2 to 8 P.M. Then to start the next twenty-four-hour cycle, we go on again at midnight, off at 4 A.M., on from 8 to 2 P.M., then on again for the last watch from 8 P.M. to midnight. Then we go back on the same cycle as today's.

Unlike the dreary midnight-to-four watch, we have something to look forward to on the four-to-eight watch: sunrise and breakfast. This morning sunrise seemed late in coming, probably because of a heavy layer of trade wind clouds obscuring the horizon. But once the sun climbed above the clouds we could enjoy its drying warmth. Then came breakfast. Mau cut up a couple of *mahimahi* (mah-hee-mah-hee, as both Hawaiians and Tahitians call the glittering dorado) caught late yesterday afternoon. First we snacked on chunks of the tasty raw flesh, then feasted on fillets Mau roasted over coconut husks. Mau is proving to be much more than just our navigator. As the only genuine canoe sailor among us, he is our teacher in all things to do with living aboard the canoe, including cooking.

An attempt in Honolulu to construct an authentic Polynesian cooking box lined with sand produced a bulky monstrosity that took up so much deck space it had to be discarded. Mau then came to our rescue with the type of stove he and other Micronesian canoe sailors now use: a five-gallon kerosene tin with the sides cut and perforated for efficient combustion.

Coconut husks provide the fuel, although our navigator-cook has many other uses for the hundreds of coconuts we carry on board. To Mau and to other Pacific islanders still close to nature, the coconut is a source of drinking water, food and craft materials as well as fuel. After removing the husk and laying it aside for fuel, Mau cracks the hard inner shell with a machete, drinks the water within, then pries out chunks of the oily white meat for an energy-packed snack. Then he files the edges of each half of the shell and cleans them to make serviceable bowls for eating and drinking.

Although coconuts are plentiful in Hawaii, they are now virtually ignored. Our crewmen have never seen anything like this, and several of them have apprenticed themselves to Mau, who has put them to work husking coconuts, scooping out the meat and manufacturing a collection of bowls.

After breakfast all of us on Kawika's watch would normally have turned in to catch some sleep before we had to go on watch again at 2 P.M. But this morning we had work to do: the cluttered decks needed reordering. Cheerfully all hands turned to, organizing the sacks of coconuts, sweet potatoes, taro and sugarcane; coiling the extra lengths of line; putting flares, life rings and other safety items in the handiest places; and stowing our personal gear. Everyone seems to be in a good mood. On the eve of our departure David Lewis had proposed that the conflict between "crew" and "leaders" would be forgotten "once we face the common challenge of the sea and work together to get the canoe to Tahiti." Bucking head winds and the short, steep seas off Maui and Hawaii has certainly not been any fun. But that, plus getting our sea legs and trying to keep dry from the near constant spray, has kept everyone busy—too busy for much talk or reflection about past differences or about what lies ahead in the weeks of hard sailing it will take to reach Tahiti.

14
Rescue

Around noon, right after finishing our housekeeping chores, we heard a roaring in the distance, coming closer, fading, then coming closer again. Finally a four-engine aircraft broke through the low clouds, heading straight for us. Zoom. Right over our heads, hardly 500 feet above the masts. We recognized it as a Coast Guard C-130, a turboprop search-and-rescue aircraft. What was it doing out here?

"It's probably just a search, locate and report exercise," volunteered Dave Lyman. But the C-130 kept circling, and twenty minutes later a Coast Guard helicopter showed up. What for?

Then the *Meotai*, the big steel-hulled motor sailer that is trailing us, pulled up parallel to our course and let out its Zodiac rubber boat with two figures aboard. With difficulty the helicopter hovered directly over the towed Zodiac. A basketlike contraption was lowered to the bouncing rubber boat, then raised with someone in it. It was lowered again and someone jumped into the

Zodiac. All this was a great mystery, for we were too far away to see who was involved.

Finally we contacted the *Meotai* over the little hand-held citizens' band radio we carried.* Dale Bell had been hoisted aboard the helicopter; a substitute film maker had been lowered to replace him aboard the *Meotai.*

The film team is paying a major share of the cost of chartering the *Meotai* (their only financial contribution to the project) so that they can use it as a base for their filming operations. Dale Bell insisted on going along despite his inability to sail more than a few miles in open ocean without getting seasick. What is more, he had left with a recently broken foot bound up in a cast. Now, after three days at sea, the violently ill and hobbled film producer has requested and received medical evacuation to Honolulu.

Having the *Meotai* trail behind us is also essential to the navigation experiment. Their navigator, a Voyaging Society board member, is tracking us, fixing our position each noon so that once the voyage is over we will have an exact record of where we have sailed. Merely arriving in Tahiti will not settle the issue of the worth of noninstrument navigation methods over long distances. It might be possible to blunder to Tahiti, arriving at the island through a freak combination of navigational errors that somehow canceled each other out and put us on target. We need a day-by-day record of our course so that once the voyage is over we can sit down—wherever we land—and plot our noninstrument calculations against the actual record.

The *Meotai* has another important function. The 64-foot-long, broad-beamed ketch is our safety net, capable of rescuing the whole crew if the canoe founders. We do not want to take a

---

* Unlike regular radios that can pick up standard and shortwave broadcasts from many hundreds (and at night thousands) of miles away, and thus can be used to determine the direction of the broadcasting station, our CB radios operated on a frequency limited to line-of-sight transmission—about five to ten miles between our two vessels. Useless for radio direction-finding, they did not compromise the navigation experiment. Kawika and the others who handled the CB transmission from the canoe, and the Captain of the *Meotai* and his men, were bound by prior agreement not to discuss the canoe's position, weather data or any other information that would give us an advantage over the original voyagers.

chance on losing anyone. Nor do we want to call on the Coast Guard in an emergency. Too many experimental voyages have come to grief and have been the object of massive and expensive air-sea searches. It would be bad enough to get into trouble; worse, we thought, to have to call upon the Coast Guard to rescue us.

So much for precautions.

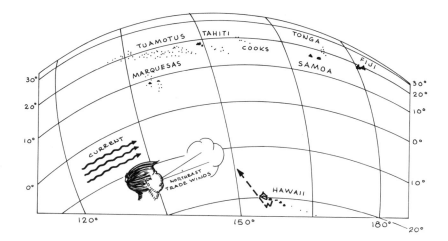

15
Southeast

May 4—Three days out (continued)

After all the excitement over the film producer's rescue died down, we spied off to starboard through a break in the clouds a mountain peak, a sharp spire with a tinge of snow showing. It looked to be Mauna Kea, the dormant one of a pair of 13,000-feet-plus volcanoes that dominate the huge island of Hawaii—although we could not be absolutely sure as the gap in the clouds closed in too quickly. Nonetheless, our dead-reckoning calculations indicated that we should be opposite Mauna Kea, or "White Mountain" to use the literal translation of the name given the peak because of the snows that often cover the summit during the winter. Thus we took the identification as positive.

This means we are pulling abeam of the island and should clear Cape Kumukahi sometime tonight. According to legend, this easternmost point in the Hawaiian chain was named after one of the first voyagers to sail up from Tahiti. Once clear of the cape we will truly be on our way back to where he, and many other legendary voyagers, had come from.

No more strikes on the three fishing lines trailing astern, so by late afternoon we reluctantly snacked on hard sticks of salted fish and the naturally sweet slices of dried banana. Not a very satisfying fare for the second, and last, meal of the day. Especially not when you are hungry for more fresh fish and are thinking about sitting down to a full-course dinner. But enough of such visions. The ancient voyagers got along on dried foods, and we are pledged to do the same.

May 5—Four days out

Darkness came quickly last night; too many horizon clouds for a lingering sunset. Around eight o'clock Lyman and his crew relieved us. I wasted no time going forward to set up the air mattress and sleeping bag on deck. I had been up since 4 A.M.; clearing the deck and then the ruckus over the Coast Guard visit had prevented any nap.

No sooner had I lain down, it seemed, than Tommy was shaking my shoulder, announcing that it was midnight and time to go back on watch. This watch from midnight to 4 A.M. is the dreariest of them all. You are at your sleepiest then, and there is usually nothing to do but stand in the chill wind and mark time till four hours pass and you can hit the sack again. But last night was different. Our vigil was rewarded by a welcome sight: the faint loom of a light sweeping over the horizon well off to starboard, the Coast Guard lighthouse indicating that we were clearing Cape Kumukahi with a good number of miles to spare.

At midday the Coast Guard plane showed up again, this time to drop a load of gamma globulin serum. We learned over the CB radio from the *Meotai* that back on Maui our host Sam Ka'ai was critically ill with hepatitis. Because he had personally prepared and served the food at our farewell feast, we were all supposed to get shots of the protective gamma globulin. It seemed a bit farfetched to us that we would come down with hepatitis in the middle of the ocean. Nonetheless, the specter of anyone con-

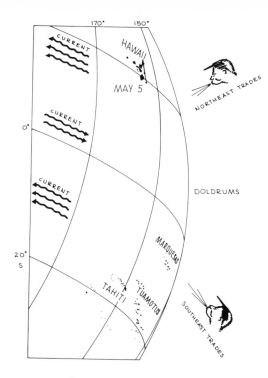

tracting this debilitating disease en route, not to mention the possibility of a total epidemic on board, made us agree to take the serum. Once the *Meotai* crewmen retrieved the air-dropped serum and brought it over to us in the Zodiac, David Lewis used his medical skills to do the honors. Dave Lyman revenged us by giving Lewis his shot.

By now, late in the afternoon at the end of this fourth day at sea, we should be pulling abeam of Hawaii Island's South Point— at least according to dead-reckoning estimates. No land is in sight. Hawaii's massive volcanoes must lie well to starboard, hidden in the haze and clouds. The strategy of tacking north around the islands has apparently paid off. We are leaving Hawaiian waters with a good measure of easting already won. Now our job is to drive the canoe southeast against the trades to gain as much easting as possible before we reach the equator.

Before us lies 2,500 miles of sea road curving to the Tuamotu Islands, coral atolls flanking Tahiti from the northeast and east. If we can reach the Tuamotus, it will be a short and easy sail from

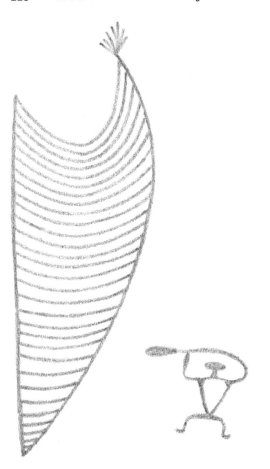

there on to Tahiti. But that means we have to make a good 800 miles of easting—400 to cancel out the miles lost to the current that will be pushing us westward an average of 20 miles each day we are in the trades, and another 400 to make it to the meridian of the Tuamotus. We have to gain most of that easting sailing southeast against the trades, or even east-southeast if the wind allows. The eastward-flowing countercurrent in the doldrums should allow us to gain some more easting. But once through the doldrums, it will be next to impossible to make any more easting. From then on the trades will be blowing more out of the southeast than the northeast, forcing us onto a course that at best will be slightly west of south. So if we have not made the required easting before then—too bad; we will end up pushed somewhere to the west of Tahiti.

A lot depends on how well *Hokuleʻa's* shallow hulls track through the ocean and resist the sideways push of the wind. Even more important is how well the new sails lift the canoe to windward. Our first set of broad, baggy sails would never have taken us to Tahiti. The tall crab-claw sails now arching high above us are our hope. A few months after the swamping, Kawika, David Lewis and I flew to Hawaii Island to visit a remote lava field. There etched into the smooth surface of the once molten lava are the outlines of elegantly curved sails, stunning works by some unknown Hawaiian sailor-artists. Our sails patterned after them look even more magnificent, silhouetted against the blue trade wind sky and tautly curved in the wind. We only hope that the ancient Hawaiians who developed this crab-claw shape were as good at aerodynamics as they were at art.

Our sailmaker, a young part-Hawaiian whose sails are in much demand among Hawaii's yacht racers, thought so. "Those old Hawaiians had something," he exclaimed after looking over the petroglyph rubbings. "They were working toward a high-aspect ratio sail hundreds of years before yachtsmen got around to it." What he meant was that the ancient Hawaiian sailmakers had developed a tall, narrow sail that, since lift is concentrated along the forward part of a sail, made for windward efficiency—a principle that has only recently come into vogue among modern designers.

There are, of course, great differences between the crab-claw sail and the tall Marconi mainsail of a modern yacht. Although both are triangular, compared to the Marconi sail the Hawaiian one is upside down, the apex of the triangle being at the foot of the sail. Furthermore, swooping curves at the head of the Hawaiian sail give it the crab-claw appearance so alien to modern sail design. Exactly why Polynesians developed the inverted triangular sail, and why Hawaiians added the distinctive upper curves that distinguish their sails from those elsewhere in Polynesia, is lost in the unwritten history of Polynesian naval architecture. Our best guess is that the old canoe masters developed this design as the way to combine island woods, coconut fiber line and matting woven from the saltwater-resistant leaves of the pandanus tree to make an efficient, durable sail.

The art of weaving long, narrow strips of sail matting, then of stitching them together to make a sail, has died out in the Pacific on all but a few remote atolls in the western Pacific. We went to considerable trouble and expense to commission weaving masters from two of those islands to make enough sail matting for a set of woven pandanus sails. But the actual fabrication of these sails from the rolls of matting shipped to us was delayed by the change in sail design after the swamping. They were not completed until just before departure, and with all the troubles we never did have a chance to try them out properly. So we are sailing with a cheap set of canvas sails originally made to be models for the mat sails. Lashed under the shelter built over the windward hull are the untried mat sails—to be tested along the way and perhaps, if they work out well, hoisted for the return trip.

We sometimes refer to the sails as the "mainsail" and the "mizzen." But these terms grate on the ear; they belong to the *haole* sailing world. Mostly, following Kawika's lead, we call them the *la mua* (lah moo-ah) and the *la hope* (lah ho-pay), Hawaiian for "foresail" and "aftsail."

Even though the sails are Hawaiian in name and shape, their master is from the tiny Micronesian atoll of Satawal, thousands of miles west of Hawaii. While Kawika has overall command of the canoe, Mau controls the sails—how the masts are raked fore and aft or canted over to one side, and how the sheets are trimmed to set the angle of the sail. This is consistent with indigenous navigational practice. In the absence of instruments so much depends on the precise control of the canoe that the navigator takes personal charge of setting and trimming the sails.

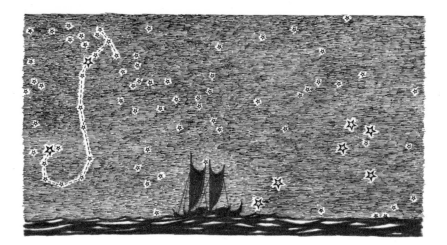

16
Sailing by the Stars

May 5—Four days out (continued)

Mau has staked out his territory on the canoe—the port, stern corner of the afterdeck where, since the sails stream out to starboard, he can feel the uninterrupted wind and enjoy a clear view of the sea and the horizon stars ahead. Mau is almost always to be found there. His round, impassive face and thick, muscled body seem as much a fixture of that part of the canoe as the buxom female image attached to the sternpiece just behind his post.

It is a rare privilege to see this master navigator at work. I have read much about noninstrument navigation and how the old Polynesian sailors employed it on their long voyages. But until now the closest I have come to seeing it applied was when sailing on Tahitian copra schooners, watching consummate island seamen combine parts of two navigational systems: using compass and charts, but also relying on noninstrument observations of wind, sea and stars to sail unerringly from island to island.

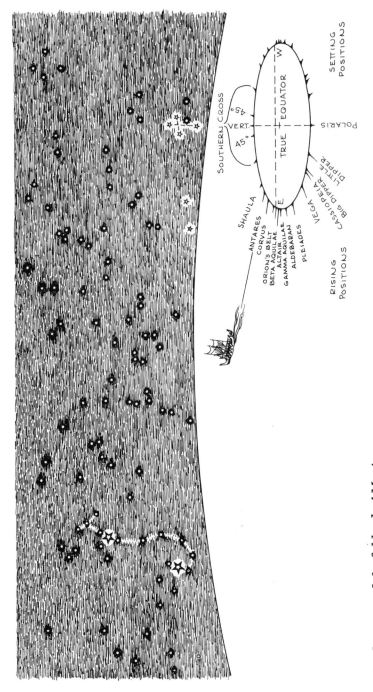

Heading toward the fishhook of Maui

Mau sets course by the stars. He carries a star compass inside his head. Where the navigational stars that form the points on his compass tip the eastern horizon upon rising and the western horizon upon setting mark the points of a star compass that is further defined by Polaris in the north and the Southern Cross in the south. The particular point on the eastern horizon toward which Mau is now aiming the canoe is where the star Tumur rises. Tumur is Satawalese for Antares, a red giant of a star 285 times larger than our sun. Its reddish glow dominates Scorpius, the constellation Polynesians call the "Fishhook of Maui," after the demigod who fished up islands out of the sea, including the one that bears his name. Antares bears east-southeast. Mau wants to keep *Hokule'a* pointed directly at its rising point so that the resultant course allowing for leeway and current will be to the southeast.

The exact angle of the wind is crucial, and it is already apparent that the wind is not cooperating. Using Mau's star compass, we can see that instead of blowing from the northeast (or north-northeast as we had wildly dreamed), it is coming mostly from the east-northeast. That prevents us from always holding the canoe pointed as high as Antares. Much of the time we are heading for the next star compass point over from Antares —the rising point of Shaula, the bright star at the end of the Scorpion's stinger, or the point on Maui's fishhook. The resultant course with leeway and current figured in often looks to be more toward the south-southeast than straight southeast. But that is not too bad. We are still making easting, just not as much as we would like.

Antares is of course not always conveniently on the horizon when Mau wants to make a star sight. It does not rise until an hour or so after dark, and toward midnight it is already too high in the sky to give an accurate bearing. But Mau is not stymied when Antares is not in the right position. He knows the sky well enough after three decades of practice to tell at a glance where Antares should cut the horizon. He can look, for example, to those stars that have the same general declination as Antares but rise before or after it. To use the Polynesian terminology, he sights on those stars that rise out of the same *pit* on the horizon and follow the same arching path across the heavens. Even if a star is several degrees to the right or left of Antares' *path*, it makes no difference; he can easily make the necessary mental adjustment.

Should the horizon be so cloudy that no horizon stars are to be seen, Mau can still get his bearings by sighting on whatever stars are visible. A glance at Polaris, or the Southern Cross (he divides

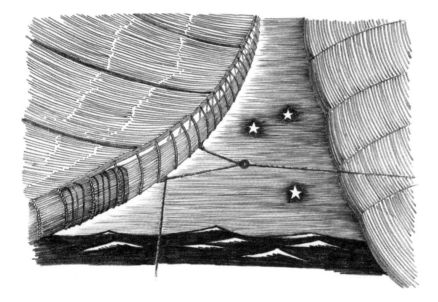

its rotation around the South Celestial Pole into five separate star compass points) or any number of other stars and constellations in his repertoire is sufficient. Mau knows the shape of the sky so well that he has only to see the smallest portion to find his way.

It is said you can spot a traditional island navigator by his bloodshot eyes. Mau looks the part. He seldom sleeps. Most of the time he stands leaning on the deck railing, or sits perched atop it, checking the sea, the sails and at night the stars. When he does sleep he takes only brief naps lying on the bare deck, huddled against a sack of coconuts. He has to stay awake as much as he can to monitor our speed and heading, as well as keep track of the force and direction of the wind and the swell pattern.

When the sky is totally overcast and the moon is either below the horizon or too high up to be useful, Mau looks to the trade winds and the ocean swells for orientation. During the day he uses these same cues, as well as the bearing of the rising or setting sun, to get his bearings.

This is not for the amateur. However steady the trade winds might be by reputation, in fact they periodically shift at least a few degrees to one side or the other. Mau watches for these shifts by constantly checking wind direction against the swells. The dominant trade wind swells striking the canoe are steadier in direction than the local winds; they have been generated by trades blowing over thousands of miles of ocean stretching to the northeast and are not affected by the daily shifts in wind direction we experience. Reading the swells is an art. Most of us amateurs aboard the canoe can make out the main trade wind swell and also see that it interacts with a number of other swells coming from different directions. But we cannot really separate out each swell and form a coherent picture of all the swell patterns. Mau can. Although not at all given to showing off, today he took the trouble to point out to us how five separate swells, each with a different direction, strength and period, were striking the canoe.

Day steering by the sun is also tricky. Because the rising and setting points of the sun shift markedly each day as we move from the northern hemisphere late spring toward the winter of the southern hemisphere, Mau has to recalibrate his solar orientation daily by checking each dawn and dusk to see where the sun has risen or set along the points of his star compass. That feat, plus his ability to use the sun as a directional guide even when it is high in the sky, comes naturally to Mau, although not to the rest of us.

Mau's ability in solar navigation is even a little unusual on his home island. He learned to navigate before the magnetic compass was introduced to Satawal. Although all Satawal navigators steer by the stars at night, those navigators who learned their craft after Mau rely on the compass for daytime steering rather than trying to keep track of the sun. Thus when those few masters senior to Mau are gone, he will be the last of the truly traditional navigators of Satawal.

Orientation and course setting are only part of Mau's navigational repertoire. To keep track of where we are at any given time, as opposed to the direction in which we are heading, calls for other skills.

A modern navigator uses a sextant to measure the angle of the sun and stars, a chronometer to give him the exact time, and star tables and other aids to enable him to use this information to compute his exact position in terms of latitude and longitude. Or he may use one of several electronic systems depending on radio beams from land transmitters or navigational satellites to fix his position. There is no way Mau can determine our position in terms of latitude and longitude coordinates. Indeed, although he is acquainted with the concept of coordinates, the idea of fixing his position in terms of so many degrees of latitude above or below the equator and of longitude east or west of the meridian of Greenwich, England, is totally alien to his navigational system.

Mau's way of keeping track of our position is solely a dead-reckoning one that depends on exquisitely precise judgments of speed and course made good. Estimates of speed and course made good are the building blocks of any dead-reckoning system. All but the most electronic of modern navigators still keep close track of course and speed between position fixes (with the aid of a magnetic compass and a log to record distance covered). It is the way Mau uses this information to conceptualize our progress that is so unusual.

In his home waters Mau plots his progress line in relation to the movements of a "reference island." First he picks an island well out of sight that lies to one side of the course, between his canoe and the rising and setting points of familiar horizon stars. Then, as he sails toward his destination, he imagines that it is the reference island, not his canoe, that moves. As the island "moves" from the bearing of one horizon star to another, this marks the completion of a predetermined segment of the voyage. Once the island has "moved" past all the preselected horizon stars, all the segments have been traversed. If the navigation has been accurately performed, the destination should therefore be in sight. Of course, Mau knows full well that it is his canoe, not the reference island, that moves. This mental plotting system is simply an ingenious conceptual device to relate his estimates of speed and course made good to a series of horizon stars in order to break the voyage into manageable segments for keeping track of progress en route.

This is why Mau's attempt to apply reference-island plotting to our voyage seems like such an impossible task. In his home waters, trips between closely spaced atolls average under 100 miles. Using five or six horizon stars for plotting, this means segments 10 to 20 miles long. Not only is our voyage much longer than those Mau is used to, but there are few islands parallel to our course that can be used as reference islands. Mau is thus forced to choose not single islands but whole archipelagoes parallel to, but some distance from, the course line. For this first leg from Hawaii to the doldrums, he says he is employing the Marshall Islands, a Micronesian archipelago lying 2,000 miles west of the course line. Using five horizon stars for plotting this means segments averaging over 200 miles in length. Yet Mau is confident that he can keep track of the segments. After traversing the fifth one we will be at the doldrums, he says. Once out of the doldrums he will be using a second archipelago, the Marquesas, hundreds of miles to the east of the course line from the doldrums to Tahiti, to plot our progress for that portion of the voyage.

David Lewis follows a Western system of dead reckoning. Like Mau he estimates our speed (Lewis mentally times bubbles moving down the length of the canoe while Mau just looks at the sea rushing past) and course made good. But instead of using reference islands and horizon stars to break the trip into conceptual segments, Lewis attempts to transfer his mental estimate of our progress into latitude-longitude fixes. Each noon he estimates where we are in terms of so many degrees and minutes north of the equator and west of Greenwich.

The height of Polaris, the North Star, above the horizon gives Lewis a fairly accurate measure of latitude. Its angle with the horizon corresponds almost exactly to the observer's latitude. Thus at Honolulu, which lies slightly over 21 degrees north of the equator, Polaris stands a little over 21 degrees above the horizon. Through his years of sailing Lewis has learned to judge the angle of a star, without using any instrument whatsoever, with a fair measure of accuracy. Particularly with Polaris low on the horizon he has no hesitancy about calling its position to within half a degree.

But Lewis has no way to judge longitude from the stars. That requires a chronometer or complicated electronic gear. All he can do is keep track of our heading, then estimate how much leeway and current set deflects us to the west to come up with an idea of how much easting we are making. The most critical variable in his calculations is the current. Lewis has no way to tell by direct observation how strong it is flowing westwards. Thus he readily admits that his longitude figures, unlike those for latitude, contain a large element of guesswork.

Actually, there seems little need for Lewis to calculate our position each noon so painstakingly, unless he anticipates that the *Meotai* will lose track of us during a storm or on some dark night. His primary task is to document, step by step, exactly how Mau is guiding the canoe to Tahiti.

Mau's navigation of *Hokule'a* is an experiment within an experiment. Can a noninstrument navigator use skills adapted for navigation between closely spaced atolls in a corner of the western Pacific to guide a strange canoe over thousands of miles of unfamiliar eastern Pacific waters? We thought so when we recruited Mau—providing he could learn a good portion of what an ancient Polynesian navigator would have known about the route between Tahiti and Hawaii, and especially about the pattern of prevailing winds and currents.

Imagine a Tahitian navigator many centuries ago who has sailed up to Hawaii, following traditional navigational instructions. He would certainly know his way home, both from his teachings and from his own experience of sailing from Tahiti. In comparison, Mau is at a great disadvantage, neither knowing the traditional sailing instructions nor having had the personal experience of sailing the route before. That is why we have tried to provide Mau with the same sort of information—gleaned from maps, star charts, oceanographic reports and interviews with yachtsmen—that a traditional navigator would have carried in his head.

The plan was for Lewis to work closely with Mau, tutoring him in the pattern of islands, winds and currents along the route and helping him to calculate the various star bearings to be used at each stage of the voyage, including alternates for various wind and current conditions. We knew that Lewis's tutelage could not entirely substitute for Mau's lack of personal experience in eastern Pacific waters, particularly since Lewis had never sailed over the route and therefore could not speak with firsthand knowledge. However, we did have use of the planetarium at Honolulu's Bishop Museum to help bridge the experience gap. By setting the planetarium projector for the desired dates and positions, we could simulate the night skies along the projected route to give Mau a feel for how the appearance of the skies would change as we sailed from the Northern to the Southern Hemisphere.

Unfortunately this procedure did not work out as well as planned. Lewis and Mau never did become fast friends and confidants. Although they seemed to hit it off at first, tension soon developed between them. Mutual friends attributed this to professional rivalry, pointing out that Mau could not readily accept tutelage from a man who was not as expert a navigator as he, yet who had published a book on noninstrument navigation (based, to make matters worse, partly on the testimony of navigators from a rival island). The situation was even more complicated than that. The way Lewis approached the task, plus all the troubles that developed in Honolulu before departure, contributed to their estrangement.

By nature Lewis is a lone voyager, a man who enjoys sailing alone in a small boat, pitting himself against formidable natural obstacles—as witness his near-fatal attempt to sail singlehandedly around Antarctica in 1974–75, when his tiny yacht was rolled over twice by 60-foot-high seas. Nonetheless, when we were planning the project Lewis was enthusiastic about the prospect of working with a large group and of having the opportunity to supervise the navigational experiment. But soon after I brought him to Honolulu in late 1975, Lewis virtually retreated into his study, an East-West Center office provided him as part of his fellowship. Although asked to help us rebuild *Hokule'a* and prepare her for the voyage as well as work with Mau, he begged off working on the canoe, pleading that he was too busy preparing for the navigation experiment and that he was no good with his hands.

The newly picked crew were quick to seize upon his apparent reluctance to join in the work, plus the tension between him and Mau, to make Lewis another object of their scorn. To them he epitomized the *haole* ripping off the islanders, getting a generous fellowship yet to their eyes doing little for it. I tried to head this off by having Lewis work with the crew on navigation and agree to participate in the preparation of a post-voyage volume of research findings to be jointly authored by a number of project participants, including leading crewmen. But by then the situation was already too far gone. The crew (or at least a vocal segment of it) really did not want to have anything to do with Lewis, and he in turn thought it an unprofessional waste of time to work with those who knew little about navigation. All this served to further aggravate crew-leader conflict and to make Lewis withdraw more unto himself.

During those last months before departure we seldom saw Lewis down at the canoe. Communication between him and Mau was minimal. It took Mau's nephew-in-law, Mike McCoy, to get the two talking—although that did not happen until three days before leaving Maui! Mike, who had flown in from Micronesia to see us off, had been shocked to learn upon arrival that, as he said with only a little exaggeration, "Lewis has never sat down and talked with Mau!" Mike then virtually forced them to get together to confer on the navigational plan.

Over the last few days Mau and Lewis have developed a formal routine of daily consultation. Usually around noon Lewis comes aft to confer with Mau on the course and to discuss other navigational matters. But the brevity of their meetings underlines the lack of any real warmth between them. Mau seems lonely. He seems to need to talk with someone with whom he would be more at ease, ideally someone who can tell him from personal experience about the route and the winds and the currents ahead.

We have just the man aboard.

17
No Problem

May 5—Four days out (continued)

"No problem." Rodo Williams, our white-haired Tahitian mariner, used that expression so often during the last months in Honolulu.

"How's it today, Rodo?"

"No problem."

"The sails aren't ready yet. We can't go sailing today."

"No problem."

And so on. For practically any situation Rodo had those words ready. They translate a common Tahitian expression that means, in effect, "Take it easy, don't worry, everything will be okay." During that troubled time before leaving, Rodo had taken to pronouncing the English version much more frequently than I have ever heard the original used in Tahiti. With his "no problem" approach, Rodo was deliberately trying to calm those who were becoming more and more upset as the time for departure neared.

Hawaiians also have an expression that carries the same reassuring message as the Tahitian one. Kawika often used to say "no problem," "no trouble," or the Hawaiian equivalent, when we were working to get the canoe ready. But I cannot remember any of the young crewmen following his lead. In fact, Kimo, after detailing all our "problems" during his dockside press conference, then denouncing what to him was an unforgivably casual attitude toward them, ended his tirade by saying, "That's the biggest word around here—no problem, no problem!"

Rodo is our old man of the sea. Countless voyages made around the South Pacific over the last thirty-five years—in fishing boats, trading schooners, yachts and even the warships of Free France—have lined and weathered his craggy face. One harrowing experience twenty years ago turned his hair snow white. That was when he spent the night swimming for his life, and that of a nine-year-old girl clinging to his back, after a giant wave capsized his boat and threw them into the sea. But Rodo is also a cheerful, jaunty man by nature. After skippering a yacht up from Tahiti last year, Rodo quickly became a favorite around the local yacht club, the man you had to have out fishing with you, or over to your house to help prepare a Tahitian feast. His popularity was evident when, upon pulling out of Honolulu Harbor, we were greeted by scores of yachts that had sailed out to see us off. It was Rodo, not anyone from Hawaii, that the yachtsmen hailed and wished a good voyage.

Rodo is my confidant, the only one aboard the canoe to whom I can easily turn for counsel, or just to share a joke or a random thought. We have a common bond: Tahitian, a language I learned during several years' residence on Tahiti and neighboring islands doing research for my doctoral dissertation. We both enjoy leaning back against the deck railing, chatting away in Tahitian, talking about fishing, Tahiti or just about anything to get our minds off the problems of the long voyage ahead.

"You have forgotten meeting me in Tahiti, haven't you?" Rodo asked me a few days out of Maui. I had to admit that although when he first arrived in Honolulu his face seemed familiar, I could not really remember meeting him in Tahiti. Rodo grinned.

"You paddled with Manu Ura, my canoe club. That is one of the reasons I decided to go with you."

Then I remembered. When starting my Tahitian research in 1961, I ambitiously joined the Manu Ura canoe racing club and paddled in one of their sixteen-men double-canoes at the Bastille Day races. Rodo was one of the club sponsors, and his son Michel had been one of my teammates.

Rodo joined our project several months back upon receiving an East-West Center fellowship. Although he set to work on a number of special projects such as making a collection of fishing lures out of pearl shell, bone and dog hair following traditional Tahitian models, Rodo's main task was to prepare for his job of piloting us through the Tuamotu Islands. This involved mentally reviewing all the many fishing and trading voyages he had made through this labyrinth of low atolls and studying available charts, to engrave upon his mind the exact location of the islands and the wind and currents that swirl through them.

Rodo had been born two generations too late to have practiced traditional, noninstrument navigation. Fifty years ago, when he was doing archaeological research in Tahiti, Kenneth Emory had seen the tail end of this old navigation tradition. In those days the Tuamotuans used to sail to Tahiti in small cutters and schooners loaded down with copra (dried coconut meat), which they were bringing to sell in order to buy cloth, soap and other trade goods. It was a rare captain who had a compass or any other navigation instruments then. To clear port authorities, however, they had to stand inspection by the French authorities. So, as Kenneth told us in class one day, just prior to leaving for home the captains would rent compass, charts and other required gear from obliging Chinese merchants—and promptly return them once the inspection was over. Then they would set sail for the Tuamotus, with only the stars to guide them.

Rodo stems from a Tuamotu seafaring family originally from Katiu, a small atoll 300 miles east of Tahiti. There for generations his forebears were renowned seafarers, and there also an American sailor named Williams married into the family, which adopted his name. Rodo's grandfather was the last traditional navigator of the clan, and was a famous trading schooner captain to boot. In the 1930s he had tried to teach his young grandson how to navigate by the stars the old way, but a teenage Rodo could muster no interest in what seemed a hopelessly antique knowledge out of a primitive past. However, when Rodo later went to sea, he did learn how to navigate in the quasi-modern way then employed by a newer generation of island sailors, a way that involved use of compass and charts but relied heavily on finely honed skills of judging current and wind, and their effect on a boat's course and speed.

Upon leaving Maui, Rodo had settled down for a long trip. His main job would not come until we neared the Tuamotus, so he thought he could relax, stand his watches and fish a bit until we were well below the equator. Mau fascinated him; as we sailed along Rodo began watching our navigator at work. At first Rodo's interest was casual, something to satisfy his curiosity and perhaps make up for his having spurned his grandfather's tutelage forty years earlier. However, since we started tracking southeast against the trades, Rodo's interest in Mau has intensified and become more serious.

Rodo now realizes that he has to understand how Mau navigates if the two are to cooperate in guiding *Hokule'a* past islands and reefs that lie along the way to Tahiti. More to the point, Rodo has discovered what a tremendous handicap Mau is operating under because of his lack of firsthand knowledge of the sea road ahead. When Rodo raised this concern with me today he was all business. Gone was his "no problem" approach.

"Mau is troubled," Rodo exclaimed worriedly. "He does not know the way!"

Rodo may be given to dramatics, but Mau truly is at a great disadvantage. Evidently he has not learned enough from his brief sessions with Lewis to be as confident as he should about the exact configuration of the islands ahead and of the shifting pattern of winds and currents along the route.

"Can you help him?" I asked Rodo. "He likes you and trusts you. You have already sailed this route, and you know all the islands around Tahiti. You talk to him and tell him what is ahead."

Rodo agreed and said he would start tomorrow.

May 6—Five days out

This morning Rodo approached me with a cheery "no problem," followed by a startling, "I have a map. I can use it to show Mau the way." Then he pulled out a National Geographic map of the Pacific. Rodo had forgotten that maps were forbidden on the voyage, as apparently had the magazine photographer who so carelessly brought this one along.

"Rodo," I said upon recovering from my surprise. "Maps are taboo on this voyage."

With that I took the map from his hands and threw it backwards over my head so that the wind would catch it and carry it astern. Now it was Rodo's turn to be startled. He stared disbelieving as the map twisted and turned in the wind and then plopped down in our wake, wondering what in the world had gotten into his friend. I explained that because of the navigation experiment we could not carry maps aboard. "You don't need a map anyway," I added. "You know the islands. You can just tell Mau about them."

Later in the day I spied the two together at the stern rail. Rodo was sketching—much as one would scratch out a pattern on the sand—a crude diagram showing the relative positions of Hawaii, the Marquesas, the Tuamotus and Tahiti, and the way the winds and currents shifted as you move south. As I approached more closely, Rodo began telling Mau that south of the doldrums the wind would shift around so that it came from the southeast instead of the northeast as now, forcing us on a course that could take us to the west of Tahiti. Mau, who is used to a southwesterly wind shift immediately below the doldrums in his home waters, was skeptical.

"How you know? You got key to wind?" he asked Rodo challengingly.

Rodo smiled and replied that he had made the trip once before and had seen the wind shift with his own eyes. Mau then asked if Lewis had made the trip, and Rodo replied that Lewis had only read about it in books. Mau chuckled and said, still with a note of skepticism in his voice, "Okay. I follow you."

18
A Little Night Music

May 6—Five days out (continued)

Now that we have left Hawaiian waters and started on the long tack southeast to the doldrums we feel more relaxed. During the day we play cards, read or just talk. Rodo tells some amazing tales, like the one about the time he sailed with a gang of men to an uninhabited atoll to harvest coconuts and make copra—only to be faced with a mutiny fomented by a hired hand who declared himself to be a *kahuna* possessed with knowledge of where Spanish pirates had buried treasure on the island.

Even quiet Sam Kalalau, the cowboy from Maui, will open up if encouraged. Unfortunately for me and my watch mates, Sam is on Lyman's watch, although at times I have stayed up to hear him spinning tales of his days as a Marine fighting Japanese troops in the jungles of the Solomon Islands in World War II, or expounding on the fine points of cock fighting, one of his current pastimes.

Playing with the animals also helps pass the time of day. Hoku (hoh-koo, star), our little Hawaiian dog that is sub-Fox

Terrier in size, has her sea legs now—although we still keep her on a leash for fear she will slip off the deck into the sea. She is a shy creature, a result of an effort by the Honolulu Zoo to breed back to the type of dog that Hawaiians once kept for food. In a way Maxwell, our lively pig, is more fun. He will eat anything we give him, and more—even his cage. However, from the point of view of authenticity, he is entirely inappropriate. We had a small black Polynesian pig and a pair of gorgeously plumed Polynesian jungle fowl set aside for us at the Zoo—until the Humane Society intervened the week before we left Honolulu. Tommy then managed to get fairly appropriate replacements from Kauai, only to lose them when the aircraft transporting them to Honolulu slewed off the grass airstrip and crashed into the brush, allowing the animals to escape. In desperation, Tommy grabbed what animals he could find: a pair of mottled gray domestic chickens and an outrageously *haole* pig, complete with white hair and pink skin.

At night there is not much to do except trade off steering, watch the stars and chat—while trying to stay awake till the change of the watch. The early evenings are nice. Everyone is on deck then, feeling satisfied after eating the second, and last, meal of the day, and enjoying the thought that one more day's sailing is over, putting us one day closer to Tahiti. That is when Kawika and two crewmen have lately taken to holding impromptu concerts, strumming their guitars and ukuleles and singing Hawaiian songs.

The two crewmen, William "Billy" Richards and George "Boogie" Kalama, are at their best when performing. Billy, a handsome young part-Hawaiian with black, shoulder-length hair, comes from a musical family—his mother has a hula troupe—and is equally adept on the guitar with Hawaiian and *haole* tunes. Back at Honolulu Harbor, Billy, who was paid to work on the canoe as a boatbuilder's helper, used to entertain the others down at the canoe with his guitar and pleasant singing voice. But he had never been content just to do his job, play music and enjoy his popularity. Billy, a part-time community college student before

Kimo pushed him forward as an ideal crewman, was definitely Kimo's man, his foremost protégé in all the protesting and foot dragging before departure. It was Billy, for example, who had so vigorously championed Kimo at that last confrontation on the beach at Maui just before the departure ceremony.

Boogie is a big, heavy Hawaiian—a good-looking man despite his bulk—whose lively face, set off by large dark eyes and wavy

Boogie steering

black hair, can look impishly jolly one moment, devilishly malevolent the next. Although nominated to the crew by Kimo, Boogie was not in his inner circle. In fact, we hardly ever saw Boogie down at the canoe those last months when there was so much work to be done. And, when he did show up, his major contribution was in providing entertainment—cracking jokes and expertly picking his guitar in the distinctly Hawaiian slack-key style. That is why he is sailing with us now—as a morale builder by popular demand of the crew. Boogie was slated to sail back on the return trip, not this one, and was only put on the crew list at the last minute to replace Kimo. Although we did not need an extra hand, certainly not so heavy a one, Kawika had wanted to placate those crewmen disgruntled over Kimo's firing by acceding to their demands to have Boogie come along to keep up their spirits.

Kawika is painfully aware that he does not command the respect of the crew—especially Billy and Boogie, whose sometimes cutting remarks reveal the depth of their hostility. That is why he is so delighted that the three can sit down in the evening and play music together. Their evening concerts are rare moments of unity—for the three of them and for all the rest of us who enjoy listening—giving Kawika hope that conflict will stay in the background for the rest of the voyage.

Kawika and the two crewmen can play together in harmony but they have different musical tastes. Billy and Boogie delight in playing modern songs, some of which are not in Kawika's repertoire. The lyrics of one of these are telling. "Waimanalo Blues" is a plaintive song of protest that sums up what many Hawaiians think about modern change. Its English lyrics express the feelings of a Hawaiian youth from the suburban Hawaiian community of Waimanalo against tourism, high rises and all the other developments seen by young Hawaiians as ruining their islands and their lifestyle.

Kawika, too, has his favorites, mostly older Hawaiian songs except for one entitled simply "Waʻa Hokuleʻa" ("Canoe Hokuleʻa"). It was composed to honor the canoe, and Kawika, on the occasion of his appearance on Hawaii's only Hawaiian-language radio program to explain the canoe project. Although newly composed, the song sounds old-fashioned. Kawika says it reminds him of the songs he used to hear when he was growing up on remote Niihau Island—which makes sense because one of the musicians who composed the music is his cousin from Niihau. The man who wrote the lyrics, and the host on the radio program, is a colleague of mine at the University, a young part-Hawaiian poet and language professor. Kawika often plays "Waʻa Hokuleʻa" on his ukulele, singing the Hawaiian lyrics in his rich baritone voice.

'Ua 'ike maka makou	We have seen for ourselves
Ia Hokule'a	Hokule'a
Wa'a kaulua nani	The beautiful double-canoe
Mehe manu i ka holo kai	Like a bird sailing at sea
Ua poho na pe'a	The sails billow out
I ke aheahe makani	In the fair winds
Ho'okele ia a kupono	Steered on course
I ka hoe a na akamai	By the expert paddlers
I ke ala o Kahiki	On the way to Tahiti
Ka holo Hokule'a	The Hokule'a sails
Na hoku o na lani	The stars of the heavens
Kou kia'i alaka'i	Guide you on course
Ho'okahi no kia'i	There is only one guardian
Nana no e malama	He will take care of you
Ma loko no o kona mana	Within his power
Na holokai Hawai'i	Are the sailors of Hawaii
Puana 'ia mai	This is our song
Wa'a Hokule'a	For the Hokule'a canoe
'O makou pu me 'oe	We will be with you
I ka holo a ho'i mai	On your trip to and from Tahiti*

_____

19
Weather Helm

May 7—Six days out

Last night 25-knot gusts made it almost impossible to keep the canoe on course. Sometimes more than one of us had to man the steering sweep to hold it deep enough in the water to keep the canoe off the wind. *Hokule'a* is designed to have a slight weather helm—to have a natural tendency to round up into the wind, which must be counteracted by the steering sweep to keep her sailing straight to windward. In the last day or so the weather helm has been getting fierce; at times last night three of us had to wrestle the big 18-foot-long sweep.

Whenever we lost control the bow would quickly round up into the wind. Then, as the angle of the sails to the wind became too acute, the sails would collapse into a chaos of wildly flapping canvas, and the canoe would slow and then stop dead in the water.

It took everyone on watch to get her moving again by rowing the stern around and backwinding the foresail. These unwanted maneuvers are hard on the sails and the booms, and make us lose precious miles of easting.

This morning crewman Douglas "Dukie" Kuahulu was particularly worried over the increased weather helm and what our manhandling might be doing to the steering rig, his pride and joy. When *Hokule'a* first sailed we tried to control her with steering paddles held (but not lashed) perpendicularly against the side of the hull in the same manner outrigger canoes are steered. That worked fine in light airs. But in heavy weather the strain of keeping the big canoe off the wind snapped paddle after paddle, and passing swells had a nasty habit of wrenching the paddle from the steersman's grip. Although I had earlier developed a lashed steering sweep for *Nalehia* based on old drawings, our young and proud watermen sailing *Hokule'a* considered it a clumsy crutch and went on wrestling loose steering paddles—and getting their fingers mashed and their heads bashed by the flailing paddle handles for their trouble. It took paunchy, gray-haired Dukie, a senior "beach captain" at Waikiki who earns his living steering tourist-laden canoes down the waves, to make the change. Apparently not at all worried about his muscular image as a steersman, Dukie stepped in after the swamping and developed our present rig, which consists of the long steering sweep mounted between the afterdeck and the port hull,* lashed loosely to a crossbeam so that it can be easily manipulated but cannot break loose.

By light of day we could see what the strain was doing to the steering gear. The shaft of the sweep, made from the trunk of a young ironwood tree, was taking on an alarming bend. The wood where the sweep was lashed to the crossbeam to give it a fixed fulcrum point was beginning to split under the pressure. While Dukie worked to patch up the damage, we started surveying the canoe to see what could be throwing the steering so far off.

---

* This applies when on the port tack. When on the other tack, the port sweep is secured on deck and the starboard sweep goes into action.

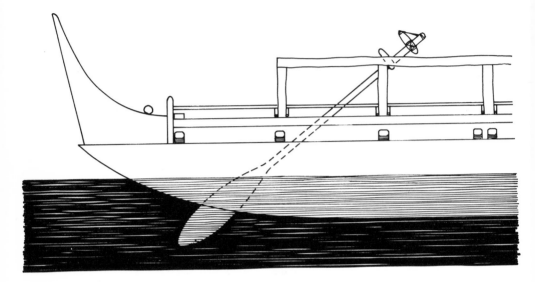

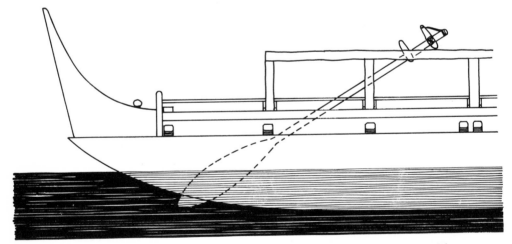

Steering sweep positions

Somehow the balance between the sails and the hulls must have been thrown out of kilter. Designing the canoe to have a slight weather helm meant locating the sails so that the geometrical center of wind force pushing against them was slightly aft of the center of resistance of the hulls to leeway movement caused by the wind push. Over the last day or so, we theorize, these points have become widely separated, either because the sails have shifted aft or the weight distribution has changed, forcing the bows deeper into the water and elevating the sterns. That is why we had to shove the steering sweep (which works on a principle entirely different from a rudder) so deep into the water: to change the underwater profile of the hulls enough to shift their center of resistance aft and thus bring the forces acting on the sails and the hulls into line.

To remedy this we first tried shifting food sacks and other items aft to lighten the bow and weigh down the stern. Then we tried raking the masts forward. Each helped a little, but even together they were not enough to take all of the heavy weather helm out. Finally Dave Lyman hit on the true cause of the heavy weather helm: water pent up in the closed compartments at the head of each hull was weighing down the bows, changing the underwater profile of the hulls to make them pivot strongly into the wind.

Once Lyman figured that out, he and a crewman grabbed a brace and bit, went forward and drilled through the plywood bulkheads separating the bow compartments from the next compartments aft (which, unlike the sealed bow compartments, could be entered through a hatch). Upon drilling through they hit a gusher, first in one hull and then the other. Water from head seas had been slowly leaking through where the lashing lines penetrated the bow compartments and had apparently built up when the small drain holes at the base of the bulkheads became clogged.

Now that the bow compartments have been drained, and the water bailed out, the lightened bows are riding over the oncoming swells instead of ponderously plowing through them. With everything back in balance, it has once more become an enjoyable, one-man job to handle the sweep and keep the canoe on course.

20
Andrew Sharp Nights

May 8—One week out

Last night was very cloudy, like the previous two or three nights, with a high overcast almost totally blanketing the sky. The horizon ahead was opaque to any navigational stars, and only occasionally did a star peep through the overcast elsewhere in the heavens. I have dubbed these cloudy nights "Andrew Sharp nights" after that arch critic of Polynesian voyaging and navigation. Maybe Sharp was not so far off when he claimed that the ancient navigators would be socked in night after night. I had always put this down to his prejudice, and to the fact that he was used to the cloudy skies of his native New Zealand rather than the fabled clear skies of tropical Polynesia. But now I have to admit that so far we have had more cloudy than clear weather, and that good star nights have lately been few and far between.

This has not stopped Mau. With no horizon stars visible ahead or astern, he can still orient himself by any stars that might briefly appear through the clouds to port or starboard. Even when, like last night, the sky is totally overcast for much of the time, he can keep track of our heading by reading the wind and studying the swells.

On these cloudy nights Mau also finds himself in demand as a human clock to call the change of watch. (We have stowed all our wristwatches in a locked box because of the navigation experiment. With an accurate timepiece and some ingenious observations and calculations, it would be possible to get a fair idea of our position.) During the day we have no trouble using the sun to estimate time. Besides, in the daytime no one really cares whether one watch is cut short and the other runs long. But at night, when everyone is anxious to sleep, it seems natural for each watch team to try to cut their watch short, either consciously or unconsciously, by overestimating the passage of time and declaring that their four hours are up. On clear nights there can be no dispute, for we can just look at the stars. They move 15 degrees every hour (360 degrees divided by twenty-four hours), a distance that can be gauged roughly by sighting, with arm outstretched and hand open, between the spread of your vertically aligned thumb and forefinger. But on a night like last night such a method was useless.

That is when Mau becomes the supreme arbiter of when the change of watch should be called. Last night after our watch had been on duty for what to our sleepy minds must have been four hours, someone anxiously went over to our navigator with the crucial question.

"Mau, midnight yet?"

Mau, hiding the amusement he must have felt at the inordinate trust placed in his judgment, squinted into the blank overcast and replied authoritatively (and with a straight face), "No, I think five minutes to."

No stars visible last night also meant that extra care had to be taken steering. Fortunately we had a steady trade wind of 10–12 knots to steer by.

Look up at the sails, particularly at where the canvas curves outward to form an airfoil. Then slowly pull the steering sweep up until the foresail begins to luff and the canoe starts to slow. Then ease the sweep back down until the luffing stops. At that point the sails begin to draw fully and the canoe picks up speed again, indicating that you are sailing an optimum wind course.

Once satisfied that the sails are working at maximum efficiency, you can switch attention to the telltales, the thin strips of cloth tied to the rigging that are so much easier to watch than the foresail arching up into the darkness. All you have to do is fix in your mind the angle of the telltales when the sails are drawing well, then steer by raising or lowering the sweep to keep the angle constant.

It takes a feel for the canoe and the wind to be able to steer without guiding stars to follow. Some of the men avoid taking turns altogether, or give up when they lose their way and allow the canoe to start running wild downwind on a southwest course. Even after all the experience I have had in steering wind courses on *Nalehia* to test her windward performance, last night I felt myself becoming disoriented when totally surrounded by an impenetrable overcast. My gut reaction was that the canoe was turning in ever-tightening counterclockwise circles and that I was powerless to control her.

I knew this could not be the case by the way the canoe continued to lope over the oncoming swells with the same rhythm: first the bow would rise, and the canoe would tilt gently one way and then the other as she climbed obliquely up the face of a swell and then slid down its back. If I was a canoe sailor from the Marshall Islands, an area of Micronesia where they literally navigate by the swells, keeping the canoe on course by maintaining that same steady rhythm of pitching and rolling would have been easy. But even though I could feel that rhythm, I could still not shake the illusion that the canoe was going around in circles.

Finally, I was able to settle down after applying Mau's trick of literally feeling the wind. Stop staring at the sails and telltales, and start trusting the feel of the wind in your face: be your own telltale. By turning your head from side to side to test the wind streaming by your cheeks you can locate the exact direction of the flow. Once the wind is flowing equally past both cheeks you are literally facing the wind. Then, set the canoe sailing at the proper wind angle as judged by the sails or telltales, and turn your head so that you are facing into the wind. Keep your head at that fixed angle, relax, and steer by the feel of the wind on your cheeks.

Once I had beaten the disorienting feeling produced by the overcast through trusting in the wind, there remained only one thing disturbing about last night: a conversation with a fellow steersman.

21
Hidden Cargo

May 8—One week out (continued)

Richard Keaulana, my burly watch mate, and I frequently trade off steering chores. Everyone calls him "Buffalo" or simply "Buff." The name is apt. His massive shoulders, thick neck and hair tinged naturally red-blond are unmistakably buffalolike. The name even fits his manner: although normally phlegmatic and slow moving, he can quickly burst into action.

Buffalo is another of Herb Kane's personal choices. Herb, and Tommy Holmes also, thought Buffalo was a "must" for the crew. They both were impressed by his great strength and his skill as a surfer, fisherman and lifeguard, and had insisted virtually from the beginning of the project, "We have to have Buff." Herb had used Buffalo as a model for crewman in some of his canoe paintings, much as he had employed Kimo. He apparently saw the two men in the same light: strong, ruggedly handsome watermen who would inspire other Hawaiians by their masterful handling of the ancestral voyaging canoe.

Yet the two are not at all alike in character. Where Kimo is a glib talker, Buffalo is sparing in his words, although when he speaks he does so with wry humor, expressing himself mostly in the local pidgin English idiom. Where Kimo was always thinking up new jobs that had to be completed before the canoe could sail, Buffalo was bored with preparations. He did not spend much time working on the canoe; he just wanted to get on it and leave. "No more talk, let's go!" was what he had shouted at the group gathered on the beach at Maui anguishing over Kimo's dismissal from the crew and whether or not he should have to apologize.

Buffalo and I were taking turns steering last night. As we traded the now manageable chore of controlling the sweep, Buffalo began talking about his life on Oahu's west coast, a heavily Hawaiian area of high unemployment and attendant social problems. At first he was relaxed and amiably told me about his family, his friends and the Hawaiian feasts they enjoyed together. But his open manner soon changed and he became guarded and defensive. That was when he started talking about Hawaiians getting into trouble with the law, and about how he and his friends try to control violent crime in their community. Then he blurted out, "Sure we do some things wrong. We smoke dope, but no one bothers us and we don't bother no one!"

Buffalo was putting me on notice that he had marijuana on board and that I should not interfere.

For the last few days he and several other crewmen have been going off to a corner of the deck, hiding behind sleeping bags and surreptitiously but nonetheless obviously puffing on a homemade bamboo pipe, perfuming the sea-fresh air with the pungent odor of burning marijuana.

The literal meaning of· *pakalolo*, the neo-Hawaiian term for marijuana, may be indicative of what we have on our hands. *Paka* means "tobacco" and *lolo* is popularly translated as "crazy," although the dictionary definition is "paralyzed, numb or feeble-minded." Whatever the exact meaning, the prospect of putting up with *pakalolo* smokers for the next three weeks is discomforting. What might happen in an emergency with a *pakalolo*-numbed crew is anybody's guess. Lyman, however, claims not to be too worried. It was he, I recently learned, who first spotted Buffalo lighting up right after leaving Maui. Lyman had not liked what he saw, but he did nothing. He rationalized his inaction by saying that the *pakalolo* might ease the anxieties and fears arising from tensions left over from shore disputes, and from any trouble inexperienced seamen might have in coping with their first long sea voyage.

Despite the prohibition contained in the Articles signed just before leaving Honolulu, and Rodo's warning given at the departure ceremony, the *pakalolo* had been smuggled aboard just before leaving Maui—hidden inside an empty guitar case, I was told. That load of contraband, plus the transistor radio that Billy Richards was listening to our second day out, are not the only items that have been smuggled aboard. Buffalo has a small camping stove fueled with butane cylinders, a supply of coffee and tea, plus a bottle of liquor that he has been using to spike his hot drinks ever since he broke out his stove and supplies the other evening. Others have candy bars, jars of peanut butter and jam, and caches of other high-energy foods. Their presence on board, despite the agreement to eat only Polynesian foods during the voyage, is symptomatic of how most aboard feel about the food experiment.[*]

The idea of having everyone subsist solely on those foods available to the ancient voyagers had at first been conceived as a serious effort to shed some light on past voyaging problems by seeing how well various dried and fresh foods held up at sea, and how well we could get along on them plus any fish caught along the way. But we were not far into the project before that idea got all mixed up with the cultural revival theme. Those trying to keep to the experimental plan by carefully researching and testing various voyaging foods found themselves overwhelmed by those who insisted that "grass roots" participation was paramount. The

---

[*] Not until much later in the voyage did we discover that the television cameraman had hidden in the hull compartment reserved for his equipment a large store of jerked meat, dried fruit and nuts that he ate in secret.

main thing, the latter group said, was to have volunteers throughout Hawaii work together to dry the fish, bananas, breadfruit and sweet potatoes and to prepare the other voyaging foods. This campaign left us with a tremendous store of salted fish and dried bananas, a spoiled mess of pounded taro root, and not enough fresh coconuts, arrowroot flour and other vital items.

What happened to the pounded taro root, which was to have been the main staple on the voyage, epitomized the pitfalls of this grass roots approach. It is supposed to be prepared by pounding cooked taro to a pulp, wrapping it tightly with leaves, then storing it in a cool pit or a closed container so that it ferments without direct contact with the air. The trouble was that those who had taken over the food experiment had failed to do their homework. Insisting that taro should be allowed to ferment in open air, they packed the hunks of freshly pounded taro into wide mesh sacks that they left out in the open, resulting in uncontrolled fermentation as well as infestation with fruit fly larva.

It has not taken long to bring home to us the inadequacy of our food stores. By now almost all the fresh food has been eaten, and our taro has turned into a rancid mess crawling with maggots. That leaves a lot of dried fish (tasty but much too salty for heavy consumption given our limited water ration of two quarts per day per man) and bananas (delicious but sickeningly sweet after the third mouthful), plus a few dozen eggs and a slight quantity of other preserved foods. Not ideal fare, but sufficient to keep us going, especially if we can keep catching fish almost every day as we have been. But that is not to be.

Griping about the food has been growing the last few days, and a number of complainers have been agitating to have the food experiment called off and to beg food from the *Meotai*. Chief among them is the skinniest man aboard—the young *National Geographic* magazine photographer who thinks it silly to try to live off Polynesian foods, and the fattest man aboard, Boogie Kalama, who claims to be suffering acutely from food deprivation and that he and his mates are being fed "like a bunch of birds."

The complainers have apparently got to Kawika and Lyman, particularly Kawika, who is also worried about the epidemic of constipation now raging on board. Although some of us find squatting over the side, or in the netting slung between the prowpieces, ideal for promoting evacuation of the bowels, most aboard are suffering from acute constipation. The photographer complains that he has yet to be successful. Kawika feels that some canned vegetables and other soft foods might help. Accordingly, this afternoon he called the *Meotai* over the CB and requested that they send over a load of food in their Zodiac.

Something more than food showed up. I was at the stern when the Zodiac pulled alongside for the transfer, and I volunteered to help the *Meotai* crewman toss his load aboard. After fielding a sack of rice, a big tin of corned beef and several cans of carrots and other vegetables, the *Meotai* crewman went to throw me a six-pack of beer. After the *pakalolo* a little beer was nothing. But my mind was working sluggishly. Maybe I had made too many fund raising talks where I had assured prospective donors that no beer or other alcoholic beverages would be allowed on board. Without hesitation I refused the six-pack, shouting over to the *Meotai* crewman, "No beer!"

An instant after saying that I realized how foolish I had been. The trip would not founder on a few beers. Beer is *the* essential social beverage in Hawaii, and it was silly to try to enforce the ban now, especially with marijuana aboard. But that realization came too late. The Zodiac was already pulling away, with several six-packs plainly visible on the floorboards. I glanced back at the crewmen standing on the deck above me. Disbelief turning to anger was written on their faces. But they said nothing, just turned their backs and moved away. They had been eight days without beer.

22
Offerings to the Sea God

May 9—Eight days out

At dawn this morning Kawika went forward carrying with him a white plastic jug around which he had knotted a network of quarter-inch line. He made his way out onto the narrow plank that runs from the foredeck to the crossboom connecting the twin prows. Once there, he unscrewed the lid, poured a little water into one hand and then, while speaking in Hawaiian, sprinkled the water into the sea flowing between the hulls.

I have been watching Kawika do this for the last several days. This morning I finally asked him what he was up to.

"Every morning I give an offering to Kanaloa*—to thank him

---
* Pronounced and written Ta'aroa by Tahitians, Tangaroa by Tuamotuans and Polynesians from several other groups.

for the good weather and the good sailing, for looking after the crew, and to ask him to continue his blessing."

The "holy water," Kawika explained, had been given to him by his personal *kahuna*, with instructions that each morning he was to sprinkle a little into the sea and say a prayer to Kanaloa (Kah-nah-loh-ah), the god of the sea.

As the eastern sky brightened, Kawika asked me to give him a hand taking down the strobe light from the stern. We rigged it last night to make it easier for the *Meotai* to follow us. The original plan was to have the ketch stay well astern, tracking us visually by day and with radar at night. But the *Meotai's* radar has been out for several days and they have been forced to close in at night to keep our dim, battery-powered running lights in sight. Afraid that he might lose us, the *Meotai* captain asked me to rig a strobe light as a beacon.

So yesterday Kawika and I took a man-overboard strobe light, a little safety device that throws a bright blue-white flash for miles, fashioned a reflector from half a coconut shell, and rigged our creation to one of Rodo's bamboo fishing poles, which we then lashed to the stern rail so that the light stood 12 feet off the deck and faced aft.

"Right on!" was the *Meotai* captain's reaction over the CB radio when night fell and he homed in on the strobe light, flashing brilliantly every ten seconds.

After taking the light down, snacking on some dried food from our stores and crackers from the *Meotai*, Kawika and I and the rest of his watch were relieved by Lyman's watch and turned in for a nap. Upon awaking at midday we discovered that the strobe light, reflector, pole and all was missing. Rodo had lashed it alongside the deck rail, but there was no sign of it when we awoke. When we asked some crewmen on watch what happened, they denied any knowledge of the light in a most suspiciously exaggerated way. Then Rodo discovered that his other fishing pole, which he had lashed securely to the top of one of the sleeping shelters, was also missing. Someone had gone to a lot of trouble to get rid of it after tossing the strobe assembly overboard. But no one would own up, or snitch on the culprits.

"Maybe they didn't get the message," I remarked to Kawika as we started to make a second light assembly, using another spare strobe light and a length of bamboo scrounged from the roof of one of the sleeping shelters. Kawika took the cue and began talking loudly, although to no one in particular, about how the *Meotai* was having a hard time following us at night, and about how we would miss the rice, corned beef and other staples should the ketch lose us one dark night and we not get together again until Tahiti. That seemed to do it, for when it came time to lash the assembly to the rail, Kawika had some willing volunteers from the crew helping him.

We have a fair idea why the light, and Rodo's spare pole, were tossed into the sea: delayed fallout from the self-conscious spiritualism and posturing that blossomed around the canoe when it was being campaigned around Hawaii as the ancestral space-ship.

The two images attached to the twin sternpieces are at the root of this curious incident. Sam Ka'ai, the Hawaiian sculptor from Maui now ill with hepatitis, made both *ki'i*, or *tiki* (tee-kee) to use the Marquesan form of the word that Westerners have seized upon as the Polynesian name for anthropomorphic sculptures. Carved from dark hardwood in the flexed-legged style of ancient Hawaiian sculpture, the two compelling figures are our constant companions, ever staring with wide-open eyes over the length of the canoe and the sea ahead. The powerful male figure attached to the starboard sternpiece portrays a navigator reaching up to the star Hokule'a, represented by a large pearl disk held in his upraised hands. Ka'ai carved this *tiki* to symbolize how all those who had planned the project, raised money and built the canoe, as well as those who have the honor of sailing to Tahiti, are reaching for something greater than themselves. Ka'ai meant the buxom female *tiki* on the port sternpiece to stand for a Maui chieftess of prehistoric times, a mothering, loving yet disciplining figure who represents all past generations of Hawaiians, and who is their witness of all that happens on the voyage.

Ka'ai had insisted that the images always be treated with respect and not be used for showing off. Nevertheless, back in

Hawaii Kimo and one or two of his disciples used to parade the *tikis* about for dramatic effect. For example, they would show up at Voyaging Society meetings conspicuously cradling the sculptures in their arms and acting as though they were the high priests caring for the tribal gods.

Last night the strobe light caught the *tikis* head-on. Although the coconut cup reflector shielded the deck, the images were exposed, especially the female one almost directly in line with the light. Her wide, staring eyes of pearl shell picked up each flash, glowing blue-white when the current surged through the unit with an audible electronic snap and heated the xenon gas within to a brief incandescence. The effect was eerie, especially against the backdrop provided by the dark rushing sea and the black night sky. Two crewmen, disciples of the absent Kimo, were most affected. For the longest time they stood staring at the periodically illuminated image, fascinated yet obviously disturbed by the electronic display. It must have been one or both of those two who, imagining that they were protecting the sanctity of the *tikis*, chucked the strobe gear over the rail.

23

A Makeshift Jib

May 10—Nine days out

During his watch yesterday Lyman made a cryptic entry in
the official log telling of his casual alteration of the sail plan.
"Bent stormsail onto foremast (only fool around)—left up for
remainder of watch."

I was asleep off watch at the time and did not see this
unauthorized innovation. That is why what happened this afternoon so caught me by surprise. An annoying snapping and popping
of canvas flapping in the wind woke me. Automatically I looked
up at the sails. Nothing wrong there. Then I spied Buffalo and
a few of his pals up forward wrestling with a small triangular sail
that had been made early in the project as an emergency stormsail
and stowed on board ever since. They were trying to raise it on
the forestay to make a jib. After much effort they finally got their

sail up, then stood back to admire it fill in the wind.

That topped everything I had seen so far on the cruise. Adding a jib, a type of sail unknown in these waters until introduced by Europeans, to our two crab-claw sails was like putting keel fins on the hulls. It had to come down or the sailing experiment would be ruined and, once we put into Tahiti and word got around, we would be the laughingstock of the sailing world.

What was even more maddening was that no one seemed concerned except me. Kawika and a number of others were napping; the rest looked on admiringly, or were not paying the least attention.

I went over to wake Kawika and ask that the jib be taken down. He roused himself slowly and, once awake, seemed exasperatingly impassive about so important a matter. He did agree that we should not be carrying a jib, but all he would commit himself to doing was to "talk to the crew about taking it down."

"Talk!" I retorted. "Why can't you just order them to take it down!"

So intent was I on getting the jib down that I momentarily forgot how little control Kawika exerts over those on board who have a penchant for doing what they want. After more reasoned entreaties on my part, Kawika did say he would take the jib down, but he insisted on holding a crew meeting to explain. Calling them together on the afterdeck, Kawika spelled out how the jib was a *haole* sail and how it ruined my research on canoe performance. Fair enough. But that was like waving a red flag at those to whom research was a dirty word.

Buffalo, enraged to be told that my research took precedence over his jib, confronted me. We stood facing each other, only the narrow width of the deck separating us.

"You think Ben, you think we Hawaiians are ten feet tall? Tahiti is a long way and we're having a hard time getting there. We need all the help we can get—and this jib helps us!"

Other crewmen joined in the attack. "First the beer, now this," was one line of complaint. Another was that I had no right to tell them that their ancestors did not have a jib.

As in the affair of the keel fins, I certainly did not relish playing the role of the *haole* conservator of Polynesian tradition against this modern Hawaiian penchant for innovation. But there was not much I could say other than repeat that the jib was a *haole* sail that wrecked the Polynesian sail plan and would ruin the voyage if it went back up.

The attack then shifted to my having complained to Kawika directly. I should have "gone to Mau, not Kawika," they argued, reminding me that Mau had told them before leaving that if they had a problem they should come to him first and then he would go to the captain.

Lyman then spoke out, admitting that it was he who had made the mistake of first raising the jib yesterday. "It was wrong. We're supposed to ask Mau before making any sail changes. I didn't ask Mau if I could raise the jib and I don't think Buffalo did either."

Lyman then turned to Mau, who all this time had been staring out to sea trying to stay out of the quarrel, and asked whether the jib should be up or down. Mau scowled.

"Take down!" was all he said.

The irate crewmen had been right on one score. This trouble might well have been avoided, or at least muted, had I gone to Mau instead of Kawika. The sails are Mau's special province, and when he speaks everyone listens. His two words had settled the immediate issue. Yet Buffalo was not through with me.

"After two *ho'oponoponos*, the same old thing," he said disgustedly, harking back to the two ritual attempts to allay tension that had failed. "*Haoles* telling Hawaiians what to do! Kawika is not the captain, Ben is. Ben tells Kawika something, then Kawika tells us."

"But its my job as president of the Voyaging Society to see that we stick to our plans!"

We were talking past each other. Our differences had not been left behind in Honolulu or on the beach at Maui. The same old conflict over whether the voyage should be an ethnic experience or an attempt to re-create an ancient voyage was still very much with us.

Buffalo continued his harangue, concluding with a threatening boast. "When it gets rough, when the big waves start coming over the canoe, we're going to be standing here steering the canoe and you're going to be down inside hiding."

That released the tension and the meeting broke up. The jib came down, but at some cost. I went forward to sit alone. It had been a most humiliating experience having to defend my right to speak out to preserve the sailing experiment, and realizing how little support I have.

Soon thereafter the crew, still gathered aft, cooled down and began talking together amiably. The *pakalolo* was broken out and openly passed around. Guitars and ukuleles made their appearance, and the soft sounds of Hawaiian music rather than those of angry voices greeted the dusk.

Sitting up forward alone in the growing darkness, I wondered again, as I had so many times before we left, if it would not have been better to have bowed out of the project when the ethnic lines were drawn after the launching.

Then a figure loomed over me. It was Buffalo. He had come forward on a friendly mission. We mutually apologized, *ho'oponopono* style, for the hard stands we had taken. Buffalo explained how he always wanted to try new things, such as adding a sail to make the canoe get to Tahiti faster. I responded by explaining how it was my concern to keep the canoe as Polynesian as possible, which made me seem so rigid. Then we started talking about a more pleasant topic: Tahiti. He volunteered that I must be anxious to get there and see all my old friends. I talked about how I had heard that it was his lifelong ambition to sail to Tahiti, and that he had once been scheduled to go but had been drafted before he could leave. After we had exhausted our friendly small talk we shook hands, and Buffalo asked me to come aft and join the group, which I did gladly.

Their Hawaiian songs sounded melancholy yet soothing. They went well with the mild night. The wind was down to a gentle breeze and had lost much of its chill, indicating we were entering warmer waters. Overhead a three-quarters moon shone through the light overcast.

No one spoke to me further about the incident, although it was obvious that it had not been forgotten. As I stood there leaning against the rail listening to the soft music, I realized what a tenuous position I was in. It was time to hunker down, keep mum on the canned food, beer, marijuana and other "imports" that did not directly affect the main experiments, and avoid taking any actions that might further rile the crewmen. Only if the jib went back up, or something else happened to compromise the voyage, would I act.

May 11—Ten days out

Later last night and into this morning it became progressively harder to hold the canoe on course. The fierce weather helm of a few days back was with us again. We were stumped. We had been regularly pumping out the compartments into which water was slowly seeping from the drain holes Lyman had drilled through the bulkheads blocking off the closed bow compartments. So what could be the cause?

The sails were briefly suspect. When the makeshift jib had been up, the steering was easier. When it came down, the steering sweep had to be shoved down immediately to keep the canoe from rounding up into the wind. Although the jib had no significant effect on our speed, it apparently had altered the balance of the canoe enough to overcome some of the weather helm. Realizing that led to suggestions about raking the masts, or sliding the mast steps forward, to try to balance out the weather helm.

Before we got around to experimenting, Kawika sent Buffalo and Boogie forward to check Lyman's drain holes to see if they, like the regular ones, had become clogged. After much banging and sawing, another gusher. Water came pouring through a fist-size hole Buffalo hacked through the bulkhead on the port bow, flooding the open compartment to knee level. After the water was bailed out and the operation repeated on the next hull, the canoe was lighter by at least 150 gallons—over 1½ tons of seawater that had been weighing down the bows, throwing our steering off.

I was steering while the water was being bailed out, and found that I had to keep inching the steering sweep out of the water to prevent oversteering. Finally, when both bows had been completely cleared of their liquid burden, the steering sweep had to be pulled clean out of the water. The canoe stayed on course without an inch of blade in the water. With the center of gravity shifted aft, *Hokuleʻa* was so well balanced that we could lash the steering sweep onto the deck and let the canoe sail herself to windward.

If only our other problems could be so neatly solved.

24

Through a Curtain of Rain

May 12—Eleven days out

When will we reach the doldrums? That question is on everyone's mind as we move south toward the equator. The nights are becoming milder. The trades feel softer, tinged with a moist warmth that makes us literally feel we are about to leave the trade winds and nose into the humid, still doldrums.

The sun beating down on the earth's equatorial bulge heats the sea, which in turn raises the temperature of the air above it. The warmed, moisture-laden air rises to a high altitude, divides and then flows north past Hawaii and south past Tahiti to the midlatitudes, where it descends and flows back toward the equator as surface wind. The earth's rotation twists these winds, our trade winds, curving them so that they flow from the northeast in the Northern Hemisphere and from the southeast in the Southern

163

Hemisphere. Usually the two wind streams do not meet at the equator but are separated by the doldrums, a transition zone ordinarily a few degrees north of the equator. There the trades are replaced by calms and light variables that mark where the heated equatorial air rises to initiate the cycle. There also the westward-flowing ocean currents disappear, replaced by the strong, if at times fitful, Equatorial Countercurrent flowing east toward South America.

We have no sure way of knowing when we will pass out of the northeast trades, or even if there will be much in the way of doldrums to cross. Sometimes this zone is 200 or 300 miles wide and sometimes it shrinks almost to nothing, allowing sailing vessels to pass from one trade wind zone to another with only a day or so of slow sailing. Not enough is known about the doldrums to allow a prediction as to exactly when they will be wide or narrow, although meteorological experts consulted before leaving indicated that the zone was more likely to be narrow in the early spring than in the late spring. Hence one more reason for an early April departure. Had we left then we would have had a better chance for an easy passage. Just before we finally did sail, the crew of a yacht newly arrived from Tahiti reported they had been able to sail quickly from one trade wind system to the other without encountering much in the way of doldrums. But they were sailing when we were still stuck in Honolulu. Now it was anyone's guess what lay ahead.

Usually the doldrums are found somewhere between 9 degrees and 4 degrees north of the equator. Our position, judging from what Lewis and Mau have been saying, is somewhere between 9 and 7 degrees north. Lewis is the more conservative of the two. But Polaris, his guide to latitude, has been obscured by clouds for four nights running, so he does not set much store in his estimate and defers to Mau's more optimistic view of our southward progress. Whichever estimate is right, both authorities put us at the northern edge of the doldrums range. As yet there is no sign of calm weather or of the characteristic thunderheads that often herald this zone.

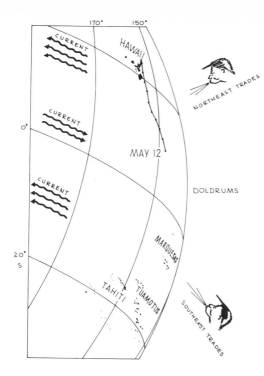

"Porpoises! Porpoises!" At dawn today the sea was filled with hundreds of them, swimming alongside, cutting back and forth across the twin bows. A magnificent spectacle, the first such treat of the voyage.

Our dog Hoku was upset by the sight. She started prancing all around the canoe, barking vigorously at the cavorting porpoises as if she objected to the intrusion of these air-breathing sea creatures into her domain. This was the first time I have ever heard her bark. With her crooked legs, long back, pricked ears and short hair, she certainly looks like the little barkless dogs sketched by the artists on the first European expeditions to reach these islands. I guess the Zoo was not quite able to breed the bark out of her.

Wheeling in the air above us all through this excitement were half a dozen birds, brown boobies from the look of them. What they are doing out here is a mystery.

Birds are the island navigator's friends, although not the albatross and other pelagic species that range far from land. Those species that stay close to land and habitually return each night to their island to roost are the navigator's favorite, for when he sees them he knows land must be near. In his book *We, the Navigators*, Lewis lists the booby as among the species used by island navigators to find land, and he cites various authorities who give its maximum flight radius as 30 to 50 miles from land. Rodo confirmed this before we left; based on Rodo's testimony, he and Lewis drew up a chart showing the flight radius for boobies, terns and other birds still used by old-time sailors such as Rodo to help find their way through the Tuamotus and in Tahitian waters. That is why it is so startling to see boobies out here. According to dead-reckoning estimates, the nearest land should be the barren atolls of the Line Islands, some 500 to 600 miles to the southwest.

Lewis is plainly perplexed by this sighting and can offer no explanation. Mau does not seem at all concerned; when queried, his only comment was a cryptic, "Not navigator birds."

Rodo, however, was ready to explain the sighting to anyone who would listen. "Those birds are juveniles. They have no babies at home to feed, so they fly far out to sea and stay away from their island for many days." An ingenious explanation from an expert which, if correct, should find its way into books on Pacific navigation. Or was Rodo kidding?

At noon we had a double strike on the trolling lines and hauled in two tunas, weighing 24 and 28 pounds on Rodo's fish scale. So far we have had fresh fish most days, sparing us from having to depend totally on salted fish or on the corned beef from the *Meotai*—although I am not alone in admitting that a little beef, even if canned, tastes good after a steady fish diet.

Around 1:30 the wind shifted abruptly to the north. Mau ordered the sheets (the lines controlling the angle of the sails) slackened and the steering oar (which has remained lashed on deck since pumping out the bow compartments) dropped into the water to keep the canoe on her southeast course. Otherwise we would have followed the wind around and have been headed due east. This is the first time we have not been sailing as close to the wind as possible.

I think Mau wants to keep on the same heading to simplify his navigation, or else he is just in a hurry to get south and cannot be bothered to try to gain a little easting by taking a tack due east.

There seems to be some disagreement on this matter of easting between Lewis and Mau. Lewis is extremely worried that the current may be pushing us farther to the west than we estimate, and he is always trying to get a few extra miles of easting by hauling in on the sheets to harden the sails and get a little more windward drive out of them. At least that is Mau's complaint, says Rodo, who adds that Lewis seems to want to sail the canoe close-hauled like a yacht instead of a little freer to the wind as is required with canoes given their tendency to make excessive leeway when pinched too close to the wind.

An hour before sunset Kawika had the sheets hauled in and the steering sweep secured back on deck, putting us on autopilot so that no one had to steer and we all could enjoy a delicious dinner of broiled tuna and rice. After eating we went back on a beam reach to maintain our southeast heading.

May 13—Twelve days out

Still no sign of the doldrums. Last night the wind shifted back to east-northeast, and we are again sailing automatically on a southeast course (or probably south-southeast when the current is taken into account). Given our speed of about 5 knots, we must be making a good 120 miles a day. Rodo is optimistic that this could be one of those rare times when there are no doldrums, and that we might be able to reach the equator in another three or four days of steady sailing. I have not heard Mau express an opinion on this. Lewis, however, is skeptical. He chuckles at the idea that we might escape the doldrums.

Late this afternoon the sea, heretofore barely flecked with whitecaps, came alive with a huge school of big tuna mixed with fast-moving porpoises. This time the porpoises were not playing, an indication perhaps that both they and the tuna are working a school of smaller fish.

May 14—Thirteen days out

Yesterday at dusk the sky ahead looked especially dark and brooding. Shortly after dark we entered what we first took to be an uncommonly warm rain squall. But the rain and the wildly fluctuating wind kept up all night. We took advantage of the rain to use a tarpaulin to collect eleven gallons of rainwater to add to our supply, and we tried to cope with the wind shifts and keep the canoe heading southeast. Dawn found us barely sailing, with a light breeze that lasted hardly half an hour before dying completely, leaving us drifting on a dull gray and formless sea. All was quiet, damply still compared to the rush of wind and water in the trades. We had passed through a curtain of rain to enter the doldrums.

We have a little wind, enough to allow *Hokuleʻa* to creep along for a while but never enough to make for steady sailing. Typically a slight breeze from the north heralds the coming of a spell of wind. As the limp sails begin to fill, we come alive to trim the sheets and use the smaller steering sweep, swivel-mounted between the hulls, to row the stern around to align the canoe properly to take full advantage of the breath of wind granted us. The breeze is never steady; it always shifts, usually veering around to the south. Sometimes it keeps veering clockwise, forcing us to tack or to jibe in order to keep on course. Sometimes it just shifts back and forth, veering clockwise and then backing counterclockwise, and so on. After anywhere from a few minutes to a few hours, it always dies.

The calm that follows may last for minutes or for hours, but the wind always returns. First a line of ripples approaches, breaking the oily calm of the sea. Then the air stirs, the limp sails swell and the canoe starts moving again, making half a knot, maybe up to 2 knots with a stronger puff. Then the wind drops and the canoe goes back to drifting. Then another spell of wind, and so on. Nothing like trade wind sailing. We are moving, but not very fast.

Keeping the canoe on course becomes a real chore in these conditions. No longer can we simply sail hard into the trades.

With the trades gone and the stars hidden by high overcast, we have only the swells, the moon and the sun to guide us.

Steering by the swells is an almost impossible job. The regular trade wind swell from the northeast has flattened out and is now lost amidst the welter of cross-seas to all of us, except Mau. He can still read the confused ocean surface for directional cues. The rest of us have to use sun and moon, and we are lost when these are below the horizon, obscured by clouds or too high in the sky.

"We've got wind from a squall and we're heading southeast."

Cheering words to be greeted with upon coming on duty for the watch from 4 to 8 A.M. After half an hour the squall passed to reveal the moon dully glowing through the overcast—on the wrong side of the canoe! The watch going off duty had entered the squall heading southeast, locked onto the wind and then, without realizing, had followed it around the clock until we were sailing north.

Embarrassing incidents like these occasionally happen when Mau is asleep. Usually those on duty realize when they are becoming disoriented and ask Mau for help, waking him if necessary. Then Mau blinks his bloodshot eyes open, surveys the dark sea and overcast sky and renders his verdict: sometimes the hoped-for "Okay," but more often a deflating statement such as, "I think we go north. Turn around."

Fortunately we are never off course for long. Nor do we stray far; we are moving too slow.

May 15—Two weeks out

We celebrated the completion of two weeks at sea by having a Hawaiian lunch: poi and salt fish. Earlier, when it was discovered that the pounded taro root was spoiled and maggoty, most of it was chucked overboard in a fit of disgust. (Some was held back for Maxwell the pig, who did not at all mind the maggots or the rotten taste.) Today, however, someone discovered a small sack of taro hidden away in the starboard hull. Because it had been wrapped in solid plastic, it was not spoiled and was free of maggots. Some hard work was necessary to mix the dry, hardened mass with water to make an edible poi, the Hawaiian staple tourists liken to library paste, but it was worth it. The poi was sour as the dickens, but the salty fish balanced out the sourness to make a tasty combination and a welcome variation from fresh fish and dried bananas, or corned beef and rice.

An hour later the film team aboard the *Meotai* sent over a "gift" that made us furious.

During our initial planning we had stipulated that any photographer or film cameraman aboard the canoe should be self-sufficient; he should take enough film with him to last the duration of the voyage and not have to receive fresh supplies from an escort vessel. However, later we agreed to allow periodic transfers of film between the *Meotai* and our canoe when Dale Bell pleaded that he could not afford to risk losing exposed film to dampness while stored on board, or risk losing it altogether as happened to the cinematographer on the canoe that broke up between the Marquesas and Hawaii last fall. But we did stipulate that no messages about our position or the weather ahead should be included with the fresh film.

This afternoon, however, the film team from the *Meotai* sent over a cassette tape with the fresh film. In an effort to further ingratiate themselves with those crewmen whose "struggle" was their main cinematographic focus, their sound technician had recorded messages to the crew that had been broadcast over shortwave radio from Honolulu to the *Meotai*. We should never have agreed to accept the tape, but it seemed harmless enough. Besides, our officers felt it might help cheer up those men who were already showing signs of acute homesickness.

As soon as the tape came aboard, a crewman grabbed it and shoved it into his tape recorder so that he and the others could hear the messages from their friends and relatives. Midway through the tape the messages were interrupted by the voice of the shortwave operator in Honolulu reading a newspaper account of our progress for the benefit of the *Meotai* crew. Before we realized what information might be disclosed, we heard him read that *Hokule'a* had "reached the doldrums 900 miles southeast of Hawaii yesterday."

Lyman started swearing and got on the CB radio to chew out the film team for this unauthorized transmission of position information. After the ruckus over the CB had died down, David Lewis tried to rationalize that the transmission had not been that disastrous. Mau had supposedly not heard it. And it was only a vague reference to the canoe being 900 miles from Hawaii at the point of entry into the doldrums. Mau had already figured out through his own system of reckoning that we were 1,000 miles from the island of Hawaii and that Tahiti was 1,500 miles distant.

I basically agreed with Lewis, although my attempt to accept this breach in the experimental plan as a minor slipup was shaken when I later learned that the last part of the tape included a recording of a conversation in which the *Meotai* radio operator told the Honolulu radio operator that our position was then "about 5 degrees north of the equator." When I heard that I started swearing. The transfer of position information of that sort, no matter if Mau heard it or not, seriously compromises the navigation experiment. Damn those film makers!

25
Doldrums

May 17—Sixteen days out

The overcast finally cleared this morning. Our spirits rose as the dull gray cloud cover broke up to reveal blue skies. But we soon discovered the penalty for being caught in calm weather under equatorial sun: it was hot. Only the sleeping shelters offered shade—a stifling one that made you sweat as though in a steam bath. The still ocean alongside beckoned, and most of us dived in to enjoy the coolness only it could offer.

After swimming away from the canoe we stopped, almost involuntarily, to look back at our home, now floating immobile on the glassy sea. "Looks like a Chinese laundry," someone cracked. Soggy clothes, sleeping bags and other gear were hanging out to dry in the rigging and atop the thatched sleeping shelters. Those of us with diving masks also took time out to stare down into the sea, following the shafts of sunlight until they disappeared into a blue-black nothingness. The effect was hypnotic, and a little frightening, for it brought the realization that miles of cold, dark water lie between us and the ocean floor. However, swimming, not sightseeing, was our object. Around and around the canoe we went, stretching cramped muscles and idly floating in the cool sea.

Upon clambering back on board we lathered with dish detergent (which works as well as expensive saltwater soap), rinsed off with buckets of refreshing seawater and then, after drying, oiled our chafed and salty hides with *monoi,* Tahitian coconut oil scented with fragrant flowers. Soon thereafter a light breeze got us sailing again, ending this brief interlude in the boring round of sitting, standing and sleeping that has been our lot so far in the doldrums.

May 18—Seventeen days out

Clear skies last night gave us the first good view of the stars in over a week. The Southern Cross is climbing higher in the sky while Polaris is low on the northern horizon. It looks to be about 4 to 4½ degrees high, indicating (as one degree of elevation equals one degree of latitude, or 60 miles) that we are around 250 miles north of the equator. That puts us at the southern edge of the normal doldrums range and gives us hope that we might be back in the trades within a day or so.

Early in the evening a light wind was moving us along, feeding that hope. But the wind soon died like all its doldrums compatriots and we spent the night drifting in circles. Although we knew that we were moving aimlessly in the current, it was still disconcerting this morning to see bobbing ahead of us a coconut shell cup that had been dropped overboard during the night.

Today has been a repeat of yesterday. Clear, hot and bright. But only a few went swimming again. Mau, we learned, disapproved of our swim the previous day. Water is a problem, and he believes that swimming in the heat of day only increases thirst. Although we have augmented our dwindling supply from doldrums showers, we could still run into trouble if the voyage goes much longer than thirty days. It was easy to stick to the limit of two quarts a day when sailing in the cool trades. Now our daily consumption is way over that.

But we do not feel any great need to crack down, for we are ever hopeful that we will soon be sailing in fresh southeasterly trades. The leaden skies are now far behind us, and a scattering of small white clouds on the horizon ahead looks like the fore-runners of more robust trade wind cloud formations. Maybe tomorrow the trades will be back.

May 19—Eighteen days out

Last night the wind did pick up. A light but steady northeast breeze allowed us to run south on a broad reach. South is now the preferred course, the most direct way out of the doldrums; this is the first time we have had enough wind to sail consistently in that direction. Steering a southerly course is a treat. To keep the canoe headed south, all you have to do is face aft and manipulate the sweep so as to keep Polaris centered between the two sternpieces and their staring *tikis.*

That fine breeze continued throughout the night and into this morning, only to falter and then die early in the afternoon. Since then we have gone back to poking along, sailing a bit when the wind stirs, drifting when it disappears, and so on.

At this dreary time the film team intruded on us again. Late this afternoon they sent over another message tape with the film transfer. As before, the cassette was eagerly grabbed and shoved into a tape recorder to hear the messages from home. And as before, the tape also contained the recording of a voice reading a newspaper article about our voyage. I was disturbed to hear the article being read but thought that surely, after the problems with the first cassette and the assurances we had received that the mistake would not be repeated, the article would have been censored for any position information. Yet once again we heard our position announced, this time in the more exact terms of miles covered from Hawaii and miles to go to Tahiti!

More cursing on the afterdeck and another chewing out by Lyman of the film team over the CB followed. Lyman's harsh words apparently made as little impression on the film team as when he chewed them out after the first tape incident. Soon thereafter the film team blithely motored over in the Zodiac, tied up alongside and, before we knew it, hopped aboard. They had not come to apologize. They came bearing gifts and greetings for their fellow cameraman and their crew favorites. They seemed surprised that we were so upset over the tapes and hurt when it was pointed out to them that they had violated yet another rule by boarding the canoe. And, before we could get them off, one of them even managed to rub it in by disclosing our position above the equator!

I wrote off the first cassette incident as a careless error. No such charity is warranted now. The only excuse offered was a lame, "It doesn't really matter." That summed it up well. The experimental basis of our voyage does not apparently matter to the film team. They are out to make a dramatic film, and they are more concerned about currying favor with those crewmen they find dramatically interesting than they are in keeping to the voyage plan.

What a mess! Bound to the doldrums by the vagaries of shifting wind belts and pestered by an inanely intrusive bunch of film makers. And, as if that were not enough, now half a dozen crewmen are feeling depressed and persecuted.

We can deal with the film team—by refusing all message cassettes and by having the *Meotai* captain keep them out of the Zodiac. Even the doldrums seems relatively tractable. We will eventually get out, and with a good bonus of easting. The sole comfort of being stuck in the doldrums is knowing that we are in the grip of the Equatorial Countercurrent which, according to the oceanographic figures we studied before leaving, must be pushing us east an average of 20–25 miles a day.* But what can be done about the increasingly despairing crewmen?

---

* Unknown to us, from May 15 to May 16 we drifted west, not east. The Equatorial Countercurrent is not a monolithic flow; it is composed of separate streams and gyres. When we drifted west we were probably caught in the westward-flowing sector of one of those gyres.

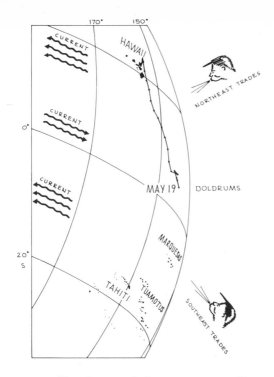

Half a dozen of them are mentally stuck in the doldrums—to use the original, psychological sense of the term that gave rise to the nautical expression. More and more these men have taken to sleeping through their watches, and even when awake they are given to lounging about morosely and muttering about their tough lot and the incompetence of the "leaders."

One man, Clifford Ah Mow, a young part-Hawaiian fisherman, is depressed almost to the point of incapacitation. The only time I have seen him come alive was a few days back when David Lewis dropped his journal overboard. Fortunately it was enclosed in a buoyant plastic bag, although Lewis was most alarmed to see his precious notes on Mau's navigation disappearing in our wake. Even before we had finished heaving to, Clifford had grabbed his surfboard and was paddling toward the bobbing plastic bag. He triumphantly grabbed the bag, paddled swiftly back and presented it to the grateful, if embarrassed, Lewis. After that, however, Clifford lapsed back into his routine of inaction, spending most of his time either lying quietly on deck or standing alone at the side rail staring out to sea.

The other affected men are less incapacitated, although their activities are far from constructive. They seem to go out of their way to gripe about the food, the difficult sleeping arrangements, and above all the lengthening time at sea. Boogie Kalama, whose bitter tongue rivals that of Billy Richards, recently exploded on the latter, challenging Tommy and Lyman with, "Jesus Christ! Why didn't you guys tell us the trip was going to take so long!"

Mau thinks the problem is that these men have never taken a long sea voyage before, and that they believe we should be in Tahiti by now. Everyone was informed, verbally and in a written document, that we would probably be at sea for thirty days or more. But this bunch apparently chose to ignore that information. Mau says that earlier he overheard them talk about setting a record by reaching Tahiti after only ten or fifteen days of fast sailing. No wonder they feel depressed. We left Maui 2½ weeks ago and we have not even crossed the equator yet.

Even the music of Billy Richards and Boogie Kalama has been affected. They seldom play together with Kawika anymore, and their selection of songs transparently betrays their mood. They are working on a new song, "The Doldrum Blues," to express their feelings, although their favorite is "The Queen's Jubilee," an old song with Hawaiian lyrics that celebrates a proud event in the Hawaiian monarchy: the visit of Hawaii's Queen Emma to the Jubilee of Queen Victoria in London. Tommy tells me that it was sung after the canoe swamped in the Kauai Channel, to keep the crew's spirits up while they sat in the Channel awaiting rescue. However, the way they and their friends now drag out the words is hardly uplifting. They sound mournful enough to be singing a funeral dirge.

Billy and Boogie may be the vocal leaders of the dissatisfied crewmen, but they and their friends all look up to Buffalo, the strongest among them. Buffalo has not been doing that much griping; he is more the man of action. His response to the frustration of sitting in the doldrums has been to try to muscle us out. Just as before when he raised the jib, Buffalo wants to do something physical to get the canoe moving faster. Given the Hawaiian pride in paddling, I have been expecting that he might propose that we paddle our way through the doldrums. That would be thoroughly wasteful in terms of the extra food and water we would have to consume in order to move our heavy craft, but it might improve morale by exhausting people and making them feel they are personally contributing to moving *Hokuleʻa* toward Tahiti. Instead, Buffalo tries to manhandle us out of the doldrums by periodically commandeering the canoe and sailing it all by himself.

When a breeze is stirring, and when the mood strikes him, Buffalo rouses himself and races forward and then aft to adjust the sails to his liking. Then he grabs the steering sweep and shoves it deep into the water to make the canoe fall off and gain speed. As *Hokuleʻa* picks up what speed it can in the light airs, he yanks the sweep clean out of the water to make her round back up into the wind. Then, as the canoe turns into the wind and starts to slow, Buffalo jams the sweep back down into the water. The flowing water catches the deeply thrust blade and smashes it against the hull with a resounding clunk. After falling off, he pulls the sweep out again, repeating the noisy sequence until the wind dies or he tires.

"You know," he said upon relaxing after one of these workouts, "this canoe is like one big toy!"

The two other crewmen in this group, Dukie Kuahulu (the developer of our steering rig) and John Kruse (a young part-Hawaiian who was a paid worker on the canoe while it was in Honolulu), are much more reasonable and constructive than the trio of Buffalo, Boogie and Billy. For example, Dukie tries hard to be cheerful, and has voluntarily taken over most of the cooking duties. John Kruse, a man who though easily swayed is not himself given to taking strong positions, similarly tries to make himself useful around the canoe. Still, these two men do follow the lead of the other three. The five of them, plus retiring Clifford Ah Mow, form a faction that increasingly stands apart from the rest of us, acting independently of the captain and those rules of the sea we are all supposed to follow.

All six are husky watermen. That may be a large part of their problem, for the surfing, beach-oriented lifestyle with its quick and easy gratifications is probably the worst possible preparation for a voyage such as ours. It is not just that they are unaccustomed to long sea voyages. Discipline, particularly self-discipline, has not been part of their life experiences. That, plus all the talk before leaving about how the "leaders" were oppressing the "crew," makes these watermen prey to feelings of despair and, increasingly, rebellion.

It is a question of lifestyle and experience, not race. The other Hawaiians aboard do not share the despair and anger of these watermen. Neither Kawika, who long ago left the beach life, nor Lyman, a former Merchant Marine officer and now a harbor pilot, find the doldrums and our slow progress to be a cause for despair. Neither does Sam Kalalau, the ex-Marine turned cowboy, to pick a Hawaiian crewman who is not a professional seaman. Sam acts in the doldrums much as he did earlier in the trades. He stands his watch, minds his business and stays aloof from the despairing crewmen. Sam displays the qualities of patience and self-discipline so lacking among our urban-bred watermen. He is the best possible crew choice; Herb Kane was "right on" when he nominated Sam.

Sam has been urging Kawika to crack down on these guys, to make them quit smoking their *pakalolo*, stop fooling around with the sails and steering, and start working with the rest of us. But Kawika seems to turn a deaf ear to Sam's urgings. The two are worlds apart. Sam swears that he would never allow his cowboys to get so far out of line. True, Kawika has had command experience at sea, but on racing craft crewed by dedicated yachtsmen and on tourist catamarans where employees lose their jobs if they neglect their duties. Neither this experience, nor his easygoing temperament, has prepared Kawika for dealing with these crewmen.

It is tempting to think that cracking down is simply beyond Kawika, for he seems to ignore so studiously the antics of these men and to turn the other cheek when they berate him or usurp his authority. But that assessment is not fair to Kawika. Nor does it do justice to the realities of the situation. Kawika has an incipient rebellion on his hands, a rebellion of a group of fellow Hawaiians against the plans for how the voyage should proceed, and particularly against the *haoles* aboard responsible for those plans. I have long realized intellectually what an unenviable situation Kawika is in. But only now do I feel it at a gut level—all because of a curious mix-up over names.

For the last day or so I have had to catch myself from not addressing Kawika as *Tavana*, a modern Tahitian word (derived from the English "governor") for the chief of an island or district. I have been involuntarily confusing Kawika with my old friend, the chief of Maiao (My-'ow), a small island west of Tahiti where I lived for a year doing research on Tahitian culture. Both Kawika and the chief are handsome, heavyset men with the same rich bronze-brown Polynesian coloring. But similarity in appearance is not the basic reason for my confusion.

The two men are alike in that both are trapped between the conflicting forces of those whose directions they are supposed to execute and those whom they are supposed to lead. To put it bluntly, they are caught between *haole* officials and Polynesian brothers.

In the chief's case it is the French colonial government and its administrators that give him his orders, and it is the Tahitian people of Maiao whom he has to call upon to obey those orders. He is not a hereditary chief; the French long ago removed the Tahitian aristocracy from power. He is only the chairman of the Maiao island council. Although locally elected, the French administration treats him more as their agent than as an autonomous leader of his people. Still, above all he is a Tahitian, and Maiao is a Tahitian island. This means that despite the power of the French administration, the chief cannot force his people to obey French edicts. Although empowered to run the island, he has to do so with a light hand. Were he heavy-handed, were he to appear to favor French over Tahitian interests, he would lose all control over the community.

I did not understand this when I first came to Maiao. My education in local political realities began one fine sunny morning when the men of Maiao went on strike against their chief. He had set aside that day for community work, as directed by the administration, to clear the village pathways and drainage ditches.

All able-bodied men were required by law to join in the work. These nonpaid work days are hardly popular on Maiao, but the men usually answer the call to duty. However, that morning they had other ideas. The copra boat from Tahiti was due soon, and they wanted to go out to their coconut plantations and make copra that day. So they defiantly marched past the chief's house without a word of explanation or excuse. To my astonishment, the chief said nothing to them. He just sat inside his house fuming.

"Why don't you stop them and tell them to get to work?" I asked naïvely.

"I can't. They would get mad and would never do anything for me again."

In our sea drama the majority of the crew see the Voyaging Society, and those of us on board the canoe responsible for running the Society and planning the voyage, much as Tahitians and other colonized people see their colonial administration and administrators. These same crewmen, in turn, see themselves as subjugated people forced to do someone else's bidding. Kawika truly is the man in the middle.

The crewmen are constantly pressing Kawika to join them and follow their lead.

"Hey, why you listen to the *haoles*?" they ask him. "You listen to us, follow us Hawaiians."

"I listen to everybody. I don't know what you guys are thinking about. We all got to work together," is his standard reply. And that is about as far as Kawika will go. Although he remains aloof from the gang's siren song of Hawaiian unity, he still will not crack down on them as Kalalau would have him do. Kawika plainly fears the open conflict he believes would almost certainly follow.

There is wisdom in Kawika's stance. Despite the split in our ranks, despite the differences of race, class and goals that have given rise to that split, despite the crowding and the limited food and water, despite the fatigue and lack of sleep, there has not been a single outbreak of violence. A captain bent upon enforcing his will, no matter how right he was, might well provoke a pitched battle into which we all would be drawn. Then what? Would the winners throw the losers overboard? Keelhaul them? Lash them down to the deck for the rest of the voyage? Kawika has little room to maneuver between extreme options. His strategy is probably the wisest course to follow: let these crewmen be, and concentrate on getting to Tahiti with the canoe and everyone on board intact.

Our first mate takes a parallel stance, although not because he and Kawika see eye-to-eye. They do not work well together. Lyman complains that Kawika is not providing him with the proper leadership, and Kawika in turn is disappointed that Lyman does not always support him. From early on in the voyage, Lyman seems to have taken an independent initiative to placate the crewmen, to let them have their *pakalolo*, their beer or whatever else they need so long as they let the rest of us get on with the voyage. As in Kawika's case, this seeming lack of firmness is partly rooted in the complexities of *haole*-Hawaiian relations, although for Lyman anxiety over his Hawaiian identity may further complicate the situation.

"I'm five cents Hawaiian," Lyman is fond of saying. That is his way of both claiming Hawaiian ancestry and of apologizing to those more Hawaiian than he for his minuscule one sixteenth share of Hawaiian blood. Lyman is a well-known island name. The clan founder was a pioneering American missionary; our first mate is descended from the missionary's son and the Hawaiian chieftess he married. Despite this slight fraction of Hawaiian ancestry and a middle-class American upbringing, Lyman favors his Hawaiian side and is a sincere supporter of Hawaiian causes. His Hawaiian sentiment seems to make him much more sympathetic to our independent-minded crewmen than one would think a professional seaman of his training and experience would be. Yet, as in Kawika's case, Lyman rejects the gang's entreaties to join them. He too tries to walk that line between doing his duty and letting the gang be, a policy my old friend the chief of Maiao would understand.

26
The Gang

May 20—Nineteen days out

Last night lights appeared way off in the distance. They were not coming from the *Meotai*, still following close behind us, but from some vessel below the horizon with lights bright enough to cast a glare into the sky. After puzzling over what a brightly lit ocean liner might be doing in these waters, we finally decided that the lights must be coming from a Japanese fishing boat using arc lamps to illuminate nets or long baited lines being set or brought in.

Lyman says that Japanese fishing boats work the doldrums because the nutrient-rich waters fed by upwellings in the counter-current attract a greater concentration of fish here than is found elsewhere in the tropical Pacific. Unfortunately, we do not have the technology to catch those fish swimming below us. We have only our trolling lures, useless now that we are just barely moving through the water. So, amidst plenty, we are forced to live off our stores of salt fish.

I do not mean to knock the thought and effort that went into procuring the literally thousands of pounds of marlin and tuna—donations from successful fishermen in the international fishing tournament held in Kona on the island of Hawaii—and the hundreds of hours spent cutting the fish into strips, covering the strips with special Hawaiian sea salt from Kauai, then drying them under the hot sun on the parched lava fields just north of Kona. The finished products in the form of leathery strips about the size of an overly large, flattened cigar are tasty. Ask Dave Lyman. He always seems to have one stuck in his mouth. But the dried fish is just too salty and stringy to be totally satisfying as the main course at dinner, now the only formal meal of the day since our fresh food supplies have been exhausted and the *Meotai* is running low on canned goods and other foods to supplement our diet.

Dukie Kuahulu has been trying his damnedest to make the fish strips more palatable by frying them or, as he did last night, boiling them in a pot scrounged off the *Meotai*. The limp result of the latter effort was more chewable than the original, but it substituted an unwelcome soggy saltiness for the former biting tang.

This morning Tommy tried his hand at cooking. He, Boogie and a few other men have a great craving for sugar in any form. That is why he was up so early fixing his idea of a dream breakfast: banana fritters made by dipping the naturally sweet dried bananas into a sweetened flour batter, then deep-frying them in oil and rolling them in sugar and cinnamon. (The flour, sugar, oil and cinnamon were all bummed off the *Meotai*.) "Those who snooze, lose," was the little jingle Tommy kept repeating as he happily prepared his sugary treats.

Despite whatever mental relief sighting the lights and enjoying these culinary efforts affords, calms and light airs remain our lot. Today marks our seventh day of drifting about. A week in the doldrums seems an overly long time, especially to our impatient crewmen, who have become desperate to find some way to get us out.

That is why late this afternoon they gathered together in a tight circle on the foredeck, as far forward and as far away as they could get from the rest of us. After a brief conspiratorial caucus, they broke their circle and marched aft with steps as resolute as can be managed treading barefoot over the undulating deck of a canoe. Dukie Kuahulu was in the lead. In the name of the "crew" he demanded a meeting. What a surprise. I never expected that congenial Dukie would be the spokesman. But this was no joke; Dukie looked furious. His darkly sunburned face, ringed around by his graying hair now matched by newly grown and similarly graying whiskers, was set in a fierce expression, his unblinking eyes staring at us with a wild, challenging gaze.

We feared the worst. For the last few days these men have been talking among themselves about getting the *Meotai* to tow us out of the doldrums. Their rationale, judging from what could be overheard, was that since the food experiment had been "blown" and the navigation experiment had been "blown," nothing mattered now but to get to Tahiti as quickly as possible.

To our relief Dukie did not demand that we take a tow. Instead he started berating Lewis for supposedly changing the course set by Mau. Then he focused on the main crew demand.

"The *hales* (hah-lays) are too heavy," Dukie declared, using the Hawaiian word for house to refer to the long sleeping shelters erected over each hull. "They're what's holding us back. We got to cut them off!"

Billy vigorously seconded his demand and amplified Dukie's argument that it was the weight of the shelters that had been holding us in the doldrums. Then Dukie asked Mau if it was okay to dump the *hales*. Mau, confused by all the quick, angry words, replied by asking what he was talking about. After receiving an explanation, a look of incredulity spread over Mau's face. Then, frowning deeply, he finally said, "Okay."

Dukie next turned to Kawika and demanded his approval. Kawika shrugged and unenthusiastically gave his consent. The rebellious crewmen looked triumphant. In a way the rest of us were relieved. It was absurd to think that a few hundred pounds of bamboo, thatching and line could hold back our 12-ton canoe. But in light of what these men might have demanded, removing the shelters seemed almost reasonable. Demolition is set for tomorrow morning.

May 21—Twenty days out

Several hours after the confrontation over the *hales*, we ran into a series of squalls, after which a warm rain began falling. Light, variable winds and the warm trickling rain continued throughout the night. At dawn the wind died completely and we were once more becalmed. Then, as the eastern horizon brightened, the wind stirred and the sky began to clear. Soon we were sailing along with a light but steady wind blowing from the southeast. We had passed through another curtain of rain, this time to exit the doldrums and enter the southeast trades.

The rebellious crewmen were not satisfied with this turn of events. They still had their minds set on demolishing the shelters. After a spartan breakfast of crackers, dried bananas and salt fish, the action started.

Machetes and knives flashed through the air as the men slashed and hacked away at the lines binding the bamboo and thatch. Unsmiling, with a determined relish that belied their feelings, they tore the structures apart. Soon the shelters were gone. *Hokule'a's* wake was littered with debris—scraps of thatching, bits of line, lengths of bamboo and even the two spare masts that had been lashed on the outboard gunwales at the base of the shelters.*

Once the demolition spree was over, the wreckers paused, exhausted yet pleased. Their pleasure could not have stemmed from a surge in speed. There was none. The canoe continues to poke along in the light trades at the same deliberate pace she was making before the shelters and masts were jettisoned. But the wreckers have not noticed. They believe that *Hokule'a* is lighter

---

* Those aboard the *Meotai* watched all this with consternation. Their first garbled radio message to Honolulu caused even greater dismay there. It was heard as, "They are throwing the *haoles* overboard!" Not until the radio operator eventually realized that the key word was not *haoles* but *hales*, meaning shelters, was the confusion cleared up.

and more lively, and they are exultant that they are the ones who seized the initiative to rid the canoe of her burden.

The six men have indeed rid themselves of a burden, a psychological one that must have been on their minds since before the voyage began. They apparently always regarded the shelters as structures unfairly imposed upon them and *their* canoe by unfeeling outsiders.

Before swamping in the Kauai Channel, *Hokule'a* had carried a single sleeping hut lashed onto the foredeck between the masts. Although comfortable, it could only accommodate four or five crewmen at a time. It also took up much valuable deck space, making it difficult to raise and lower the sails, an important consideration especially in an emergency. In order to provide more sleeping space and also to clear the deck, after the swamping I proposed that we put a long hut over the windward hull (port hull sailing to Tahiti, switched to the starboard hull for the trip back) to provide accommodations for at least eight men at a time sleeping in hammocks. Honolulu's Bishop Museum had an example of such a structure, although in miniature form. It was part of a finely crafted model of a Tuamotuan double-canoe that had been collected early in the last century before those sleek craft disappeared from the seas.

The plan fell victim to disputes over design and some expert foot dragging by crewmen who favored rebuilding the old deck-house. Finally, after a virtual sit-down strike a few weeks before leaving, a compromise proposed by Kimo was accepted: a pair of simple lean-to structures built over the midsections of the hulls. These were supposed to provide shelter from rain, spray and boarding seas for the men sleeping in the cramped bunks located below—between the decking sealing off the lower two thirds of the hull and the canvas spray shield stretched over the hull. Four bunks, separated by crossbeams running through the gunwales, were under each shelter. Each space measured 5 to 6 feet long, 2½ feet wide and 2 feet deep. That gave us eight bunks, enough for the two watch groups "hot bunking" by trading places at the turn of the watch.

Almost everyone disliked these coffinlike bunks. Not only were they cramped, but they were also unbearably stuffy when it was calm, and constantly wet when it rained or when the canoe was driving hard through the sea. The now-demolished lean-to shelters only kept out the worst of the rain and spray, some of which always found its way through the ill-fitting canvas covers over the hull and into where the crossbeams penetrate the gunwales and the lashing holes are drilled through the gunwale side boards. Even when wearing foul weather gear for pajamas, we could not shut out the drips, dribbles and spurts of water that found their way into ears, down necks and into pants.

Except for Kawika, Sam Kalalau and David Lewis, hardly anyone has been regularly sleeping in their assigned space. Kawika and Sam, who are on opposite watches, have managed to keep their common bunk fully occupied. No sooner does one climb out than the other dives in and is quickly snoring away. They remind me of Tahitian sailors on trading schooners who can lie down atop smelly, lumpy copra sacks and fall instantly asleep. However, of this trio of sound sleepers, David Lewis takes the prize for having the wettest bunk, the forward one in the starboard hull where the waves funneling between the bows strike. Lewis not only sleeps there regularly, he manages to make light of the cascades of spray that periodically drench him through the torn canvas cover over that section of the hull. After sailing in frigid Antarctic waters in a 30-foot boat, getting soaked in the tropics is nothing to Lewis. I swear that once when a particularly large wave peaked up between the hulls and then inundated his bunk, I heard Lewis splutter and then let out a hearty belly laugh.

Tommy and I have hardly ever slept in our common bunk in the port hull opposite to where Kawika and Sam sleep in the other hull. Although it is one of the drier bunks, the double crossbeam at the foot makes it way too short for my long frame, and Tommy is too given to claustrophobia to be able to sleep there comfortably. So we have loaned the space out to others while we sleep on the roomy, airy but spray-drenched deck.

The rebellious crewmen have also been sleeping out on deck, but not just because they have found their quarters too cramped or too wet. It was poor psychology to have them bunk separated from one another in a line of individual niches. The old deckhouse from the interisland cruise days, we now realize, was a kind of clubhouse to them, a place to "talk story," play music and just be together.

That is why this afternoon, after the demolition had been completed, the crewmen went to Mau to request that he make them a deckhouse out of the little bit of bamboo, line and matting saved from the old shelters. Although plainly annoyed by what to him was nonsense, Mau nonetheless set to work laying out a low semicircular hut which, with the aid of Tommy and Lyman, was finished before dark. The rebellious half-dozen then happily moved into their new home with their air mattresses, sleeping bags, guitars and other gear.

Now, at nightfall, the new deckhouse presents a cozy scene with the six crewmen jammed in, lying so that their heads come together in the center. A battery-powered camping light bathes them in soft yellow illumination as they idly talk. Occasionally Boogie picks his guitar, between puffs on the *pakalolo* pipe that is being passed around and around the group.

That leaves the rest of us out in the weather to make whatever sleeping arrangements we can in the now even more exposed hull bunks, or on what little deck space is left. Yet I think we are all happy to trade some discomfort for the relief of physical separation. In one important sense it has been helpful to demolish the hull shelters and build the deckhouse. To have seventeen men crowded together for weeks on a canoe is bad enough. But to have them also divided into factions with such opposed ideas has made for constant tension. The rebellious crewmen have reduced that tension by staking out their own turf—and a clubhouse to boot.

Their actions also have made it clear that we are dealing with a gang, not just a collection of rebellious individuals.

Gang. Billy Richards is fond of using that term among his mates, as when he says, "Let's go gang," or "Hey gang." The deckhouse gang is, I now realize, a classic example of what sociologists call a peer group—a group bound together by common status and outlook. Such groups, sociologists tell us, are prominent in Hawaiian neighborhoods, particularly working-class neighborhoods in and around Honolulu. There it is the peer group —not the family, work or any other institution or activity—that is the main focus of life for so many Hawaiian men. Typically they spend what seems like an extraordinary amount of time together drinking, fishing, surfing and engaging in other male pursuits. This may be partially a carry-over from ancient patterns of sexual segregation and male solidarity. But it probably has more to do with the collapse of the rigidly hierarchical ancient society wherein a man's status was largely determined by birth and regulated by custom. That collapse, plus the other shocks experienced by the Hawaiians in the last two centuries, has been particularly hard on the men, so many of whom now find themselves adrift in a society in which status is determined by formal education, business success and other alien criteria. That is where the peer group comes in, for it is within the tight circle of his fellows that the Hawaiian deemed unsuccessful by the outside world can shut that world out and gain the mutual support, sense of belonging and measure of self-esteem he needs.

I tried this long-winded analysis on Rodo, explaining how it was the gang's need to be together and to shut out the rest of us that really prompted their demolishing the hull shelters and building the deckhouse.

"Now I understand. I'll go tell Mau. He thinks they are just crazy," responded Rodo, adding, "Why didn't you tell me this before?"

"I couldn't. I only just figured it out."

It has taken a long time to put two and two together, to connect sociological analyses of Hawaiian peer groups to the crew situation. Maybe that is because of this corollary: if these six men form a tight little peer group, a gang, then they have a separate reality that will not be shaken by appeals to reason or authority. Beyond their circle no one, no ideal, really matters.

But so what. Now they have their own clubhouse and can do what they want within its confines. As long as they leave us and the canoe alone, we can get on with the job of sailing to Tahiti.

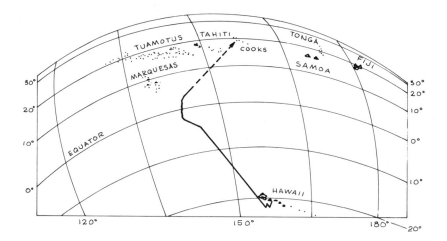

27
Head Winds

May 22—Three weeks out

Dazzlingly clear skies, a steady breeze and calm seas have been ours since we exited the doldrums yesterday—by far the best cruising weather of the voyage. *Hokule'a* sails on smoothly and serenely. The sun is warm but never too hot because of the fresh breeze. And the sea has come alive again, sparkling as sunlight glints off freshly formed wavelets. To top off our good fortune, we are back to sailing automatically to windward just as we did before the doldrums. The steering sweep is lashed up on the deck; nothing cuts the water but our twin hulls. With the bow compartments drained of water, and with what remains of our fast-dwindling food and water supply stored well aft, the canoe is trimmed stern down for self-steering.

Actually we do steer the canoe, but only by occasionally adjusting the sheet controlling the aft sail, letting it out to make us fall off a bit, pulling it in to bring us closer to the wind. The aft sail is the key, for it is the one which, when the wind force is concentrated on it, can pivot the canoe into the wind and cause a heavy water helm. The sacrifice of some sail area accomplished by reducing the size of the aft sail is now paying off. Before the swamping, when we sailed with two sails of equal size, the canoe always had a weather helm. Only in very light airs, with the aft sail slacked out till it was virtually flapping in the wind, could we make the canoe sail to windward without using a steering paddle to keep her off the wind. Now, with the small aft sail barely slacked, we sail steadily and automatically to windward, never too close to the wind and never too far off it.

Personally, I have never been so comfortable at sea. Tommy and I have rigged a small shelter atop the canvas cover over the starboard hull out of life jackets, a leaky air mattress and a small tarpaulin. It is an ideal bunk for sleeping or just for resting and watching the sparkling sea dance by a scant 18 inches below. But we are not about to brag of our good fortune to those who displaced us from the deck—especially since they are being such poor sports about sharing their new quarters.

Now is the time to sit back, relax and enjoy the trip for once. With the gang happily settled in their clubhouse and the afterdeck largely ours, tension has eased greatly. Even Mau seems more relaxed. He sleeps through much of the night now, and by day he sits atop his stern rail perch, staring out to sea and dreaming—I would like to think—of past landfalls on strange islands, and of future landfalls in the Tuamotus and on Tahiti. Kawika keeps busy painstakingly copying the official log in a slow but nearly perfect hand. Lyman, too, has his project. He is covering a small flask with ornate lashing patterns and fancy knotwork, a favorite sailor's pastime. Lewis and I have become bookworms, relishing a collection of soggy paperbacks to while away the now pleasant hours.

Tommy is occupied with his plants and animals. The chickens, although molting, are doing well, pecking up all the coconut meat we can grate for them. Hoku is off the leash, enjoying her freedom by scampering around the canoe.

Our pig Maxwell still takes the prize in the eating department. He is getting enormous, so big and strong that we fear he may break out of his cage—suspended so perilously between the stern-pieces for automatic disposal of wastes—and fall into the ocean. One day last week we thought Maxwell was done for when morning light revealed him flat on his back with legs stiff in the air, a victim, we surmised, of sun and sailcloth. The day before, the voracious animal had eaten the nylon sailcloth rigged over his cage as a shade to protect his tender, *haole* skin. That left him exposed to the equatorial sun. The resultant sunburn, together with the mass of indigestible sailcloth in his gut, almost finished

Hoku asleep in the deckhouse

him. It took some tender care by Tommy to bring him back to health.

"Roast pig tonight, Tommy?" Our keeper of plants and animals has to endure a lot of that kind of ribbing. But he accepts it with good grace, and even seems to invite it to inject some humor into our divided situation. Tommy's ready smile, his quick laugh and his knack for avoiding confrontations have so far helped him escape the gang's ire and keep the plant and animal part of our experiment relatively free from hassles.

He has had a few close calls though. Some time back a bored crewman was tormenting Maxwell, poking him with a short stick thrust between the bars of his cage. Fortunately Tommy did not have to intervene on behalf of the enraged pig. Maxwell was too fast for his tormentor, drawing blood when he nipped the crewman's hand with his sharp teeth.

Then, right after the original sleeping shelters were demolished, Tommy had to think fast and act coolly to save the plants. Before leaving the islands he had spent months gathering a comprehensive collection of roots, cuttings, seedlings and other plant materials. He painstakingly wrapped them in special moss and salt-resistant leaves to keep them moist and to protect them from the salt air. Because Tommy could not pack them in waterproof containers without exposing them to rot and mold (and without going beyond the original Polynesian methods as well), the plants are extremely vulnerable to sea spray. That is why Tommy lashed them close underneath the shelters, and why he was in such a quandary when those shelters were demolished. The only spray-free place on the canoe was the gang's new deckhouse, but they wanted no part of the plants. Tommy, undaunted, took their refusal without comment and waited until they had all gone aft to eat. Then he slipped into the deckhouse and lashed the packages to the ridgepole. When the gang returned to discover the new additions to their quarters, he managed to talk and joke them into letting the plants stay.

Only one thing is wrong with this otherwise idyllic time: head winds. We are in the southeast trades all right, but they are too light and have too much south in them. These trade winds of 5 to 10 knots are forcing us onto a course slightly to the west of south. *Hokule'a* is at her worst in winds like these. Her sails are meant for heavy trades; they are not big enough to give such a heavy canoe enough speed to allow her to point high in light airs. For the first time since the voyage began we are losing easting. But we are not too concerned, hoping for more favorable winds within a few days. Before leaving Hawaii, an oceanographer warned me to expect a spell of light head winds upon leaving the doldrums.

"They panic all the yachtsmen heading for Tahiti," he said.

"Don't worry, though. Past the equator the winds pick up and turn more easterly. Then your course will straighten out."

We can afford to lose some easting. After the long drive to the southeast through the northeast trades, and our drift to the east in the doldrums countercurrent, we have at least a couple of hundred miles to spare. Lewis puts us almost 200 miles east of the longitude of Tahiti. Rodo thinks we are another hundred miles farther east, an estimate which, as near as I can tell, given the difference in position-reckoning systems, is closer to where Mau puts us. If the wind picks up and backs to the east after the equator, we will be in a good position to make a landfall on one of the Tuamotu atolls northeast of Tahiti. Even if the winds do not cooperate and we are forced to stay on this heading, we might still have a chance of hitting Tahiti directly, or of fetching up on one of the smaller islands immediately west of Tahiti—that is, if our position estimate is realistic.

Last night was brilliantly clear, almost totally without clouds or haze of any sort to block our view of the stars. For a brief moment an hour after sunset Rodo and I caught a glimpse of what appeared to be the Pole Star barely shining through the thickened atmosphere just above the horizon. At first we doubted that it was Polaris; because of the usual layer of clouds and haze on the horizon, it is practically unheard of to be so close to the equator and still be able to see the Pole Star. Yet the star we saw had the same quiet gleam as Polaris, and was spaced at just the right distance along an imaginary line drawn from the two pointer stars in the Big Dipper. It looked to be slightly less than 2 degrees above the horizon. Allowing for a slight increase in apparent elevation because of refraction, this means we are within 100 miles of the equator.

Rodo is now paying extra close attention to our speed and course, recording his estimates in a journal I have encouraged him to keep. He has a good-natured competition on dead reckoning going with Lewis, and is determined to estimate exactly when we are going to cross the line in order to impress us that he, too, is a navigator of note.

May 23—Twenty-two days out

Today, Sunday the 23rd, marks the start of our fourth week at sea. All three of our navigators say we will cross the line today, but only Rodo has publicly called the time of crossing. At about eight he cockily announced that we would cross the equator at eleven. Kawika then merrily raised the *Meotai* on the CB, telling them, "We're expecting a visit from King Neptune about 11 o'clock."*

We skipped a line-crossing ceremony. A few of us who had been through the pageantry, as well as the bottom-paddling and other hazing that usually accompanies it, had idly talked of having Rodo dress up as King Neptune to preside over the initiation into his realm of all those who had never sailed across the line. But the idea died. We were crossing the great ocean domain of the Polynesian sea god Kanaloa, not that of a Roman god from a near landlocked sea. Besides, any hazing efforts would be easily misunderstood because the gang formed the majority of those who would be eligible for initiation. And, as someone put it, "Who's going to paddle Buffalo?"

We are all delighted to be at last sailing in the Southern Hemisphere, the true South Pacific, and this afternoon we celebrated the occasion with a fine meal. The cuisine, a cross between the Oriental and the Polynesian, even got Clifford out of his bunk to join in the effort. While Tommy boiled the rice, a suddenly cheery Clifford soaked strips of dried fish in his version of teriyaki sauce, then fried them in oil in the upturned lid of our cooking pot. We even had a dessert, the first real one of the trip. John Kruse grated the meat from some of our last coconuts, squeezed the rich milk from the grated meat, then cooked the milk together with arrowroot starch (the Polynesian equivalent of cornstarch) to make a tasty pudding.

That probably is our last such meal. The *Meotai* is running

---

* Later in the day when the *Meotai* navigator finished working out his noon fix he was amazed to find that Rodo had been off by only two hours, or about six miles at the slow rate we were then sailing. We could not, however, share in his amazement. Only when we reached land was word of Rodo's accuracy passed to us.

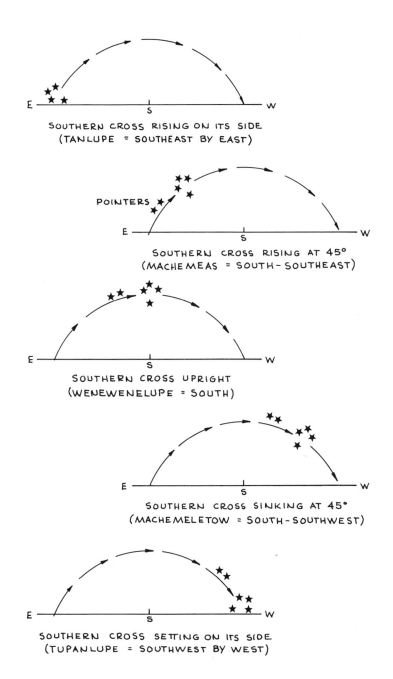

SOUTHERN CROSS RISING ON ITS SIDE
(TANLUPE = SOUTHEAST BY EAST)

POINTERS

SOUTHERN CROSS RISING AT 45°
(MACHEMEAS = SOUTH-SOUTHEAST)

SOUTHERN CROSS UPRIGHT
(WENEWENELUPE = SOUTH)

SOUTHERN CROSS SINKING AT 45°
(MACHEMELETOW = SOUTH-SOUTHWEST)

SOUTHERN CROSS SETTING ON ITS SIDE
(TUPANLUPE = SOUTHWEST BY WEST)

THE FIVE POINTS IN MAU'S STAR COMPASS
INDICATED BY THE POSITION OF THE SOUTHERN CROSS

very low on rice and has no more soy sauce or vinegar (the vital ingredients of our homemade teriyaki sauce) to give us. Furthermore, we are out of arrowroot. John's effort took what was left after our small initial supply had been raided by those suffering from sitting around in damp, salt-encrusted bathing suits. (They discovered that the arrowroot starch worked as well as the finest of talcum powders to soothe their itch.) It would certainly be timely now for the wind to pick up so that we could get enough speed to pull our lures through the water and catch some of the fish that must be out there. Otherwise, some extra hungry times are coming up.

May 24—Twenty-three days out

The promised wind shift is right on schedule. Last night the wind picked up to a reasonable 10–12 knots and backed to the east. The canoe speeded up and automatically followed the wind around until the bows were pointed slightly to the east of a star compass point Mau calls *Machemeas*, which is marked by the half-risen Southern Cross lying at an angle of 45 degrees. When leeway and current drift are taken into account, that heading gives us a resultant course of due south, or close to it. If this wind holds, as it seems to be doing this morning, we could reach the Tuamotus in less than a week.

May 25—Twenty-four days out

The wind held its strength but not its direction. Late yesterday afternoon it veered sharply to the south-southeast, putting us on a course that looked disastrously close to straight southwest. Last night the compass point *Machemeas* was far to the left of our port bow. We were heading well to the west of the upright position of the cross that marks due south on Mau's compass. Most of the night our bows were pointed to the next compass point over, *Machemeletow*, made by the half-set cross leaning over at 45 degrees.

Then, to make matters worse, this morning the wind died to

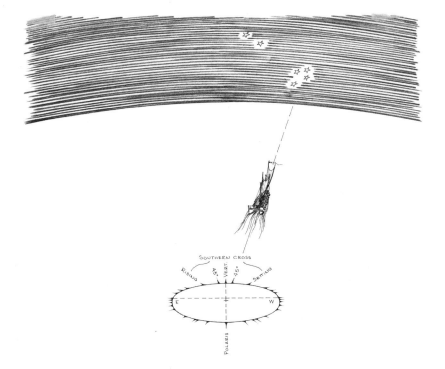

Sailing toward the Southern Cross setting at 45°

a whisper, slowing the canoe until she was barely moving. Kawika and Lyman thought it was time to clean off the barnacles flourishing below the waterline of our two hulls and undoubtedly slowing us down. A dozen of us, armed with machetes, knives and blocks of wood, dived in and set to work knocking off the barnacles and scraping the hulls clean.

We had not painted the hulls with an antifouling compound; we could have been accused of having an advantage over our ancient predecessors who had no such chemicals. Had we done so, the hulls would have stayed smooth and clean for the whole trip, and perhaps we would have sailed a fraction of a knot faster. Inadvertently, however, our handicap had been increased. The plan to scrape the hulls clean just before leaving Maui was another casualty of the predeparture troubles. We therefore had sailed with a bright green ring of sea grass at the waterline and a multitude of sharp little bumps below, which had by now grown into a formidable collection of sizable barnacles.

After banging and scraping away for a good ten minutes, John Kruse, who was working right next to me at the stern, grabbed my shoulder and yelled, "Sharks! Sharks! Get out of the water!"

Four long sharks with white-tipped fins were swimming in formation below and slightly astern of our dangling feet. We did not wait to find out what they wanted. With much thrashing and grappling, we hauled ourselves on board.

"That shark no good. Bite." Mau, who had prudently stayed on deck, gave us the benefit of his knowledge. He knew the sharks as a variety that sometimes attacks swimmers from below without warning. Mau was only slightly amused by our hasty retreat into the canoe. It turned out that he had quietly advised a number of men not to scrape the hulls; island fishermen who snare sharks bang on the resonating hulls of their canoes to attract the beasts. In addition to cleaning the hulls, we had done a good job of shark calling.

May 27—Twenty-six days out

A few hours after the shark adventure the wind picked up again. By late that afternoon we were making a comfortable 5 knots. But the wind still had more south than east in it, forcing us back onto a course significantly west of south. That unwelcome wind has lasted for two days and still shows no sign of shifting.

We are now losing easting at the rate of maybe 2 or 3 miles for every 10 traveled. Should this slide westward continue, we might well lose all our hard-earned store of easting and end up passing well to the west of Tahiti. If that happens we might be lucky enough to fetch up on one of the islands in the Society Group that trail off to the leeward of Tahiti for a few hundred miles, or we might miss them as well and end up hitting one of the Cook Islands, the next archipelago to the west of Tahiti and its outliers. That would be embarrassing, although not fatal. The Prime Minister of that tiny Polynesian nation located 600 miles southwest of Tahiti has invited us to call. After a layover there to wait

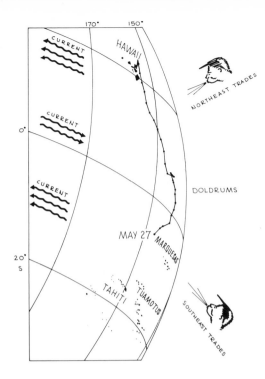

for the right winds—the westerly winds that occur periodically from November through February—we could sail back to Tahiti. According to tradition, that is what the old canoe navigators did when they wanted to go to Tahiti. But that was long ago in the days before modern work schedules, when voyagers could afford to wait for months, even a whole year, to catch the right wind shift. If we got stuck waiting in the Cooks, I am afraid that many of us would lose our jobs for being gone so long.

We really do not figure on having to go all the way to the Cooks if driven past the westernmost islands in the Society Group. Mau, in consultation with Rodo, has worked out a contingency plan. Should we miss all the islands in the Societies, we will continue sailing on the same tack for a few days to get well south of the islands. Then we will tack back up to the northeast to intersect the chain from the south. Once we make a landfall on one of the islands, we can work our way up the chain to Tahiti.

"HOKULE'A OFF COURSE." The headline of the May 28 edition of the Honolulu Advertiser *proclaimed our predicament to its readers. In the story that followed, the news broke that*

those members of the Voyaging Society board left in Honolulu had met the night before to discuss the canoe's alarming westward slide, and that they were considering ordering the Meotai to notify us that we were off course.

A day earlier my wife, Ruth, had heard that these deliberations were to take place and had tried to head off any attempts to

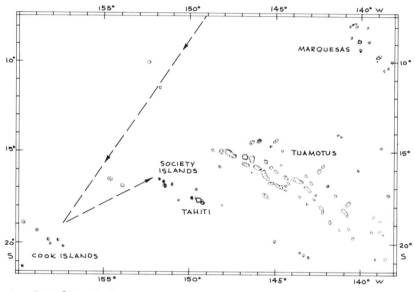

Mau's tacking strategy

interfere. She found board members worried that we would miss Tahiti and would run out of food and water before finding land. Some also thought we were disoriented and had lost our way; they wanted the Meotai to notify us of our position so that we could get back on course. One even went so far, after reminding Ruth that she was not a sailor, as to advise that a tow to the east was in order. Nonetheless, Ruth's efforts may have had some impact; at the meeting the board deferred action to see if the canoe kept sliding west. Still, one man was not satisfied; he decided unilaterally to call the Meotai on a radio-telephone hookup to direct the boat's captain to tell us over the CB that we were off course.

Fortunately, the sailing orders gave Kawika the sole authority to call off the navigation experiment—although, when we wrote them, we never imagined that one of our own board members would try to interfere. The board member in question, it turned out, had not read the sailing orders. The blunt-spoken Meotai captain, a retired Air Force colonel, read them over the radio, then dismissed the interfering board member from the airways.

28

Lost on the Great Ocean

May 28—Twenty-seven days out

"There is one big problem with Mau's plan," Rodo tells me confidentially in Tahitian. "The crew. The men from the deckhouse will never be able to take it."

Rodo does not think they would be able to cope with the disappointment of missing Tahiti, then of enduring the week or two of extra sailing it would take to pass south of the Society Islands and tack back up the northeast to intersect the chain from below.

The euphoria of having their own home has worn off. Dukie and John Kruse, the marginal members of the gang, have moved their bedding out of the deckhouse and have set up hammocks slung from opposite side rails of the afterdeck. "Its too hot in there, there's no air," was John's rationale for leaving the deckhouse, but there was more to his move, and Dukie's, than that. Although they remain partially under the sway of the gang's leaders, basically neither of them can stand lying around all the time. Dukie loves his cooking too much, and recently has branched out into giving haircuts and making model canoes. John, a skilled carpenter, has busied himself with numerous little repair jobs that need to be done. And, although they have not exactly gone back to standing watch, they have assured Lyman, their watch captain, that they will turn out of their hammocks if called in an emergency.

This partial defection of Dukie and John leaves the hard core: Billy, Boogie, Buffalo and Clifford. This gang of four spends most of their time lying within the deckhouse—sleeping, talking idly, picking a guitar or just smoking and staring vacantly. Sometimes they leave their shelter to wander about, or to sunbathe on the deck immediately forward of the deckhouse. Often they eat separately from the rest of us, coming aft only to grab their food, then retiring immediately to the isolation of the deckhouse or to the little patch of deck forward of it. They have also been supplementing their meals with eggs they swipe from the last ones we have, saved for a treat in buckets stowed too conveniently close to the forward entrance of the deckhouse.

These four seem to grow more despairing by the day. The canoe may have left the doldrums, but they are descending further and further into that mental state. Judging from their long faces, their lethargy and some stray comments overheard, they fear that we are lost on this great ocean and that we may never get to Tahiti.

Our slow but continual slide westward has unnerved them, as has the incredibly lonely sea over which we slowly travel. To be sure, *Meotai* still follows us, but except for the sight of her bobbing astern, there is nothing out there to remind us that the watery surface we sail over is that of an inhabited planet. The latitudes we are now crossing comprise a vast oceanic desert—at least to our eye. For a week now we have not seen a single fish, porpoise or bird, or even a sign of living creatures in, on or above the ocean. That the days have been so sparkling clear, and the sunrises and sunsets so spectacular in their red-and-gold pageantry, probably does not help those feeling lost. A little bit of pollution, a stray oil slick, a floating plastic bottle or the roar of a jet passing high overhead—anything to break the pristine monotony of the clean blue ocean and clear skies—would help to remind them that they are not lost forever to the world they left behind.

Sometimes these men seem curiously agitated, only to lapse into their usual somnolence after a period of frantic movement or animated talk. Their supply of *pakalolo* is said to be disastrously low. Could that be causing occasional wild swings of mood and action? Perhaps, but more potent drugs may also be involved. There seems to be a lot of pills being passed around, and Sam Kalalau has witnessed the young magazine photographer and some crewmen inhaling a white powder into their nostrils. Some surmise that the photographer, who came aboard with a supply of pills that he claims are necessary for his health, and who goes out of his way to curry favor with the gang, is the source. However, the gang certainly had plenty of opportunity back in Honolulu, were they so inclined, to obtain anything they wanted.*

Mau's attitude toward the gang is one of silent contempt. They have managed to break all the rules of the sea that he laid down at the ceremony on Maui. He does not speak out against them, although his private comments to Rodo about them are scathing. Maybe he feels it beneath his dignity to admonish them again; maybe he believes it would do more harm than good.

Mau has been more than patient. He has truly wanted to help the Hawaiians recover their lost seamanship skills, and he has taken seriously the obligation to do so under his East-West Center fellowship agreement. Yet Mau has only one really apt pupil, Milton Bertleman, a slight, young part-Hawaiian everyone calls "Shorty." One of the few crewmen with any sailing experience

---

* One of their numerous friends who used to hang around the canoe in Honolulu was reputed to be a big-time drug dealer. He was a huge man who, with his wild tangle of hair, his tattoos and boar's tooth necklace, looked like some sort of fierce Polynesian giant. But at the canoe he always played the part of a gentle one. He would go out of his way to smile at me, although he never volunteered why he was there. In court testimony following his murder in 1977, a witness alleged that this man's involvement with the canoe was mainly a "cover-up" of his cocaine dealing designed "to keep the police and feds from watching somebody who was doing good for the community."

before signing on the canoe, Shorty has chosen to be Mau's understudy and personal servant. He behaves as an island navigator's apprentice should. He keeps quiet, is attentive to Mau's every need and sticks close by him, even to the point of sleeping out on the open deck at his master's feet. Most important of all, Shorty watches Mau's every move, trying to absorb in the island style of nonverbal learning all he can of our navigator's knowledge and skill.

I admire Shorty, but not just for his devotion and zeal to learn. Shorty is a little like Sam Kalalau. He too comes from a rural ranching area (on the island of Hawaii, across the channel from the eastern coast of Maui where Sam lives), and he also does his duty even though he may not agree with all the policies and decisions. Before we sailed, Shorty made it clear that he was dead set against the idea of *haoles* sailing on the same canoe. Yet, since the trip started he has been all business, shunning those of like mind about *haoles* and concentrating on the job of sailing the canoe and learning from Mau.

The gang believes that they are the true followers of Mau. They have been able to disregard Mau's pronouncements at the departure ceremony, or at least those they disliked, by choosing to believe that Mau never really said the words Mike McCoy translated. "That's the *haole* talking, Mau doesn't talk like that," is how they have managed to invert reality.

In this respect, Boogie's performance this morning when he deigned to join us for breakfast was typical. Upon emerging from his nest, he unsteadily made his way aft where, bracing his bulk against the side rail, he commanded our attention. First he blessed the food, then he delivered a "sermon" on how the rest of us had not been following Mau and how: "We Hawaiian members of the crew really respect Mau and follow him. We know he has had thirty to thirty-five years of experience at sea and we respect him. We wish that you others would follow him."

Upon completing his "sermon," Boogie quickly ate his breakfast and then slipped back into the deckhouse—not to emerge again until late afternoon, despite his obligation to stand watch with the rest of us on Kawika's watch from eight until two.

Never mind Boogie and his ravings. The rest of us do not feel lost or disheartened. In fact, today our spirits could not be higher. In the predawn hours the wind started to pick up—first to 12 knots, then 15 and finally to 20, with squalls bringing gusts of 25 knots. After two weeks of drifting and slowpoke sailing, *Hokuleʻa* came alive, her twin wakes hissing, a sure sign we were making 6 knots.

As the sun rose to illuminate the blue ocean, now flecked white with the tumbling crests of the building seas, we received further proof that we were back to good sailing: near simultaneous strikes on all three trolling lines. One got away, but we landed a 30-pound bonito and a 32-pounder, the first fish caught since we entered the doldrums two weeks back. In the doldrum calms, and in the light trades that followed, the canoe just had not been moving fast enough to troll the lures through the sea with sufficient speed to attract predators.

The fresh trades pulled *Hokuleʻa*'s bows around until she was heading almost due south. The wind had not shifted direction that much. The improvement in heading was as much a function of wind strength; our sails work more efficiently in strong winds, automatically bringing the canoe several degrees closer to the wind. Still, we knew that with leeway and current drift added, our course was somewhat west of south, and that we needed a marked shift in wind direction to get us onto a southerly course.

We got the hoped-for shift this evening. The wind backed sharply to the east, pulling the canoe onto a south-southeast heading and giving us a course that must be close to due south. If this wind holds, we could hit Tahiti on the button, or fetch up on one of the islands immediately to the west—assuming the estimate of our position as being approximately due north of Tahiti is correct. We should only have some 600 miles to go, which could mean land in four or five days.

Rodo is especially jubilant. He is almost willing to bet that we will make our landfall on Raiatea, a high island 120 miles west-northwest of Tahiti. This is his feeling, not the result of any dead-reckoning calculations. Underneath Rodo's jaunty manner runs a strong mystical streak—or should I call it religious?

"Remember, Ben, those four sharks you saw below the canoe? Those were my guardian spirits from the Tuamotus."

Rodo surprised me with that. He went on to explain that since we were approaching his home waters, the sharks were now guiding the canoe. Was he pulling my leg? With Rodo you never know. Anyway, Rodo says he has the gut feeling that we are being magically drawn to Raiatea, the sacred island which, according to legend, was the ancient center of Tahitian culture and the starting point for Tahitian expeditions to the far corners of Polynesia.

29
Bioluminescence

May 29—Four weeks out

Last night, starting an hour or so after sunset, we were treated to a wondrous display. First, wave crests began to flash luminescently as the fresh trades tumbled them over. Then the whole ocean came alive. Every breaking wave, every agitation of the ocean's surface, brought forth a sparkling shower of bioluminescence as tiny plankton lit up in the dark, moonless night. That was not all. Where the two hulls furrowed the sea, some sort of larger creatures joined in the show. Glowing spots of luminescence an inch or more in circumference danced alongside the canoe, then swirled round and round in the twin wakes, winking on and off as we sped through the night.

Later, at the midnight change of watch, someone spied a glow on the deck coming from a one-gallon plastic water jug we had cut down to make into a bucket. A steady, blue-white light shone through the thin, translucent sides of the bucket, and within was a shimmering mass of velvety luminescence. At first we thought that a concentration of whatever creatures had so entertained us earlier might have found their way into the bucket from the spray of passing waves. Then we realized that raw fish left over from the morning's catch was the light source. We had not quite consumed all the 60-odd pounds of bonito; after immediately wolfing down sashimi slices, then later feasting on fillets roasted over coconut husks, and drinking bowl after bowl of fishhead soup, a little of the flesh had remained. That was what we had put into the bucket, and that was what was now so eerily lighting up the afterdeck.

None of us had ever seen anything like it. Tommy put a magazine beside the glowing bucket and found it gave out enough light to read by. Had the bioluminescence of the plankton been passed up the food chain to be concentrated in the flesh of the bonitos we had so recently preyed upon? If so, what about the two or three pounds of fish inside us, the same fish now giving off that cold, chemical light? No one was glowing, but the thought that we had eaten tainted fish was inescapable.*

"Get rid of that spooky thing!" someone yelled before our speculations had advanced very far. An obliging hand reached down, grabbed the bucket and tossed it over the side.

---

* The luminescence we saw earlier in the evening, and that given off from the fish, may not have been directly connected. The glowing fish was probably indeed tainted in the sense that a luminescent variety of bacteria found in the humid tropics was feeding on it. By then the fish had been dead for eighteen hours. We had apparently eaten the fish raw, and cooked it for our evening meal, early enough in the day to have avoided any taint from this or other bacteria.

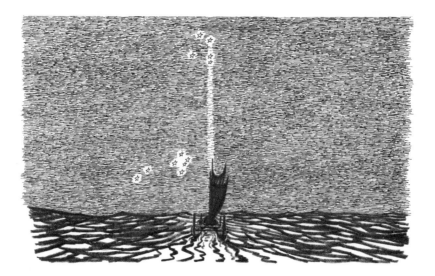

30
Zenith Star

May 30—Twenty-nine days out

The brisk, east-southeasterly winds have been blowing for over twenty-four hours, speeding us southward and feeding our hopes of soon seeing land.

The previous evening's luminescent display was muted last night, overshadowed by the multitude of stars shining brilliantly against the blackness of space. Gone was Polaris, now far below the northern horizon. To the south was the Southern Cross, its circumpolar rotation now edging higher and higher above the line between sea and sky. This Southern Hemisphere sky looked so familiar; it should after all the hours I used to spend—to the amusement of my contemporary-minded Tahitian friends—lying on my back on the beach in front of my Tahitian home, staring up at the night sky and wondering how the old navigators used those stars to guide their canoes. The whole length of the "White Shark," as Tuamotuans call the Milky Way, was clearly visible, as were the mysterious Clouds of Magellan, galaxies beyond our own that can only be seen from southern latitudes. But our attention was not focused solely on this galactic spectacle, or on the familiar horizon stars and constellations. We were also watching David Lewis as he peered directly overhead at the bright star Spica, watching it as it rose toward its zenith, the highest point in its arc across the sky.

Lewis was trying to determine our latitude by observing whether or not Spica passed directly over us when it was at its zenith. For once Mau was the interested spectator. Although he understood the principle of zenith-star sighting, he himself did not systematically use the method.

The zenith-star method is based on the principle that a star crosses the heavens along a particular parallel of latitude. For example, observers stationed around the world along the parallel of 11 degrees south latitude would see Spica pass directly overhead. Thus a mariner at sea can judge whether or not he is 11 degrees south of the equator by watching to see if Spica passes directly overhead. The ancient Polynesians apparently memorized which stars passed over the various islands in their voyaging realm. Then, by observing these stars to see which one passed directly over their canoe, or close to it, they could gauge their relative north-south position—although in terms of islands, not degrees of latitude.

Lewis has a preselected list of zenith stars to be used in succession to plot our progress southward on this last leg when the Pole Star is lost to view. Although Spica is not the first star on his list, last night was the first time on the voyage that Lewis has seriously tried to use the zenith-star method. It had suddenly become important for him to know our exact latitude: whether we were 10 degrees below the equator or 11 degrees below. At the time Lewis's dead-reckoning calculations showed us to be very near Caroline Island, a tiny atoll almost due north of Tahiti and 10 degrees south of the equator. Although Rodo had dismissed Lewis's concern with a good-natured, but pointed, "Bullshit, we're east of Caroline," Lewis was worried. His calculations showed that we were within 30 miles of the island's longitude. On the chance that we might be within range of the atoll's fringing reef, Lewis was mounting his watch on Spica to determine our latitude. If Spica proved to be directly overhead at its zenith, then we were in the clear, one degree south of the island's latitude. However, if Spica was not yet overhead, we might still be in the danger zone.

The after mast was Lewis's sighting instrument. He had adjusted the stays to compensate for the canoe's slight heel and to bring the mast to the perpendicular. All of us on deck at the time watched as Lewis crouched at the base of the mast peering upward along its length to the sky above. Finally, after what seemed like a good hour of mysterious observations, Lewis left his post and told us to relax. He reported that at its zenith Spica had been half a degree in front of the waving tip of the mast. This meant that we were at 10½ degrees, some 30 miles south of the atoll's latitude.

Lewis is confident that he can judge latitude to within half a degree, 30 nautical miles, by the zenith-star method. He is no amateur; in 1965 he sailed a catamaran from Tahiti to New Zealand using horizon stars for orientation and a series of zenith stars to plot his latitudinal progress southward. Although he once allowed himself to get off course near the Cook Islands, when he foolishly decided to follow the vapor trails of a high-flying jet rather than the stars, overall his star navigation proved remarkably accurate. When he arrived off the North Island of New Zealand, his landfall was within half a degree of that predicted by his last zenith-star sight!

When news of Lewis's voyage to New Zealand reached me I had been building *Nalehia* in preparation for my first canoe experiments. At the time I remember trying to find out which stars passed directly over Santa Barbara by going out in my backyard and trying to sight directly upward. All I got for my troubles was a stiff neck. Not until Lewis published his results did I learn how he had used the mast of his catamaran to sight on a zenith star.

This evening I had a chance to try the zenith-star method. With Lewis's help I located Spica well before it was at the zenith.

As the star mounted higher and higher, I began practice sighting up the mast. The base was too cluttered with coils of line, food bags and other items to lie down, so I had to crouch beside the mast, hold on as best I could to steady myself against the pitching and rolling of the fast-moving canoe, and press my head against the mast to get an accurate sight of the weaving masthead and the stars above. It was worth all the contortions. Once Spica finally did reach its zenith, it appeared right on the after (northern) edge of the rough ellipse circumscribed by the masthead. The difference between the center of the ellipse and the position of Spica looked to my unpracticed eye to be between 1 and 2 degrees, which put us between 12 and 13 degrees south of the equator. This means we are not more than 5 degrees, or 300 miles, north of Tahiti, which lies at 17½ degrees south latitude. (Although, of course, it does not tell us whether we are right on Tahiti's longitude or to the east or west of it.)

This welcome proximity to Tahiti's latitude is also evident in the arc of an otherwise insignificant little star called Gienah. Early in the planning phase of the project we thought we might use Sirius as Tahiti's zenith star. It passes directly over the island and is the brightest star in the heavens. But one session at the Bishop Museum planetarium showed us that during the months scheduled for the voyage, Sirius would reach its zenith in daylight hours and thus would be useless to us. At the same time we discovered that dull little Gienah, in the constellation called the Crow (Corvus)—an arrangement of stars that looks more like a gaff-rigged sail to us—is in just the right position, passing directly over Tahiti at night during the voyage months. We also discovered that Gienah has the additional virtue of being easy to spot. The long axis of the Southern Cross points almost directly at the star. Furthermore, just before the long axis of the Cross reaches the perpendicular in its nightly rotation, Gienah is at its zenith.

Tonight was not the first time I have watched Gienah. Since leaving Hawaii I have taken advantage of every clear night to look for the familiar outline of the gaff-rigged sail to get a rough idea of our southward progress. At the beginning of the trip it was arching across the sky well to the south of us. Gradually its arc has moved higher in the sky, until it is now to within 5 degrees or so of passing directly overhead, giving us further proof that we are getting close to the latitude of Tahiti.

At the same time I have been watching the arc of the bright star Arcturus, Hawaii's zenith star. While the gaff-rigged sail has been rising higher in the sky before us, behind us Arcturus has been slowly falling away to the north as we sail southward. Mentally reversing our direction of travel allows me to realize vicariously why Hawaiians called this star Hokule'a, their "Star of Joy." What Hawaiian sailor would not have been overjoyed to see his zenith star rise higher and higher in the sky as he sailed for home?*

---

* "You know, Ben, *le'a* can mean a special kind of joy," an elderly Hawaiian woman had once told me with a hint of a girlish giggle in her dignified voice. *Le'a* can refer specifically to sexual joy—all the more reason for a homebound sailor to call Hawaii's zenith marker the "Star of Joy."

31
Northeast Is the Wind

May 31—Thirty days out

After observing Spica we ran into a series of light squalls. An hour later, at midnight, I went off watch, roused Tommy and turned in, thankful for a dry bunk and a chance to catch a few hours of sleep.

It seemed as if I had hardly closed my eyes when Tommy was back, shaking me and shouting, "Four o'clock. It's blowing hard and raining like hell!"

"Heavy squalls, stand by the sheets with me," Kawika shouted as soon as I stepped on deck.

Gusts of gale-force wind were sweeping over the canoe. *Hokule'a* was sailing hard to windward, and the steepening swells made her roll violently. One moment the entire 60-foot length of the canoe would be canted sharply to the right as her twin hulls climbed obliquely up the face of a big swell. The next moment she would suddenly rotate to the left as she plunged down the swell's backside. At first it felt as if the least added push from the wind would lever the canoe over, especially at the critical moment when we were heeled way over climbing up a swell.

Kawika and I had loosened the sheets from the side rail and were holding them with a quick release grip ready to let go if the canoe reached the point where it felt as if she was starting to go over. Releasing the sheets would spill the wind from the sails, relieving the tremendous levering pressure and bringing the canoe onto a more even keel.

Hokule'a showed her mettle. We never had to let go of the sheets. The winds, gusting upwards of 40 knots, were not strong enough to push the canoe over given her modest sail area and heavy weight. She rushed along throughout the night at a good 7 knots, corkscrewing over the swells, giving us a wild, roller-coaster ride.

I glanced back at Kawika. We both grinned as best we could in the pelting rain. For once Kawika looked as if he was enjoying himself. It was more like he was back standing watch on a sleek racing catamaran than skippering a heavy, problem-burdened double-canoe.

I too was enjoying myself as we raced through the squally night. My thoughts went ahead in space and back in time. In May 1956 I had been aboard the *Tamara*, an old copra schooner converted to government use, sailing through the Tuamotus on a medical and administrative tour of the Archipelago. I was twenty-two then, fresh out of college, and had sailed to Tahiti while waiting to go in the Navy. After a few weeks in Tahiti I had jumped at the chance to sail to the Tuamotus on the *Tamara* as a deck passenger in exchange for surveying the islands we visited for cases of elephantiasis, then a common disease in Tahiti. Little did I dream that twenty years later I would be approaching the Tuamotus in a double-canoe bound for Tahiti.

I knew that should this wind keep up for long, and the sea build further, we would be in trouble. Rodo feared that a prolonged spell of wind like this might strike us near Tahiti, battering the canoe and driving her to the west, far off course. Periodically during the approaching Southern Hemisphere winter, high-pressure zones settle over the cold waters far below Tahiti. Winds of almost gale force then sweep up from the south, blowing for days—sometimes weeks—on end, chilling the air and building up huge seas before them.

With dawn came clearing skies and moderating winds. The danger passed as quickly as it had come. We are back to ideal sailing conditions.

Upon going off watch at eight I dove for my bunk but could not fall asleep. I was too keyed up by the fast sailing to relax. In addition, someone in the deckhouse was making a lot of noise. While lying there stewing over the racket, it dawned on me that it was not one of the gang who was talking so loudly. It was a radio announcer. The gang was listening to Kimo's radio.

Soon thereafter the droning radio voice was drowned out by cheers emanating from within the deckhouse. The gang tumbled out, all smiles for once. Billy Richards seemed particularly elated. He kept giggling and repeating, "Oh, how happy I am. Oh, how happy I am."

A few days back, Kawika had spilled the news to me that the gang had been secretly listening to Kimo's radio since gaining the privacy of their deckhouse. Lyman had discovered them huddled around the radio one night. When challenged, they had replied, "Oh, we're just listening to Hawaiian music." Kawika says that while tuning into their favorite Hawaiian music station (during the night long waves from standard broadcast stations can be heard far out at sea), they heard the alarming news reports that we were hopelessly off course. That, Kawika theorizes, is why these men virtually collapsed a while back.

A little detective work revealed that for the last two days the gang has been listening to the English-language news program broadcast every morning from Radio Mahina, the government radio station on Tahiti. Yesterday's broadcast had apparently brought them their first word that our course had straightened out. That must have made them realize that their despair over reaching Tahiti had been groundless, and that they have behaved ridiculously over the last weeks. Perhaps that is why yesterday evening Billy Richards made a curious speech, ending with the demand, "When we get to Tahiti let us not say things about other crew members, let us not make accusations." This morning's broadcast must have really contained good news to have the gang come bursting out of their lair in such good humor.

We were to learn later that all Tahiti was now caught up in our venture. The Tainui (Taee-noo-ee) Association, a group formed by my Tahitian friends to welcome us, had been receiving daily position reports via shortwave radio and were charting our progress daily on large maps tacked up around Papeete (Pah-pay-ʻeh-tay), the port town and capital of Tahiti. In addition, they had the newspapers, the government television station and Radio Mahina spread the word of how we were closing in on Tahiti.

The Tahitians were excited to learn that after wandering so long toward the west we were now headed directly for Tahiti. To them it was as if after fooling around we were finally getting down to the business of heading straight for our target, thus proving the worth of their ancestral navigational methods as well as voyaging canoes. Little did they realize that our peregrinations over the ocean were at the behest of the wind. The steering sweep remained lashed to the deck and the wind was still in command of our course.

Some European residents of Tahiti were strangely offended by the Tahitians' enthusiasm. A few cried foul. A navigational instructor, a French expert who apparently saw himself as the bearer of all navigational enlightenment to the Polynesians, was particularly incensed. He went to the press and appeared on television to declare that it was impossible to navigate so far and so accurately without instruments. He even accused us of having a compass secreted aboard.

We knew nothing of all this excitement and controversy. Nor were we fully aware that at the time we were headed directly for

Tahiti. Our three navigators had somewhat differing opinions as to exactly where we were and where we were headed.

Rodo tells me he reckons that as of noon we are 13 degrees, 47 minutes south of the equator and at the meridian of 149 degrees west longitude. His estimate puts us about 250 miles north of Tahiti and a dozen miles east of the island. But Rodo does not wholly trust his pencil-and-paper calculations. He feels that we may be even farther to the west, and still has the premonition that we are being magically drawn to the sacred island of Raiatea.*

David Lewis puts us at about the same latitude as Rodo but places us one degree, or 90 miles, to the west of Tahiti. Yet, like Rodo, he does not seem to trust his figures. Once when discussing the voyage before departure, Lewis had let the remark slip, "But I have my professional reputation as a navigator at stake." It was as if he felt that he, not Mau, was the navigator, and that the world was watching his performance. That is why, I believe, he does not trust his longitude figure. There is no way he can ascertain our longitude by observing the stars. In reality he can only make an educated guess, one that depends largely on his estimate of the strength of the westward-flowing current. That is what has been bothering him. Lewis is haunted by the thought he might be underestimating the strength of the current, and that therefore we might be even farther west than his figures indicate. That would explain why he has been talking with Rodo about the possibility of fetching up on Scilly (Manuae) or Bellingshausen (Motu One), the two small westernmost islands in the Society chain.

In contrast to his assistants, Mau seems calmly confident that we are on course, approaching Tahiti from an angle just slightly

---

* Incredible as it may seem, after thirty days at sea Rodo was within one minute, or one nautical mile, of where the *Meotai* navigator placed us at the time —13 degrees, 46 minutes south, 149 degrees west longitude! Furthermore, since there is no reason to believe that the *Meotai* navigator's calculations were accurate to within a mile, for all purposes Rodo placed us exactly where we actually were.

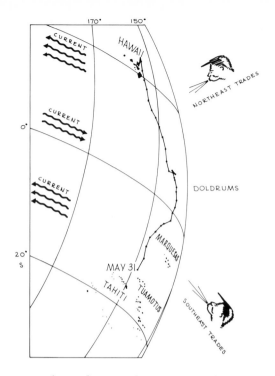

east of north. He thinks we will pass the Tuamotus sometime tomorrow and see Tahiti the day after.

At about one this afternoon we went through a squall, only to come out of it a few minutes later to find that the wind had backed clear around to the northeast. The canoe, still on self-steering, automatically followed the wind around until it was on a southeast course. We are now definitely making easting for the first time since leaving the doldrums. Any miles we can gain to the east are welcome. If we are west of Tahiti, the favorable winds might allow us to regain Tahiti's longitude. If we are east of Tahiti, the extra miles of easting will be insurance against any later wind shift that might put us back onto a southwest heading.

"'O maoa'e te mata'i," a Tahitian phrase meaning "maoa'e is the wind," popped into my head after the wind shift. Maoa'e (mah-oh-ah-'eh) is Tahitian for the northeast wind. As near as I can recollect, the phrase was the opening line of an old Tahitian song. Unbidden, it keeps running through my mind, although try as I might I cannot remember the rest of the song. Only the phrase " *'O Tahiti te fenua,*" or "Tahiti is the land," comes to mind. Does that mean that the northeast wind is blowing us to Tahiti?

I went to Rodo. He, too, can recollect the song only vaguely, and cannot remember if Tahiti or some other island was the land specified in the lyrics.

An hour later Rodo cried out, " *'Itata'e! 'Itata'e!*" pointing to some small white birds darting over the waves. Earlier, Mau had seen one far off but had kept his counsel. Rodo was more than willing to talk. He was in his home waters and had instantly recognized the birds to be *'itata'e* ('ee-tah-tah-'eh), or fairy terns, sure signs that land was near. Rodo assured us that these were not wandering juveniles like the booby birds we had seen north of the equator. They were adult birds which, according to Rodo's experience, ordinarily do not fly out more than 20–25 miles from their atoll roost.

Late this afternoon came another sure sign of land nearby. The regular trade wind swell from the southeast faltered, then died altogether. Except for the chop generated by the northeast wind, the sea is now flat. *Hokule'a* sails along serenely as if she is moving through the protected waters of a huge lagoon. An island lies out there somewhere to windward, cutting off the trade wind swells. But which island? And how far away?

Most likely a coral atoll in the Tuamotu group has blocked the swells and is the home for the terns we just saw. If so, we will not be able to see the tops of the coconut palms before we are within 10 or 12 miles of the island—and then only as long as the sun stays up. Once night falls we will not be able to spot the atoll until we are almost upon it.

June 1—Thirty-one days out

Darkness came without sight of land. Sometime in the night, we thought, we would see an island—hopefully in time to avert crashing onto its fringing reef. An old name for the Tuamotus, *the Dangerous Archipelago*, came to mind, as did the many tales of shipwreck in this labyrinth of atolls and hidden reefs. In all my dreaming about sailing a canoe to Tahiti there had been one nightmare: speeding through a dark night, suddenly breakers ahead, then smashing onto the reef where the canoe breaks up as pounding surf grinds it over jagged coral heads.

Almost everyone was up at the beginning of the eight-to-midnight watch eagerly scanning the dark horizon ahead for land. But by midnight most had turned in, leaving only three of us on watch: Kawika, Rodo and I. The moon was not out, and low

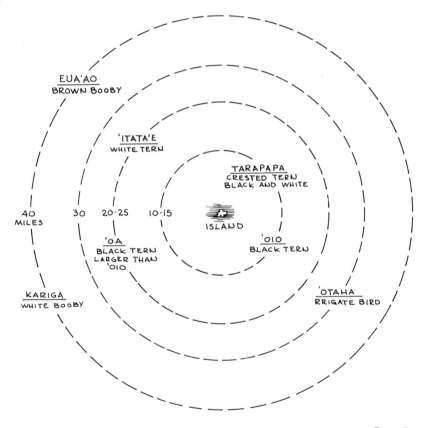

MAXIMUM NORMAL FLIGHT RANGE OF TUAMOTU BIRDS
AFTER RODO WILLIAMS

clouds blocked the horizon. I was glad to have Rodo with us to help with the difficult task of spotting a low atoll. But he was strangely subdued. After only an hour or two on watch, he asked to be excused because of illness, and unsteadily climbed into his bunk under the port hull covers. That left only Kawika and me on watch. The two gang members who were also supposed to be on duty were bedded down in the deckhouse, and the sixth member of the watch, Shorty Bertleman, was sleeping on the afterdeck near where Mau lay snoring.

When Rodo had been on duty I had stationed myself on the deck forward of the masts in order to have an unobstructed view of the horizon. After Rodo left I came aft to be with Kawika, taking a post at the rail watching the horizon off the forward quarter of the port hull. I assumed that with our present southeast heading, land would first appear in that direction. I searched and searched until my eyes ached. So dark and murky was it that I repeatedly imagined that I saw an island ahead, only to have it dissolve into a dark cloud before my straining eyes. Finally, Kawika said it was getting near four and asked me to go forward to wake the other watch. I was disappointed that we had not spotted land on our watch.

Upon stepping forward to go around the after sail, which had been blocking the view to starboard, I saw it: a long, black line curving off in the distance. A quarter moon was rising, making the sea glitter dully in contrast to the thin, dark curve. I called Kawika over to confirm the sighting.

"That's an island all right," Kawika said as he came around the sail. "Wake up Mau!"*

I called to Mau and started blowing my man-overboard whistle to wake the rest. Mau sat up, blinked, focused on the black line

---

* Although the first to raise the alarm, I was actually the fourth person to see the island. Earlier the photographer had spied a dark line on the horizon while standing on the outer gunwale of the starboard hull, urinating to leeward. But he thought nothing of it at the time and slipped back into his sleeping bag. Dukie and Buffalo had just gotten up and were leaning against the starboard rail, wondering out loud what that funny wave or cloud was doing out there, when I came around the after sail.

and gave the order to come about. The atoll was not far off to starboard and we were closing fast. Within a few minutes everyone was up. We brought the canoe into the wind and then over to the starboard tack to stand out from the island. Once we were a safe distance away, we hove to and pulled the booms and sails against the mast to drift and wait for the dawn, a maneuver that was marred when Clifford inexplicably challenged Kawika to a fight.

Then the guessing game began: what island was out there?

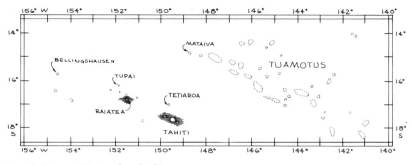

Candidate atolls for landfall

The way the shore curved away so abruptly in both directions indicated that it was a small atoll, smaller than all but a few of the atolls in the Tuamotu chain. That, plus the belief that we could be no farther east than the western edge of the Tuamotus, made for three obvious candidates: Mataiva, a tiny atoll at the northwestern tip of the Tuamotus, and two other small atolls farther to the west: Tetiaroa, 30 miles due north of Tahiti; and Tupai, 120 miles west of Tahiti. Rodo, now back on deck though obviously in pain from some ailment, thought that the island must be Mataiva, but he was not sure. Mau thought we had reached the Tuamotus, but lacking personal knowledge of the archipelago he declined to guess whether the island was Mataiva or not. Lewis believed we were farther to the west and favored Tupai. He even went so far as to ask Rodo anxiously, "How about Bellingshausen?" Evidently Lewis feared that the current might have swept us to this little atoll lying almost 300 miles west of Tahiti. Rodo, too, was worried about what the current might have done to our course. Despite his calculations which indicated that the island out there in the darkness must be Mataiva, Rodo could not shake the feeling that we might have fetched up on an island lying farther to the west.*

---

* That made Rodo also consider Tetiaroa and, as an outside chance, Tupai, although he was bothered by the fact that both were far to the south of where his figures indicated we were. Lewis was less concerned, however, about the southerly position of these atolls as well as that of Bellingshausen. A zenith-star sighting earlier in the night had made him revise his latitude estimate a degree or so to the south, although he was rightly suspicious that the canoe's heading toward the southeast (instead of toward the south, as when he made his previous zenith-star sights) might have led him to overestimate our southerly progress.

32
The Nine Sentinels

June 1—Thirty-one days out (continued)

A light was moving along the shore—probably a lantern carried by a fisherman. Then it disappeared. It was tempting to think that the light ashore knocked Tupai and Bellingshausen out of the running, for neither of them is permanently inhabited.

Then someone thought he spotted a glimmer of light off in the distance to the south of the atoll. Rodo and I strained to look. If the island were Tetiaroa, we might have seen a faint glow behind it from the city lights of Papeete or from the Point Venus light-house on the northeast coast of Tahiti. But it was a false alarm. The sky was dark and uninformative in that direction.

Dawn. No sign of the peaks of Tahiti or any other high island behind the atoll. That ruled out Tetiaroa and also Tupai, which lies immediately north of the stunning volcanic island of Bora Bora.

In the spreading light the dark line changed gradually into the curve of an atoll ringed with surf and green with dense vegetation. We were off the northeast end of the island. Mau started to give the order to tack to port and sail south down the eastern shore. Rodo stopped him, explaining that for most atolls in these waters the pass into the lagoon was on the northern or western side. So we went over to the starboard tack instead and headed west along the northern shore.

The light wind pushed us slowly along as we sailed parallel to the island. Only surf breaking on the reef could be heard. We stood mute, gazing hungrily at the first land seen for a month. As the sun rose higher, we could see clearly the narrow coral sand beach beyond the surf line and could make out the coconut palms and other trees and shrubs that formed a solid green wall behind the beach. Not a soul was in sight ashore; not one sign of human life.

After another fifteen minutes of following the shore, we spotted something way ahead where the coast curved out of sight. As we drew closer, first one building then several appeared, indicating that we were coming to a village. By now Rodo was almost certain that the island was Mataiva (Mah-tah-ee-vah); the village was in the right location at the northwestern tip of the atoll. Rodo could not be absolutely sure, for it had been twenty years since he last called on Mataiva. If he were to identify the island as Mataiva and it turned out to be another island, he would never be able to live it down. So all he would say was, "Not sure yet."

As we sailed closer, two skiffs powered by outboard motors came buzzing out the pass to meet us. Rodo called out to them but did not ask the name of their island. That would have been like admitting he was lost.

Earlier Lewis had related a case in point. After having been battered by a severe storm, two Micronesian navigators from an island near Mau's were wandering the sea, lost, when they fetched up on a strange atoll. It was Kapingamarangi, a small Polynesian outlier hundreds of miles south of their island. Although from their traditional training they knew of the existence of Kapingamarangi and other islands peripheral to their usual voyaging range, they had never before visited the island and did not recognize it. But being proud navigators they could not admit they were lost. Instead they came ashore pretending they had been heading for the island all along. Then came the problem of finding out where they were so they could orient themselves for home. Instead of giving away their ignorance by asking, they took to sauntering around the village, eavesdropping on conversations in hope that

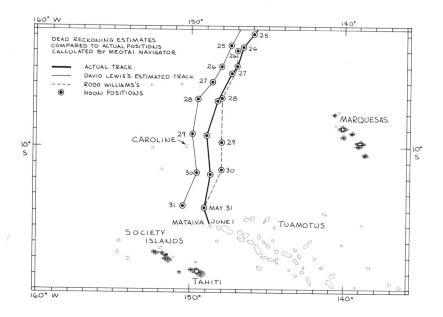

someone would mention the island's name. Finally, after many days, their efforts were rewarded when a group of playing children shouted out "Kapingamarangi!" in the midst of a game. That was all the information the navigators needed to know to sail for home.

I had no navigator's reputation to lose. So as the skiffs pulled up, I called out in Tahitian, "What is the name of your island?" The people in the skiffs looked confused. I repeated the question. They yelled back, " *'O Mataiva!*"

After a quick conference between Rodo and the leader of the group, the skiffs towed us into the narrow pass, battling the strong current flowing out of the lagoon in order to bring us to a safe anchorage in quiet water near the village.

The Mataivans then climbed aboard with great excitement. But when they came face-to-face with us on deck, they suddenly became shy. Apprehension was written all over their faces. Although their ancestors had once sailed the sea in double-canoes, *Hokuleʻa* was the first they had ever beheld. And we ourselves must have been a sight—seventeen strange men with beards, disheveled hair and a musty odor concocted of sweat, mildewed clothes and dried fish. That some among us looked like them, and some like the *haole* yachtsmen who occasionally call on their island, might have added an aura of mystery. It took the woman among them to break the ice—by popping seashell leis over our heads and then pecking us on both cheeks, French Polynesian style. The men relaxed. We exchanged greetings and started showing them around the canoe.

Then they ferried us ashore in their skiffs to meet the rest of the people waiting in the village. Our first steps on solid ground were surprisingly steady, not at all like the hesitating gait of a sailor whose legs have become habituated to the pitching and rolling deck of a monohull craft. One more reason to bless the stable ride provided by *Hokuleʻa's* twin hulls.

If any among us imagined we had touched upon some isolated outpost of old Polynesia, they may have been disappointed, at least initially. The Mataivans were dressed in modern style, the men in shorts or long pants and shirts, the women in dresses. Not a thatched roof was in sight, only red-painted corrugated iron roofs capping substantial houses of concrete or imported timber. A few cars and trucks were parked on the coral-paved streets in front of small general stores selling anything from spark plugs to Crackerjacks. For generations the islanders had been exporting copra and living in a cash economy. Yet the village was not a city, and the 150 Mataivans living there greeted us with genuine Polynesian warmth.

They were a little embarrassed, for we had caught them unprepared. Although they had heard over Radio Mahina that we might pass by their island, they never dreamed that we would stop. Polynesian custom dictated that they welcome us with a feast, the preparations for which now occupied almost everyone. One group was singeing the hair off a newly slaughtered pig; another was at work preparing a small mountain of papayas; still another was heaping wood in the large, rock-filled pit in the ground that was their oven. After burning the wood to heat the rocks, in would go the pig, the fish and all the taro, breadfruit and other local vegetable foods being prepared. Over that a thick layer of leaves (or burlap copra sacks), followed by a final layer of sand, to seal the oven so that the hot stones (volcanic rocks imported from Tahiti) within could bake the contents in the moist, airless environment.

Before we could watch that process, the Mataivans whisked us off to the village schoolhouse, where the chief of the island stood waiting with other dignitaries in front of the assembled schoolchildren. The latter's smiles and giggles faded as we approached. Faces frozen, they began to sing the "Marseillaise," the French National Anthem that they had learned by heart to intone when the island hosted important visitors. That duty completed, they relaxed and gaily sang a medley of Tuamotu songs, after which they presented us with shell leis, including an especially delicate one that Hoku accepted around her neck with her usual aplomb.

After the inevitable speeches, presentation of still more leis and the gift of one of the *Hokuleʻa*'s paddles to the chief, we piled into trucks for a tour of the island along a road that had been built to connect the coconut plantations scattered around the atoll. Every few miles the bumpy road would break out of the lush vegetation onto wide channels running from the outer reef to the interior lagoon. When the surf rises, waves sweep over the reef, through the channels and into the lagoon. Now, however, the channels were dry and we could drive right across their hard coralline surface.

"*Mata* means eye and *iva* means nine," our guide explained when we stopped at one of the channels to visit a coral rock at the lagoon's edge where in ancient times prisoners of war were slain and prepared for the earth oven. Each channel was an "eye" to the outside reef, where a warrior would be stationed to watch for invading canoes. The island's name, he explained, was derived from the fact that nine such channels cut the atoll's ring.* The thought of "nine sentinels" stationed around the island was appealing, perhaps because of a coincidence. Subtract the two photographers and the six deckhouse gang members from our complement of seventeen; that leaves the nine of us who had watched over the canoe during the last weeks.

On the way back to the village we were treated to other sights, including the remains of two shipwrecks: a large steel-hulled sailing vessel that had been washed over the reef and driven far inland during a huge storm over half a century ago, and the half-buried remains of a small wooden yacht that had run aground one calm night a few years ago. The owner and sole person aboard the yacht had miscalculated his course; he had been down below asleep when his craft sailed right onto and over the reef. That our canoe might have met the same fate was, I am sure, the unspoken thought of many of us as we examined what was left of the yacht projecting out of the sand, looking like the ribs of a long-dead whale.

From the shipwrecks we were taken to the island's now abandoned taro beds. Years ago, the ancestors of today's Mataivans had used wooden digging sticks and their bare hands to excavate pits in the infertile mixture of coral debris and sand that passes for soil on Mataiva to reach the fresh water lens that floats upon the salt water permeating the atoll's coralline base. There, in the days before trading schooners and before rice, flour and other imported foods now enjoyed on the island, previous generations of Mataivans grew their staple taro in an artificial soil, painstakingly made from leaves and other plant debris scooped off the atoll's sandy surface and transported to fill the bottom of the pits.

Our guide wanted to continue the tour and show us still more

---

* Although a folk etymology, such as this one, may make good sense, there are often alternate etymologies, even alternate names, for islands. Old written sources indicate that Mataiva was originally Matahiva, a name that may be translated as "Face of the Clan" or "Face of the Company."

island points of interest, but we begged off. We were thinking of the feast being prepared back in the village, and of using some of the villagers' store of rainwater to wash the salt out of our hair and off our hides.

What a feast it was! Feeling clean for the first time in a month, we trooped into the overlarge dining room of our host's house. Spread out before us on two long tables were platters of roast pork, chicken and steaming fish fresh from the earth oven, raw fish marinated in lime juice, steamed lobsters and crabs, breadfruit, coconut bread, platters of bright yellow papaya pudding that had been wrapped in banana leaves and also cooked in the earth oven, and lastly a supreme island luxury: bowls of canned fruit salad.

After our host, the semiofficial port pilot who had towed us into the pass, gave the blessing, we dug in—watched by practically the whole populace of the island, who were crowded around us or were peering through windows and doorways.

I heaped my plate, a large shallow soup bowl, with food in the Tahitian manner. First half an inch of coconut sauce in the bottom, then everything else piled on top. Rural Tahitians and outer islanders disdain eating with metal utensils. "How can the white man put those iron things in his mouth?" they ask. Their idea of pleasurable dining is to eat with the hands. Just grab a piece of pork, fish, pudding or whatever you want. Swirl it around in the coconut sauce. Then, using two fingers and a thumb, pop it into your mouth with a hearty smack designed both to vacuum any sauce left on your fingers and to show pleasure. To the delight of the Mataivans, several of us took to eating that way, spurning the forks and spoons customarily laid out for foreign visitors.

"Right on," "Out of this world" and " *ʻOno*" were some of our exclamations of delight. The Mataivans understood *ʻono*, for it means "delicious" in Tahitian as well as Hawaiian. It was not just that we were ravenous after our Spartan canoe fare. The feast was truly delicious, one of the best I have ever tasted.

A mellow mood spread among us as we filled our bellies with the first really satisfying food since leaving Maui. Even the deckhouse gang loosened up, seemingly calmed by the hospitality of kindred Polynesians.

Once the meal was over, our host, a tall, dignified Tuamotuan in his fifties, took the floor. Rodo was off trying to call Papeete over the government shortwave radio, so it was left to me to translate.

"We the citizens are so happy that you have come in your canoe to our island Mataiva," he began, speaking with the grave demeanor of a Polynesian orator. He went on to explain how they had followed our progress from radio reports, how they had been so disappointed that we were headed straight for Tahiti and would not stop at their island. But the position report they received from last night's news broadcast from Radio Mahina had given them hope that we might sail close by Mataiva so that at least they could see the canoe and maybe even take our picture.

"This morning we went out to the pass, and when we got there we looked and I called out, 'There's the canoe, let's go grab hold of it and pull it in.' "

At this point the Mataivans broke out laughing, as did many of our group who had figured out what he was relating from his vigorous pantomime of hauling the canoe and from the Tahitian word *huti*, which means "to pull." Hawaiians use a *k* where Tahitians use a *t*; *huti* (hoo-tee) is identical with the Hawaiian *huki* (hoo-kee), a word still heard in paddling and surfing circles.

Then he told how they grabbed their cameras, scooped up what shell leis were lying around the house, and launched their skiffs to come outside the pass to meet us. To their delight they did not have to talk us into coming into the lagoon. It was we, he related with great gusto, who asked them, "Can we go inside?"

After emphasizing that Mataivans and Hawaiians were kinsmen of "one family," our host surprised us by renaming *Hokule'a*. Hereafter our canoe was to be known as *Tearikitu* and *Heiau*, two legendary warriors from Mataiva's past who had sailed from island to island in search of adventure and battle. Another coincidence. *Tearikitu* (Tay-ah-ree-kee-too) means literally "the Chief of Tu," the Polynesian god of war. In Hawaii the god Ku (the

Hawaiian pronounciation of Tu) also guarded the great forest trees and was the deity to whom canoe makers prayed before felling a forest giant to make a canoe hull. *Heiau* (Hayee-ow), the other new canoe name, also carries a special meaning for us because in Hawaiian it means "temple" and is one of those religious terms which, along with *mana* and *kapu* (taboo), is commonly employed by those who have retained some knowledge of the ancient religion or are trying to revive the old practices.

Our host's eloquent speech, particularly after he capped it with the renaming of *Hokule'a*, brought tears to the eyes of many. It fell to Kawika to respond. He could have spoken in Hawaiian. Tahitian and Hawaiian (particularly Kawika's Niihau Island dialect) are close enough for the Mataivans to have understood the gist of whatever he said. Yet Kawika chose to speak in English so, as he explained to the perplexed Mataivans, his crew would understand.

Kawika delivered a polished speech that was hard to translate into anywhere near so eloquent Tahitian. After thanking the Mataivans profusely for their hospitality, for the warmth of their welcome and for the delicious feast, Kawika elaborated on the theme of Hawaiian-Mataivan kinship, following the same Christian theme our host (a lay minister) had employed.

"This trip was planned so long ago. Somewhere in the Pacific we had a long-lost family. By the guiding hands of our Heavenly Father we found this land. That's how we found you as our lost family. We could have found any other island in the Tuamotus, but fate brought us here."

Our host then requested that we sing some Hawaiian songs. Kawika started to lead, but to his consternation Billy and Boogie, followed by the rest of the gang, got up from the table, took their guitars and slipped out of the house. The fundamentalist religious beliefs of our host dictated that the feast be dry; a supply of beer awaited the gang across the street in an abandoned shack. Upon landing, Rodo, fearful of what might happen if the gang got drunk, had requested that the Mataivans not give us anything to drink. Undaunted by the prohibition, our gang had quickly found and petitioned the few habitual drinkers on the island to supply them with the beer now sitting in the shack along with their newfound friends. The gang lost no time making their way across the street to join the latter happily in drink. Soon sounds of raucous laughter and strains of "The Queen's Jubilee" and other gang favorites were competing with our more feeble musical efforts.

"What is this? We feed these people and they do not stay and sing for us!" was the comment that summed up the disappointment and disgust of the abstemious Mataivans who had feted us.

Fortunately the beer supplies on the island were limited. After finishing off the few bottles available, the gang retired to sleep from dusk till dawn.

June 2—Thirty-two days out

After a good night's rest—the first in a month not interrupted by watch calls—a magnificent breakfast that was a small version of yesterday's feast, and tearful songs and farewells on the beach, we took the launches back to the canoe to ready her to sail the 170 miles that lay between Mataiva and Tahiti. This last leg would be easy, we hoped; a matter of no more than 1½ days of steady sailing.

With that in mind, yesterday we talked about raising the mat sails, which so far have remained rolled up along the port hull. Although the short trial would add little to the experiment, sailing into Papeete Harbor with the sun glinting off sails of golden pandanus leaves would be a fitting gesture to conclude the voyage. But upon climbing aboard the canoe I discovered that Kawika and Mau had nixed the idea. "The wind is too strong," they said, although I suspect that the true reason is that they are still anxious about getting the canoe safely to Tahiti and do not wish to add an extra complication at the last moment.

Getting out of the narrow pass and into the open ocean was their foremost concern. A strong current was running out of the lagoon, ripping through the pass, which looked not much wider than *Hokule'a*'s beam. The gusty winds were not to be trusted. If they were to die in midpassage, the current could sweep us onto the coral. If they suddenly shifted direction, we could be driven aground. So instead of sailing out we elected to take the tow offered by our hosts, hoping that the outboard motors on the two skiffs could pull us through the water fast enough to gain steerageway in the swift current.

Everyone was tense; *Hokuleʻa* was at risk. The men from the

skiffs tossed us the towlines, maneuvered into place in front of the bow and started revving their puny-looking outboard motors. At the signal the shore line was cast off. The skiffs started pulling us slowly toward the pass, attempting to gain speed before the current fully caught us. All of a sudden the mainstream gripped the canoe, hurling us into the pass. The buzzing skiffs raced to pull us down the narrow passage, while Dukie and Tommy manned the swivel-mounted central sweep to keep the canoe sliding straight between the jagged coral banks. No problem.

Within seconds we were through the pass and safely out into the blue sea once more. We waved our thanks to the Mataivans in the skiffs, unfurled the sails and set off on the starboard tack, sailing parallel to Mataiva's western shore until we could get a straight shot to the south. A rainsquall swept over the atoll and then out to sea, blessing us with a cool shower just as we cleared Mataiva and set our course directly for Tahiti.

33
"A Dangerous Gift"

June 3—Thirty-three days out

Late this morning a cloudy beacon announcing land appeared
in the distance: a stationary mass of clouds evidently caused by
high peaks interrupting the trade wind flow. In the past such a
sign had answered the prayers of many a canoeload of wandering
Polynesians searching the ocean for a high, volcanic island on
which to settle. Assuming our navigation was on target, the
clouds were telling us that Tahiti lay dead ahead.

After a few more hours of sailing, dark shadows appeared
beneath the clouds. Gradually they took the form of mountain
peaks thrust up from the ocean. It looked as if two islands were
ahead, but that was an illusion. Tahiti is shaped like a figure
eight: two volcanic cones joined by a low isthmus. From a
distance only the widely separated tips of the eroded cones can
be seen above the horizon.

We are too far away to reach land before dark. At best we
might make it to the port of Papeete around midnight, too late
for a safe entry into the pass. Our Tahitian sponsors, the Tainui

Association, do not want us to land until tomorrow morning. Via the CB relay from the *Meotai*, they requested that we keep clear of Tahiti till daybreak and not enter the pass until nine o'clock, when we are to receive a formal Tahitian welcoming. In order to keep safely clear of Tahiti during the night, Rodo advised that we heave to in the lee of Tetiaroa (Tay-tee-'ah-row-ah) Atoll and wait there until one or two in the morning before sailing the remaining 30 miles to Papeete. So Kawika gave the orders to fall off to the southwest and head for the atoll.

That was a terrible idea as far as the deckhouse gang was concerned. "Why are we going there? Why aren't we going to Tahiti?" they demanded irately. Kawika and Rodo tried to explain that it was too late to land at Tahiti, that we must wait till daylight the next day to enter the harbor safely and, above all, to receive the formal welcome from the Tahitians. The explanation did not sit at all well with the gang. To them it was just another decision of the "leaders" designed to cheat them out of their due, which in this case was a night on the town in Tahiti.

As the coconut palms of Tetiaroa began to stand above the horizon, a sleek white sportfishing boat came racing out to meet us. None other than National Geographic's Dale Bell was aboard. After recuperating from his brief sea voyage, he flew to Tahiti and inserted himself into the welcome the Tainui Association was planning. But he could not even wait for us to appear off Papeete as Tainui had requested of all greeters. Bell had to come out before anyone else so that he could welcome us personally with a photogenic gift—a dozen bottles of French champagne that were tossed over from the sportfishing boat to anxious hands. This time his meddling had immediate, and explosive, consequences.*

The men from the deckhouse gang claimed a lion's share of the bottles and moved forward to enjoy their drinking on the foredeck away from the rest of us. Corks were popped, and after

---

* Later even Dale Bell himself acknowledged this in the narrative of his film, although he neglected to confess his personal role. "Friends," the narrator blandly announces at this juncture in the film, "toss champagne aboard. It is a dangerous gift."

the gushing foam of the sea-churned champagne subsided, the bottles were passed round and round their circle. It was not long before the champagne had its effect. The initial smiles and laughter faded, replaced by those same contorted faces and angry voices we had witnessed several times before the voyage.

All of a sudden the gang broke their tight circle and started moving aft toward the rest of us, assembled, as usual, on the afterdeck. They pushed their way between us, taking up stations

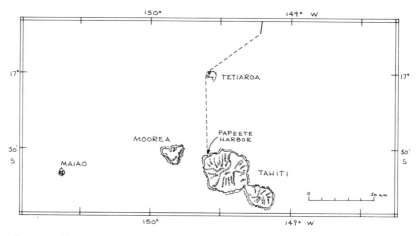

Route to Papeete

against the port and stern rails. Then, almost as if on cue, the harangue started, led by Boogie and Billy, with Dukie joining in. Lewis was accused of trying to change course while Mau slept. Kawika was castigated for not being a "strong leader"; then he was told that he should have "followed the crew." Lyman was similarly criticized for not following the crew's lead, and also for apologizing over raising the jib. I was attacked for spoiling the trip with my presence and for preventing the installation of keel fins as well as forcing the jib down.

Boogie was particularly bitter. The canoe, the food experiment, the *haoles*, the whole trip was "all bullshit." He declared that he had never wanted to go in the first place, and that once he stepped ashore he would forget the whole trip. No one challenged him with the obvious question: "Why, if you thought it was all bullshit, did you try so hard to get on the crew?"

Next Billy Richards took the floor. As he started to speak the television camera focused on him. Billy was playing his part well as Kimo's understudy. Taking the role of an abused crewman, he began a long speech with a justification of crew rebellion: "When the chips are really down, seems like nobody really behind the crew. The crew got to, got to get together so that real strong— tight, and almost forcefully do what we got to do. You know just come out in numbers and say, 'Hey, this is what we going to do. We're going to dump the *hale*, we're going to dump this, we're going to dump that—we're going to do our trip.'

"But it seems, it seems, it just seems like we don't get the backing. We don't get the backing like we should. And this crew know this canoe more than anybody else on this canoe."

Then Billy started to claim that he and his friends were the ones who had constructed *Hokule'a*. But under our stare and that of the unblinking lens of the television camera, he hesitated after saying "We built" and completed the sentence with, "we, we put the thing together. We sailed 'em between the islands."

Those who had worked hard to relash the crossbeams were rightfully proud of their work. But Billy had a habit of claiming too much for himself and others who had joined the project well after the canoe was built. To him, the high point in their experience had been the near disastrous interisland cruise:

"Like everybody in the islands, everybody, all the Hawaiians on this canoe thought in the beginning that it would be just like between the island trips, man. It was really far out. It was really together.

"We cannot. We cannot," Billy repeated to emphasize his contention that we had unfairly prevented the "crew" from recreating those conditions on this voyage.

"In the beginning, like when we did have one *ho'oponopono* at the Society office, Shorty and I were the only two that said we didn't want the *haoles* on the canoe. Because we knew this was going to happen. But you said, 'Oh, don't you want to sail with Tommy Holmes? Don't you think we just can't go without Tommy

Holmes?' Hey, I can go without Tommy Holmes. Boogie can go without. Buff can go without. We don't need him!

"What I'm saying is," Billy continued in his effort to dramatize the gang's case, "we don't get the backing. All right, so we decided okay, that's all right. Everybody else let the *haoles* come, we're going to let the *haoles* come. We'll just change the whole idea as to what we feel about the canoe. We make the canoe just like us —half-breeds!"

Again the problem of identity. Having *haoles* aboard the canoe was above all a painful reminder to Billy that he was racially and culturally part-*haole* as well as part-Hawaiian. "What does Billy think he can do—split himself in half and throw away the *haole* half?" was once asked of me by another part-Hawaiian who recognized in Billy the anguish of one who would reject his *haole* half because he felt the *haole* world discriminated against him. Billy, I recently discovered, is especially embittered because he feels that the *haole* side of the Richards family ignores his parents and other Hawaiians who bear the Richards name and have the same prominent early missionary for an ancestor. "We only hear from them when someone dies—then they send us a wreath," Billy had complained the other day to Lyman when the two were discussing their respective missionary family connections.

"You know," Billy continued, "if we thought in the beginning that this was a full-on Hawaiian trip you think Buff would bring the stove? You think we would listen to the radio, smoking all this stuff like that? I bet you not. Because it would be a full-on Hawaiian trip. But we know that it's no one Hawaiian trip. From the beginning it's not. That's why they say it's bullshit."

After an interruption from Buffalo in support of what he had said, Billy finally ended his performance by switching to the role of the stern schoolmaster.

"All right, everybody think about what was said. Remember we got the trip back. I don't like to see none of this happen again with the second crew. So again, better not have the same bullshit."

Boogie retook the stage for more recriminations. But it was not long before Billy was back in front of the television camera with a final word. This time he was out to justify their use of marijuana. His message was that when the gang felt oppressed, "We go smoke, feel good, we let it slide. Because we have to smoke. Hey, pray for *pakalolo*, man. Because that's what saved you guys' lives —long time ago!"

Boogie then seconded Billy's chilling logic: "That's the truth! Let me tell you, that's the truth!"

By now Buffalo was thoroughly riled and joined in the attack. Whereas Boogie and Billy had spoken in a calculating way, almost as if they had rehearsed their parts, Buffalo exploded with a vehement denunciation of *haoles*. Everything we did, the way we talked, the way we ate, everything was damned: "That's why I live out in the country—to get as far away from you guys as I can!"

Buffalo spat out his words, punctuating them with quick, jerky arm movements. Completely gone was his usually measured way of speaking and moving. Buffalo was losing all self-control, something he himself had been afraid might happen during the trip. Earlier he had confided in Lyman how he feared getting mad, how he went wild when his anger overwhelmed him. Their conversation had taken place some weeks back when Buffalo had complained to Lyman about the efforts of the young magazine photographer to ingratiate himself with the gang by butting into their circle to ridicule Kawika, me and others on the leaders' side. Now Buffalo's resistance was way down. The champagne, plus the effects of a foot infection now spreading up his leg, and finally the goading words of Boogie and Billy had brought him to a flash point.

Tommy, who claimed Buffalo as an old friend, saw this and wisely backed off the deck and onto the starboard hull, leaving Lewis, Kawika and me lined up against the starboard rail like ducks in a shooting gallery. Although I stayed put, I bit my tongue; it was hardly the time for defensive statements. But David Lewis, who stood only a few feet from where Buffalo perched against the stern rail, started to object. The idea that a man who had spent much of the voyage flaked out in the deckhouse, and who knew little about sailing and navigation, would criticize him was too much for Lewis.

"We're human beings too. We deserve to be treated like human beings."

That did it. Buffalo launched himself from the stern rail and in quick succession slugged Lewis, clipped the nearby photographer and bashed our captain. After Kawika, I was next in line, still standing against the rail, transfixed by the sight of blows I did not want to see. Then Buffalo was on me, delivering a right that caught me full in the face. He kept slugging and kicking as I went down. I could not fight back, even though psychologically as well as physically I needed to defend myself. Any move on my part might well have precipitated a bloody battle on *Hokuleʻa's* deck.

Lyman sprang from the port rail to pull Buffalo back. Buffalo hesitated and, as I got up, a stream of blood flowing from my nose, Mau intervened. A wave of his hand and a stern, "Buff, stop!" was enough to get the enraged crewman to go back to the stern rail. After a few more angry words from the more vocal crew members, the gang went forward. The encounter was over.

A fishing boat had been following us. Just before the gang had marched aft to begin the confrontation, Rodo had jumped aboard the boat to see the skipper, his adopted son, and to talk to Papeete via radio-telephone about the planned welcome. Now the boat pulled alongside. Rodo and the skipper, an immense Tahitian who would have been more than a match for any of the gang members, jumped aboard the canoe. Rodo strained to be jovial while his adopted son warily looked around to check out the situation.

Once the fishing boat skipper was satisfied that the assault was over, he jumped back over to his boat. Only then did Rodo tell me that they had been on the radio to Papeete while Buffalo was punching us out, and that a tug with policemen aboard was on its way out to escort us. Till then his adopted son would stand by in case of further trouble.

Although outwardly composed, Rodo was fighting mad. "I'm the best harpooner in Tahiti," he said, pointing to the harpoon he had made, following old Polynesian models, and brought along to fend off attacks of marlin or any other creatures that might try to ram the canoe. I was gratified for his show of support, but thankful he had not been aboard during the punch-out. I told him that I thought it was over. Although I could not be sure, it looked like the gang's anger was spent, or at least temporarily at ebb.

By then it was dusk. Dukie, ever wishing to be useful, had fixed a meal. But before we could eat it we had to hear from Billy once more. He came aft to bless the meal.

"To the Almighty Lord," he began. Then, following the Hawaiian ecumenical style that he had heard used at our *ho'oponopono* sessions, he continued with, "to the *akua*, to the *'aumakua*, to the *kapuna*." He was addressing his prayer to the ancient Hawaiian gods, to the traditional guardian spirits and to the ancestors, as well as to the Christian god.

"We thank you for this food we are about to eat and for the fine winds that have brought us to Tahiti. This afternoon we have taught these people a lesson. We do not feel it is wrong to have done this. We feel we have done it for you, to show them the right way."

Buffalo was silent. After the meal he came up to me and mutely shook my hand. Later Lyman informed me that Buffalo was in great pain from his infected foot and had remorsefully told him, "Dave, I'm so sorry about what happened."

By now the plan to heave to in the lee of Tetiaroa had been abandoned. We were sailing directly to Tahiti to wait offshore until morning. The escort, a large tugboat, had reached us and was steaming alongside at a distance of a few hundred yards. The police on board were in civilian clothes so no one knew of their presence except Rodo and me. If the need arose, we would signal them with a flare.

Mau came up to me after dark. "Ben," he said, speaking softly but in dead earnest. "I like go home. I no go back to Hawaii on canoe."

Mau explained how he had been thinking of quitting for a long time because of the way the gang had been acting throughout the trip. It was their violence that made him finally decide. Mau came from a small island community where peaceful cooperation is a requirement for survival. Violence disgusted him, particularly the unreasoning violence against authority he had witnessed. He had

almost decided to quit after Clifford challenged Kawika to a fight
as we maneuvered off Mataiva. When Buffalo punched me and
Kawika, Mau stopped hesitating. He knew that he must leave the
canoe in Tahiti.

I asked Mau to reconsider.

"No, I like go home."

"Okay, you've done a good job. I am sorry for all the trouble.
I'll get you home. Don't worry."

Although I hoped to change his mind later, that was all I
could say then.

The night was not restful. My head ached. But the thought of
completing the voyage under police escort, and above all of losing
Mau for the return home, hurt worse. Rodo, Mau and I were up
most of the night watching to see that we kept clear of the reef
fringing Tahiti, as well as keeping an eye on the deckhouse. All
was peaceful within. The gang had bedded down for the night.

A little after midnight we were within sight of the surf
breaking on Tahiti's barrier reef. I felt a great sense of relief—and
of accomplishment. Despite all the troubles and delays in Hawaii,
despite the doldrums and head winds that followed, despite all
the antics of film makers and crewmen—we made it.

PART III

34
Tahiti

"Look at all those people!" It was 9:30 in the morning. The high peaks looming before us had cut off the trades. We were laboriously paddling through the pass into the glassy, calm waters of Papeete Harbor. Thousands of Tahitians lined the pass and waited along the shore within the harbor.

This was why the Tainui Association had been so insistent that we not come ashore till morning. In an unprecedented move, the Governor of French Polynesia had declared our arrival day, Friday the fourth of June, to be a public holiday. Schools were closed and workers were given the day off. The Tahitians had started coming down to the waterfront the night before to spread their sleeping mats and to await the arrival of the strange canoe from Hawaii. Now they were everywhere, standing knee deep in the surf surging over the reef, jammed along the shore, perched atop waterfront buildings and weighing down the limbs of shade trees lining the water's edge.

The Tainui leaders were astounded. When they first began spreading word of our voyage, they had hoped that a few

251

thousand Tahitians might come down to see us arrive. What they got were 15,000—one out of every five Tahitians. This was the biggest crowd ever in Tahiti's history, bigger by far than that which had greeted Captain Cook two centuries earlier, or that which had more recently welcomed General de Gaulle.

Waiting within the harbor was another double-canoe, slightly longer than *Hokuleʻa* but without masts and rigging. Long pennants flew from her high, arching sternpieces. A decorated plat-

form above her deck was crowded with costumed Tahitian dancers. She was a replica of a traditional Tahitian ceremonial canoe, built fifteen years earlier for the filming of *Mutiny on the Bounty*.

Once we came closer, the double-canoe's two big outboard motors pushed the craft alongside to become our harbor tug, allowing us to rest our paddles and enjoy the welcome.

Many of the crew members who had flown to Tahiti two days previously were aboard the Tahitian canoe, including Kimo. He had apparently changed his mind about sailing on the canoe and, after convincing the Voyaging Society board members left in Honolulu of the sincerity of his motives, he had assumed leadership of the return crew.

Among the Tahitians aboard I recognized a Tainui leader, who jumped over to our canoe and made his way across the deck toward me. He greeted me with a grave face and handed me a letter with the words, "I have something you must see."

It was from my wife, Ruth, who was then waiting on the beach with our two boys. The news was that my mother had died in California the day we left Mataiva.

She had been fighting an undiagnosed case of cancer for years. Ruth had called her from Honolulu just before flying down to tell her that we were within two days of land. The way my mother repeated the words, "just two more days," had mystified Ruth. Late on the afternoon of June 1, the day we touched on Mataiva, she was rushed to the hospital. Although news of our arrival had not yet reached California, her last words to my father were that we had made it to land.

After reading Ruth's letter all I wanted was to go ashore and join my family there. But for the others aboard *Hokule‘a* and the Tahitians on shore, the slow passage through the harbor was a triumphant procession.

Yet we heard no cheering as we neared shore. Only silence; then a swelling chorus. A church choir assembled on shore began to sing in Tahitian. Soon the thousands spread up and down the beach added their voices. Although the song was a church hymn, the spine-tingling effect of the massed chorus was that of an ancient chant.

As we maneuvered toward shore, the crowd surged into the water. Hundreds tried to climb aboard, their weight threatening to swamp the canoe. It took the combined efforts of policemen and welcoming officials to make this human tidal wave subside. Ruth and my two sons waved to me from the packed crowd, but I could not go ashore until the formal ceremony welcoming us to Tahiti had run its course.

Hundreds of cameras were now trained upon us. *Hokule‘a* and

our bearded selves must have made good subjects. But the one man aboard attracting most attention from the photographers was someone who had not made the voyage.

There, perched partway up the foremast, was Kimo holding Hoku in his arms. He had come aboard from the Tahitian double-canoe and, after tearfully greeting his friends, had mounted the belaying cleats on the foremast from where he could survey the crowd stretched before him. To those who had no way of knowing that he had just flown in from Honolulu, Kimo must have looked like the veteran voyager who, clutching his faithful dog, had climbed the mast to reconnoiter the new island and its inhabitants.

The rest of the morning was a blur to me—chants, speeches and welcoming dances, followed by a procession to the Governor's mansion for an inappropriately formal garden reception. I soon separated from the rest to join Ruth and the boys and go to the hotel. My elder son had greeted me on the beach with the words, "Daddy, can we go swimming?" So right after lunch I went swimming with the boys in the hotel pool.

After the swim I tried vainly to sleep. I could not relax and Ruth, I thought, was acting most strangely. Several times I caught her staring at me with an alarmed expression on her face. Considering everything, I felt that I had come out of the trip in relatively good shape. No injuries, not even a twinge out of the cranky back vertebra that had knocked me out of canoe experimenting for so many years; the last operation and the physical therapy regime I had followed since had apparently done the job. True, I had lost a lot of weight. And my nose and cheek were swollen and my left eye blackened. But my appearance was not the main thing bothering Ruth.

It was my manner. Ruth later told me that I acted more like someone who had come out of a concentration camp than a

person who had just completed the voyage of his dreams. The unobtrusive demeanor that I had been forced to assume after the jib incident, plus the worry of seeing the voyage through to completion, had taken its inevitable toll on my psyche. The punch-out, the night's vigil and then the shock of my mother's death had served to weigh me down even further.

In the evening we were honored at a second reception, a truly Tahitian affair hosted by Papeete's Mayor. A huge crowd of Tahitians feted us with drinks, food and a magnificent display of Tahitian dancing. For the first time since arriving, I began to loosen up. The Tahitian hospitality was working its magic, and the absence of the gang helped. They were still at their hotel, sulking about something or other. But I did not have a chance to fully enjoy the reception. Kawika, Lyman, Lewis and I were whisked off to the government television station for a live interview.

After the transmission of a film taken of our arrival, we were introduced by the French television reporter hosting the show. He and the Tahitian who had chanted for us at the beach were to pose the questions. A Swedish anthropologist settled in Tahiti who had first come to the islands drifting aboard the raft *Kon-Tiki* was there to translate their questions into English and our answers into French.

The questions were general at first—about the weather, the food, navigation, how fast we sailed and the like. Eventually the subject of conflict was raised with a diplomatically worded question. News of the assault off Tetiaroa was all over Tahiti by now, and my black eye was obvious. We avoided fully divulging the problem and made only general statements about how some of the crewmen were unfortunately not psychologically prepared for the long voyage.

The interviewers had by then discovered that I spoke Tahitian. To avoid lengthy translation, and especially to have the trip explained directly to the Tahitian audience, they began directing their questions to me. Despite my fatigue and grief I enjoyed fielding the questions, answering in the best Tahitian I could extract from my tired brain.

When television had been introduced to Tahiti a decade earlier, the broadcasts were totally in French. My Tahitian friends used to sit for hours staring at the screen with only limited comprehension of what was being said. At the time I resolved that if ever I could manage to reach Tahiti by canoe I would break the ban on Tahitian by going before the television cameras to explain the voyage to the Tahitians in their own language. But I was a year too late. Thanks to an impassioned plea to French officials by my old friend Jacques Drollet, a Tahitian cofounder of the Tainui Association, Tahitian programming was already being introduced.

At one point the Tahitian interviewer asked me how I came by the idea of sailing a double-canoe to Tahiti. To his delight, and I hoped to that of his viewers, I was able to point out that the idea was originally Tahitian, going back to the 12th century or earlier when Tahitian voyagers were ranging far and wide over the ocean. I also reminded him that we had a more recent Tahitian inspiration. When I was first in Tahiti in 1956, there were two local projects being planned to build canoes and sail them to Hawaii. Although neither of these projects went very far, in effect, I pointed out, they had come to fruition with our voyage.

The interviewer was also curious about how I came to speak Tahitian. While I was telling him how fifteen years previously a retired Tahitian chief had been my teacher, my eighty-five-year-old language professor was watching me on television at his son's house. Not till I mentioned his name did he truly register that it was his former pupil behind the beard and battered face. He broke into tears and exclaimed, "*Aue, e Tumoana Tane e!*"

The old chief is known to everyone as Tenani'a Tane (Tay-nah-nee-'ah Tah-nay, literally "The Man on Top"), although that is not his legal name. He had received it upon marriage and had gone by it ever since. Following the same Tahitian custom, upon our marriage Tenani'a had rechristened me *Tumoana Tane* ("Tumoana Man") and Ruth *Tumoana Vahine* ("Tumoana Woman"), and had insisted that those were our Tahitian names for all time.

Moana (Moh-ah-nah) means the open ocean. *Tu,* aside from being the name of a principal deity, is also a verb meaning to stand erect or to stand fast. Tenani'a had picked *Tumoana* to convey my passion for the sea and my determination to find out how the migratory voyages of ancient times had been accomplished. As he watched television that night, Tenani'a was gratified to see that his pupil had tried to live up to the chosen name.

35
Unforeseen Departures

Saturday, the day following our arrival, I was scheduled to leave on the night flight to Los Angeles so I could attend my mother's funeral in nearby San Diego. However, because the question of Mau's departure, as well as the disposition of the gang, was not yet settled, I had to cancel my reservation and cable my father to delay the funeral until the following week.

The slim hope of changing Mau's mind about quitting faded that Saturday evening. Mike McCoy, his Satawalese wife (Mau's niece) and their child had flown down to Tahiti on their way home from California to Micronesia. Mau asked to return with them when they left on the Monday morning flight. After a quiet dinner at Mike's hotel—where Mau had taken refuge to avoid the deckhouse gang—Mike announced, "Okay, now Mau will talk, but we'll do it Micronesian style." That meant leaving the women and children in the hotel room, going to a thatched-roof shelter overlooking the lagoon and then spending the rest of the night talking over bottle after bottle of strong Tahitian beer.

Never have I heard anyone so bitter. On and on he went, speaking in rapid-fire Satawalese with Mike translating. Everything he had stored up during the trip and from before came out. Mau ridiculed the gang, pouring scorn on them and those who had given us trouble in Hawaii. No, he would not sail on *Hokule'a* again. Never would he return to Hawaii. Mau had had enough. He wanted out.

Get rid of the deckhouse gang and those on the return crew who sympathized with them. Probably even get rid of all the return crew and sign on experienced Tahitian sailors if extra hands are needed. Under these circumstances Mau might have agreed to stay and navigate the canoe back. But such a near total rejection of Hawaiian crewmen would have been taken as a declaration of war and might well have led to violence in Tahiti and continuing repercussions in Hawaii. Mau wanted no more conflict. For fear of what the gang might do if they found out he was going home, Mau wanted to leave without anyone from the canoe knowing but me. Because I soon had to fly off to California, I was in no position to force the issue of drastically changing the crew composition. Besides, to dismiss crewmen indiscriminately would have been tragically unfair to those members of the return crew who had nothing to do either with the troubles before we left or those visited upon us at sea. Better to let Mau go, I reluctantly concluded.

Getting Mau on the Monday morning plane to Fiji was not easy. I had to call on Tainui to help pay for the ticket as well as enlist the aid of my friend Jacques Drollet to obtain from week-ending officials the special documents Mau needed in lieu of his passport, which the East-West Center was holding in Honolulu. Miraculously, by early Monday morning all was in order. Mau, Mike and his family were ready to leave.

It was a sad farewell. Only a few Tainui leaders were at the airport to see Mau off. *Hokule'a* was losing her navigator and the only man who could be fully entrusted to sail her back to Hawaii without instruments. Mau, however, was relieved to be going. And despite his secret departure, he was quietly proud even though he had not spoken a word about his accomplishment. According to the code of behavior he followed, that was for others to say. The skillful navigator does not need to boast.

"You beat Repunglug," I had told Mau upon completion of the trip. When Mau had left Satawal to come to Hawaii, he was considered an accomplished navigator on his island, but not the top one. Six months before we left Hawaii, a more senior navigator named Repunglug had sailed 1,800 miles from Satawal to Okinawa to deliver a canoe to the International Marine Exposition being held there to celebrate that island's return to Japanese rule. Although Repunglug's trip had not been direct, having been accomplished by island hopping through Micronesia and the intervening Volcano Islands, his voyage was nonetheless the longest in modern Micronesian history and served to further enhance Repunglug's already considerable reputation. The desire to beat Repunglug by taking a longer trip that did not involve island hopping had helped to keep Mau going through all the troubles in Honolulu. Now Mau was number one. The voyage to Tahiti had been far longer than his rival's trip, and a much more difficult sailing and navigational feat.

Mau left a cassette tape on which he had recorded a message telling the crew of his departure. They had not seen him since the arrival and they had no idea that he was even thinking about going home. That evening they were called together in the hotel meeting room to hear Mau's message. Their apprehension grew when the tape started with Mau speaking in incomprehensible Satawalese.

Mau could have had Mike record a fluent English translation. But he knew better from the Maui experience. Mau's own English translation followed his Satawalese words.

"Okay now, I like go home. For what? For the crew. The crew no good. I see the first crew on, on the trip. No good—when I say on Maui don't take the trouble with you to the trip.

"Okay now, I feel sorry for the second crew. But the first crew is no good. Maybe the second crew, I think same. Okay now, I like go home. I think Rodo don't take canoe back to Honolulu. I don't know about you. Maybe you go back on airplane. But *Hokule'a*, I don't know. Maybe throw away or what."

More rapid Satawalese followed, then Mau switched back to English to translate.

"Okay, the crew if good maybe I take *Hokule'a* to Honolulu. But the crew no good. Okay, I like back home."

A short message to Kimo followed about having his father send Mau's things back to Satawal. Then came Mau's farewell.

"Me, I no like back to Honolulu. Okay, now last I see Honolulu. You don't need me anymore. Now last. Thank you everybody, I say goodbye to you. For what? For now is I say last. I don't go back Honolulu anymore. Okay, now is the last. Bye-bye."

This blunt yet poignant message had its inevitably shattering impact. For many of the crew, it was too much to have their idol so utterly reject them. "That's not Mau talking, that's the computer feeding him all this," one yelled out. They could not believe that Mau would say what he had of his own free will.*

Billy then jumped up, shouting, "The captain's the one who did all this!" and headed for Kawika. Sam Kalalau blocked Billy, but Kimo slipped by and made for the captain. Exactly what happened was lost in a blur of motion. Kawika remembers Kimo lunging toward him with one hand extended as if to shake hands and with the words "I thank you so much" on his lips. Then Kimo pulled his hand back and cocked his fist. Kawika pushed Kimo aside, hopped over a low rail to a walkway below, and got out of there while Buffalo and others held Kimo back.

This latest fracas further mystified our Tainui hosts. They could not understand the reason for such hostility or why crewmen were ignoring welcoming ceremonies, heatedly challenging Tahitians to fights and openly smoking marijuana.

The Tainui leaders were beginning to doubt the wisdom of continuing to help us, or even to associate with us. When they had been formed at our request a few years earlier, they had hoped that the voyage of *Hokule'a* would serve to stimulate the Tahitians culturally, to make them more aware of their voyaging heritage and get them to sailing canoes again. The enthusiasm our arrival had sparked went beyond their wildest dreams. But

---

* When Mau later learned that once more the authenticity of his words had been questioned, he made another tape in which he repeated the charges in detail. The transcript of the tape was made at the district headquarters in Micronesia and the translation was verified by the deputy district commissioner, Mau's fellow islander, who swore that Mau had not been forced to say anything and had not been handed a prepared script.

now they were afraid the whole *Hokuleʻa* venture might collapse before their eyes. "If *Hokuleʻa* goes down, then Tainui goes down, and with them would go our hopes for a Tahitian sailing canoe revival," was how one of them summed it up.

The continued smoking of *pakalolo* by some of the gang (thanks to a fresh supply said to have been flown in by one of their friends who greeted them upon arrival), plus the rumored use of harder drugs, particularly bothered the Tainui leaders. The police, alert to drug smuggling by foreigners because of the recent discovery of the "Tahiti Connection" involving the transport of cocaine from South America to the United States via Tahiti, began pressing a Tainui official to file a complaint against the gang. He refused to do so for fear of the international incident it might provoke and the harm that would follow to *Hokuleʻa*, Tainui and our joint cause. For the same reason I refused to make any complaints and dodged all questions from reporters who wanted to know what really had happened on the canoe.

Despite misgivings, the Tainui leaders stood by us. Their support included helping out on return air fares for crewmen as well as for Mau. We had no money to pay for the flights of our current crewmen, or anyone else who had to fly home. Kimo's "press conference" back in Honolulu Harbor had effectively cut off the flow of donations counted on to take care of air fares. We needed angels, and Tainui came through with four tickets for Honolulu to get the hard-core gang members off the island.

That left us four tickets short, two for the other gang members and two for Sam Kalalau and Dave Lyman, who had to get back to their jobs in Hawaii. Then another angel appeared in the person of a regal Hawaiian woman, Abigail Kawananakoa, who gave us money for the needed tickets. As a descendant of one of Hawaii's last kings, she had come to Tahiti to represent Hawaiian nobility at our arrival. She and other members of the Kawananakoa family had already been generous to the project; this additional gift was most timely.

Tuesday morning, the day after Mau's departure, several Voyaging Society board members flew in from Honolulu. As soon as they were through customs, I brought them together with

Tainui leaders for a conference about what had happened on the voyage and more recently in Tahiti. My testimony, as well as that of Kawika, Rodo and Lyman, was frank, perhaps uncomfortably so for some of the new arrivals who did not seem to want to believe what they heard. However, I tried to put our troubles in perspective by first writing on the blackboard "*Ua tae tatou*," a Tahitian phrase that carries the meaning of "We made it."

"That is the most important thing. Remember that. Despite all the problems, *we* made it."

I emphasized *we*, using the special Tahitian form *tatou*. Tahitians have many words for "we," each telling how many people are involved and whether or not the listeners are also included. I deliberately employed *tatou*, the most inclusive form, to mean "we all" so as to include everyone in the room—the board members who had just flown down from Hawaii and our Tainui hosts as well as those of us who had sailed on *Hokule'a*. I wanted to emphasize that ours was a joint effort by people of various backgrounds and talents, and that despite trouble along the way, all of us had made the coming of *Hokule'a* to Tahiti and her magnificent welcome possible.

That night aboard the Air New Zealand flight to Los Angeles to attend my mother's funeral I could not sleep. Buffalo, Boogie and Dukie had left a few hours earlier on the Pan Am flight to Honolulu. The unfinished business of getting the rest of the gang back to Hawaii, and of getting the canoe and the new crew ready for the return voyage, weighed heavily on my mind. In addition, I was worried about what Kimo and other Voyaging Society board members newly arrived from Honolulu might do in my absence.

David Lewis was also on the plane, leaving Tahiti and the project. He talked on and on about the gang, particularly about the inability of some to endure what he considered to be the mild hardships of the trip. Lewis spoke with the scorn of a tough New Zealand adventurer, as well as a man who had sailed with Pacific islanders who could easily suffer rough conditions and privations without complaint. He could not get over how the gang was "so American" in their craving for modern foods, beer and marijuana, as well as in their complaining about sleeping accommodations and the lack of a jib, keel fins and other modern aids. To Lewis, a question one of them posed during the harangue preceding the punch-out off Tetiaroa epitomized the gang's plight: "If *haoles* can have anti-fouling paint, why can't we Hawaiians?"

The only way Lewis could accept the behavior of the gang, and all those back in Hawaii who had caused us trouble, was to declare, "Hawaiians are not Pacific Islanders; they are an American minority group." Although callous-sounding, his remark actually shifted blame away from individuals and onto the Americanization of Hawaii, a process that has created a pool of increasingly frustrated urban Hawaiians subject to the same social ills that strike other deprived American minorities. Yet Lewis's remark was too broad. It ignored those Hawaiians who have been able to adapt to modern society without bitterness and without losing their cultural identity—in particular, it ignored men such as Kawika, Sam Kalalau and our *kahuna*, Edward Kealanahele, who had worked so hard to get the canoe to Tahiti.

Lewis also made it clear that he wanted nothing further to do with the canoe or the Voyaging Society. He advised me to pull out also and, "Let them fight it out among themselves." Tommy Holmes had already left the project, having resigned as soon as he got the plants and animals safely ashore. The day before, Tommy had warned me, "This is one *haole* face they won't see around here anymore. When we get to Tahiti I'm going to get lost in the country." Tommy's facile phrasing disguised his deep disappointment. He had tried to bridge a gap only to find that he was not wanted.

I, too, had been tempted to abandon the project upon arriving. But that feeling had not lasted more than a day or two. Yet I had decided not to sail back on the canoe. However much I wanted to be on the return voyage and see the peaks of Hawaii rise out of the sea, I realized that it would be politic to carry through on my earlier proposal to have the return home be a Hawaiian experience. We had some dedicated young Hawaiians on the return crew. It was time to pull back and work to make it possible for Kawika and his new crew to bring *Hokule'a* home in triumph.

36
Renewal

Four days after leaving I was back in Tahiti, arriving at the airport in the predawn hours of Sunday the thirteenth. I went directly to my old district, where Ruth and the boys were staying with friends. At daybreak we headed back to the airport to take a light plane to the adjacent island of Moorea. I wanted to get my family away from the tensions surrounding the canoe and to be alone with them for a few days. The project, the whole three-year long haul—not just the voyage—had been hard on them. My elder son, then five, was particularly affected. It had been the canoe and all its troubles that had taken his father from the house so many evenings and weekends, and had made him so tense and irritable when home.

Moorea (Moh-'oh-ray-ah) is a little gem of a South Seas island, complete with a fantastic skyline of basaltic spires rising thousands of feet out of the lush, green interior, a pair of deep bays big enough to anchor great ships, and that unbeatable combination of clear blue-green lagoon and dazzling white coral-sand beaches.

We were lucky: a Tainui official loaned us his weekend retreat on the lagoon's edge. The boys were in their idea of heaven, with a beach at their doorstep and a lagoon beyond to explore by canoe. Plus, to their delight, the chickens scratching around the yard had a habit of sneaking through the open windows of our cottage and laying their eggs on the boys' bed.

Even though we were tucked away in a little village across the channel from Tahiti, we could not escape *Hokuleʻa*. Many Mooreans were sporting *Hokuleʻa* T-shirts, official ones sold by Tainui to raise funds and unauthorized versions put out by an enterprising merchant on the eve of our arrival. And it seemed everywhere we went we heard someone singing one of the dozens of *Hokuleʻa* songs that had been composed in our honor. A number of strangers stopped me to talk about the trip. Refreshingly, theirs was a Tahitian "no problem" attitude. They did not want to hear of troubles, only of what it was like to sail in a double-canoe all the way from Hawaii.

Their enthusiasm was infectious. After a day or two on Moorea, I began to feel better about the experience. News from Tahiti also helped revive my spirits. Kawika flew over for the day to tell me that the situation had greatly improved. He was still captain, despite attempts by Kimo and other board members as well as dissident crewmen to get him off the canoe. It was Kimo who eventually was dismissed, once again, along with a few of his loyal followers on the return crew. That left a fresh and dedicated group of young Hawaiians who wanted nothing more than to bring *Hokuleʻa* home without incident—and in so doing to restore the honor of Hawaiians as Polynesian sailors.

After several days of rest, I started traveling daily to Papeete, enjoying one of the most unusual commutes in the world. Our benefactor, a Tahitian businessman who headed Papeete's Renault dealership, had left us a car on Moorea and another at the Tahiti airport. Off I would be at dawn to the airstrip, driving through the cool morning air, past coconut plantations and spectacular lagoon vistas, to catch the early morning flight across the channel. Then, after a day in hot, noisy Papeete on canoe business, I would catch the late afternoon plane to Moorea, arriving in time for a refreshing swim in the lagoon before dinner.

The canoe was in drydock, being cleaned and undergoing repairs. Most of the work needed was minor, except for one section of the port hull that had been cracked by the repeated banging of the steering sweep against it. *Hokuleʻa* was in capable hands. The new crew was working hard under the direction of

Rodo after arrival

Wally Froiseth, a skilled craftsman and a Voyaging Society regular who had flown down from Honolulu with his wife, Moku, a handsome Hawaiian woman who had been working on the project since its inception. Also performing yeoman service was John Kruse from the first crew. John, who had requested to stay on to help us, was completing the metamorphosis begun during the last weeks of the voyage when he had started pulling back from the gang leaders. Now he wanted nothing more to do with them or their protests, and was cheerfully working on the canoe even though he would not have a chance to sail back on her.

I saw Rodo around town during my daily visits. Rodo, a man who loves his whiskey when ashore, was the toast of Papeete. But he, too, was keeping mum on our troubles, preferring to talk of our accomplishments—and to castigate those French critics who had accused us of cheating on the navigation. In answer to the charge that he had consulted a hidden magnetic compass, Rodo gave the newspapers a ready-made headline: "I have no need of a compass. I am Tahitian!"

Rodo would also not be making the return trip. Even if he wanted to he could not, for he was scheduled to fly to New Zealand for surgery on the hernia he had sustained the day before we reached land. That was why the night we spotted Mataiva Rodo had nearly collapsed and was forced to leave the watch.

After an all too short week on Moorea, it was time to get back to Tahiti. *Hokule‘a* was out of drydock and ready to start on a goodwill tour around Tahiti and to Raiatea organized by Tainui. We flew over to Tahiti in time to meet the canoe at her first stop, a rural district some 30 miles from Papeete. After ritual greetings, dance performances, a spear-throwing contest and other exhibitions, and the inevitable and always enjoyable traditional feast, we were all driven down the road a few miles to Tahiti's botanical gardens for an unusual ceremony.

The cultural symbolism of our transport of plants and animals from Hawaii to Tahiti had not been lost on the Tahitians, particularly the schoolchildren who could relate to Hoku, Maxwell and breadfruit saplings much easier than to the problems of windward sailing and noninstrument navigation. The animals had been an immediate hit, so much so that after a few days the quarantine regulations were waived. Hoku, the public's favorite, joined the household of one of our Tainui supporters. The chickens were given to a Tahitian farm family who added them to their flock. Maxwell, whom all the Tahitians insisted was to be called Hokule‘a, found his reward for enduring a month at sea at a piggery where he was given the chore of servicing local sows to spread his pale but distinguished genes around Tahiti's porcine population.

Our task at the botanical gardens was to plant the seedlings, cuttings and other materials that Tommy Holmes had so carefully protected from salt spray and other hazards during the trip. Save for a few taro roots that had become moldy, the materials had apparently survived the voyage well. The planting ceremony started with Tahitian orations, followed by a medley of *Hokule'a* songs. Then Kenneth Emory (who had flown down from Honolulu right after our arrival), John Kruse and I did the honors, setting out the root cuttings and seedlings to leave further evidence of our voyage, and to serve as a reminder of how early voyagers had once carried life-giving plants across the ocean.

Things were falling into place for once. Although Kimo, another man also fired from the return crew and Billy (who had been given a ticket home but refused to fly back right away) were still hanging around, no one was paying attention to their absurd claims to spiritual powers, or to the talk of betrayal and impending disaster they were peddling. The absence of the National Geographic film team may have helped rob Kimo and his friends of their former influence. Right after our arrival the film team declared they had enough footage, then packed up and flew off to the United States to begin editing their television drama. Now the important thing was that the canoe was sound, that Kawika was in command and that the new crew was looking forward to the sail home—a voyage that would be free of intrusive cinematographers. All that remained was to complete the circuit of Tahiti, then sail over to the historic island of Raiatea and back, and finally to provision the canoe and be off.

37
Return to Green-Clad Hawaii

Hokule'a and her new crew could have stayed and stayed in Tahiti and have spent a good year or two touring all five archipelagoes of French Polynesia. Communities all over were begging us to call on their island. The outer islanders wanted to see the canoe, fete us, and especially meet their Hawaiian cousins.

On Tahiti and Raiatea, the only other island we were able to visit, some of our Hawaiian crewmen were singled out by earnest Tahitians as long-lost relatives. In one case the relationship was indisputable. A Tainui leader discovered that he and John Kruse were kinsmen. They both had related ancestors who had emigrated from the Cook Islands, one to Tahiti, the other to Hawaii—although in the days of sailing ships, not voyaging canoes. Both Kawika and Sam Kalalau were the objects of determined attempts by local families to declare them to be kinsmen, descendants of Tahitians who had wandered off to Hawaii in the last century. In Kalalau's case the kinship might well have been real; according to his family tradition, he is descended from a Tahitian who

270

landed on Maui off a whaling ship. In addition, some of our young, unattached crewmen found themselves the objects of attention from vivacious Tahitian girls interested in establishing a different kind of relationship.

But the canoe had to get back to Hawaii, and fast. We were a month off schedule. The late summer hurricane season was approaching. Even with a late June departure, the canoe would be at sea uncomfortably close to the most dangerous time.

The Tainui leaders were also anxious to see us go, for we were beginning to strain their resources. Two days after our arrival they had held a public lottery to raise funds to finance our stay in Tahiti and to build their own sailing canoe. But the costs of housing and feeding our large group, of arranging events all around Tahiti and Raiatea, and finally of supplying us with food for the return—as they insisted on doing—had so depleted their treasury that they had no funds left for building their own canoe.* Yet the Tainui leaders did not begrudge the expense. *Hokule'a* had served an unforeseen purpose that they, as staunch Tahitian patriots, well appreciated.

Just when we arrived, the Tahitians were locked in a bitter struggle with the retrograde French colonial administration over the granting of internal autonomy to French Polynesia.

"Then," one of the Tainui leaders later told me, "we saw the sails of *Hokule'a* on the horizon. That gave us courage. That made us think with pride of ourselves as Polynesians, and gave us strength to persist. And now we are on the road to autonomy."

He was referring to political changes set in motion by a mass demonstration in Papeete that led to changes in the structure of government, including the abolition of the French governorship and the elevation of a Tahitian to an office equivalent to that of prime minister in charge of the internal government of French Polynesia. The demonstration occurred six days after our arrival and, so the Tainui leader claimed, its success and the political reforms that have followed owed a debt to *Hokule'a*'s grand

---

* Upon returning to Hawaii, my wife and I sent *Nalehia* to Tahiti aboard an oil tanker as a gift to Tainui in appreciation of their hospitality.

entrance into Papeete Harbor and her uplifting impact on the Tahitian people.

The Tainui leaders were also pleased to have one of their own men aboard the canoe for the return voyage.

According to an old tradition, a Tahitian high priest once sailed to Hawaii, where he discovered that new chiefly blood was needed to reinvigorate local ruling lines. So he sailed back to Tahiti where he attempted to recruit a high-born chief with the words:

> Here are the canoes, come aboard,
> Return and dwell in green-clad Hawaii,
> A land discovered in the ocean,
> That rose up amidst the waves.

The petitioned chief declined the honor and sent in his stead another ranking chief who, upon arrival, married into the Hawaiian chiefly class to establish a Tahitian-Hawaiian dynasty.

The Tainui man returning aboard *Hokule'a* was not a hereditary chief, although his father was the elected chief of the island of Raivavae, 500 miles south of Tahiti in the Austral Archipelago. He was a young professional seaman whose job was to navigate the canoe back to Hawaii—with instruments. Because of the departure of Mau and Lewis, and the incapacitation of Rodo, we were forced to give up the idea of completing the navigation experiment.

Two recent recruits from Hawaii further strengthened the enthusiastic but inexperienced crew. Both were skilled sailors, the type of men who should have been on the crew in the first place. That they were also part-Hawaiian pleased everyone, for that made an all-Polynesian crew—if you overlooked the fact that one of the two women aboard was *haole*. That is exactly what everyone did—because of her sex. Hawaiian men generally regard *haole* women in a much different light than *haole* men, especially if they are as attractive and sympathetic as this statuesque crewperson.

After the return from Raiatea, readying the canoe to sail home suffered from the inevitable delays, and a scare. Late one night someone cut *Meotai*'s mooring lines, setting her adrift in Papeete Harbor. Fortunately the crew awoke before she was driven onto the reef. Thereafter we mounted a round-the-clock guard on both vessels. Nothing else untoward happened during the final preparations, and *Hokule'a* was ready to sail on July 3, just twenty-nine days after our arrival. Then, as befitting Hawaii's Bicentennial canoe, we delayed an extra day to send her off to celebrate the Fourth of July.

By then my wife and children had returned to Hawaii by air, and several days after the canoe left, I flew to Rarotonga, the main island in the Cooks, where I had been invited to give talks on the voyage. From there I went on to New Zealand to visit Rodo while he recovered from surgery performed in an Auckland hospital, and to talk to university groups.

During my travels I was able to keep track of *Hokule'a*'s progress northward through a combination of satellite reports, ham radio contacts and telephone calls to Hawaii. The news was good. Because Tahiti's location well to the east of Hawaii's longitude did not obligate them to make easting, they were able to sail due north, reaching across the southeast trades instead of beating hard into them as we had been forced to do. *Hokule'a* was making good speed. At midday on July 13, nine days out of Tahiti, the canoe crossed the equator, completing a record day's run of 185 miles (7.7 knots average). The same day the crew celebrated Kawika's forty-sixth birthday.

My reception in Rarotonga and New Zealand served to cheer me further. The Polynesians there were proud of what had been accomplished on the voyage to Tahiti and were looking forward to a successful completion of the return to Hawaii. In addition, their sense of humor added a perspective to the voyage that I sorely needed.

Through all the troubles of the last year and a half I had virtually forgotten how to laugh. Yet the Rarotongans in particular found our adventures with the deckhouse gang to be uproariously funny—and I soon found myself laughing along with them. It was ridiculous to think of a group of brawny, self-appointed heroes pining away in the deckhouse, emerging periodically to complain how they were being mistreated or to deliver a castigating sermon.

"The same thing would have happened if you had taken young men from our island. You have to go to the outer islands where people still live by the sea and have to work hard. That's where you find good sailors."

To the Rarotongans, our folly, and the primary cause of our troubles, had been to take urban Polynesians, men without sea experience or a disciplined background of any sort, and then expect them to stand up to the rigors of a long, difficult voyage. They had a good point, a serious one that indicted the whole process of modern change and how it robs Polynesians of their former virtues.

Yet the Rarotongans missed the really tragic element, how our attempt to have the voyage restore cultural pride lost through the alien takeover of Hawaii had nearly foundered because of the sentiments generated by that takeover and continued *haole* domination. The Rarotongans' former masters, the New Zealanders, were comparatively gentle. More importantly, they have withdrawn, leaving Rarotonga and the other Cook Islands to the Polynesians. The full impact of what it meant to be an American minority group was therefore lost on the Rarotongans. They could not really grasp how it was the Hawaiians' rankling resentment of *haoles* that, when combined with the unfortunate choice of inexperienced and undisciplined crewmen, had been at the root of our troubles.

Some professors in New Zealand received my talk on the achievements of the voyage with a degree of skepticism. I agreed with their attitude, but only up to a point. No single experimental voyage can prove, in the scientific sense, a migration theory. What our voyage to Tahiti did was to demonstrate the worth of the Polynesian double-canoe for making long slants to windward, and show how the ancient system of noninstrument navigation can guide a canoe over thousands of miles of open ocean.

Our efforts, I argued, had turned the tide against those who claimed that traditional canoes and navigation methods were not good enough to have allowed the ancient Polynesians to set out purposefully to explore and settle their island world. My contention was that the voyage to Tahiti had rescued the ancient Polynesians from their damnation as mere "accidental voyagers" and put them back in their rightful place among the most daring and resourceful voyagers the world has ever seen. Most of those attending my talks in New Zealand agreed, particularly the Maoris (Polynesians indigenous to New Zealand) among them, whose tribal legends tell of how their ancestors discovered and settled New Zealand after sailing over the seas from far-off Tahiti and Raiatea.

A day after crossing the equator the canoe ran into mild doldrum conditions that slowed her northward progress. But the return crew was lucky. They were spared the calms and baffling variables we had experienced. They had enough wind to keep sailing at a steady if reduced pace, and after a few days the winds picked up again. By July 18, two weeks after leaving Tahiti, they were in the northeast trades well north of the equator. From then on it was fast sailing. The canoe's position upon entering the trades, slightly east of Tahiti's longitude, enabled them to reach across these strong and steady winds, heading northwest straight for Hawaii.

By the time I flew back to Honolulu from New Zealand, weather satellite photographs were revealing a disturbing problem. An early hurricane, christened Diana, was heading west from Mexican waters on a course that could possibly intersect with that of *Hokule'a*. Kawika learned of the hurricane via the CB relay from the *Meotai*. He elected to keep on course, figuring that the canoe could outrun the hurricane and reach land before the storm intersected with the return track. He was right. Hurricane Diana slowed, weakened and then degenerated into a mild tropical depression—all well to the east of the speeding *Hokule'a*.

The island of Hawaii was spotted on the 24th, one day short of three weeks out of Tahiti. The next day was spent coasting

along the northern shores of Maui and Molokai. The canoe could
have made it to Honolulu that night, but the welcoming committee requested Kawika to heave to off Molokai till dawn, so that
the canoe would arrive the next day for the planned welcome.

The canoe appeared off Oahu the next morning, met by a
flotilla of ships, fireboats, yachts, catamarans, racing canoes and
even surfers on their boards. The grand procession made its way
around Diamond Head, past Waikiki and on to the yacht harbor,
where the canoe turned shoreward to move slowly down the
congested channel, cheered by the ecstatic crowd gathered on
shore.

Hokuleʻa was back, her triumphal return demonstrating how
superbly adapted the Polynesian double-canoe was for two-way
voyages between islands separated by thousands of miles of blue
water. Yet, she suddenly looked small amidst the big cruising
catamarans and tall-masted yachts, too small to have sailed over
almost 6,000 miles of open ocean to complete her mission. Still,
there she was, weathered but in almost as good shape as when she
had left nearly three months earlier. And there was her grinning
crew, looking at once deliriously happy to be home and be-
wildered to be the focus of so much attention after spending
almost a month alone at sea.

The return of *Hokuleʻa* had been the talk of Honolulu for the
last week. Daily reports from the *Meotai*, which included news
relayed over the CB radio from the canoe, had kept us informed
of the canoe's swift progress and made it clear that everyone
aboard *Hokuleʻa* was having a grand time sailing her home.
Those who could get off work for the Monday arrival lined the
coast to watch the canoe sail by, or crowded into the yacht basin
to witness the actual arrival, or viewed the events on television.
Conspicuous among the spectators jammed into the yacht basin
were thousands of Hawaiians, including troupes of costumed
dancers, who had come out in force to welcome with pride their
canoe and their crew home from the sea.

Yet, despite the warmth of the welcome, it was obvious that
Hawaii was no longer as Polynesian as Tahiti. The crowds would
truly have been overwhelming had the Governor, like his counter-

part in Tahiti, declared a holiday in honor of *Hokule'a*. Although we had asked him, the Governor could not stop the wheels of commerce and government in busy Hawaii for a canoe arrival. Even more telling was the treatment received by Hoku, the only one other than Kawika to have completed the round trip. Upon docking, officials seized the frightened dog and carried her off to a steel cage to begin a four-month sentence of quarantine as required by law. (A week later Kawika freed Hoku and put her aboard a jet headed for Tahiti, where obliging officials once more waived quarantine regulations and allowed the well-traveled dog to rejoin the Tahitian family that had adopted her.) Hawaii had traveled too far from its Polynesian beginnings, had become too much a part of the United States and the modern world, to be able to unbend completely for a canoe as did its South Pacific neighbor. That contrast struck me as I watched the welcoming festivities, and I found myself thinking back to a celebration a month earlier when our voyage had been honored at a sacred temple on the island of Raiatea.

38
At a Sacred Temple

"Stop the car," Kealanahele told the driver. Our *kahuna*, who had flown to Tahiti and then over to Raiatea to join us, got out and walked over to the stream where, according to our driver, the high chiefs once bathed. After a few minutes Kealanahele was back, carrying two water-rounded rocks from the streambed. "I will use these," he said, "to talk to the spirits at Taputapuatea."

The driver started the engine and we were back on the dirt road, winding along the lush coast of Raiatea, heading for Taputapuatea, the most sacred temple of the old Tahitian religion. Taputapuatea (Tah-poo-tah-poo-ah-tay-ah), which translates figuratively as "Sacrifices from Abroad," was once the center for a yearly pilgrimage of chiefs and priests from islands many hundreds of miles around. That was long ago, centuries before the introduction of Christianity and the destruction of the old religion. In 1962 I had made my own pilgrimage there as a student of Polynesian culture. It was a sad visit. The temple was totally deserted, overgrown with bushes and trees, some growing right out of the massive stone altar, splitting it apart.

The desolate sight did not come as a total surprise. I had read what Te Rangi Hiroa, a half-Polynesian, half-Irish anthropologist from New Zealand who achieved scientific fame as Sir Peter Buck, had written after his first and only visit to Taputapuatea in 1929. Tramping around the deserted ruins left him with: *

. . . a profound regret, a regret for—I know not what. Was it for the beating of the temple drums or the shouting of the populace as the king was raised on high? Was it for the human sacrifices of olden times? It was for none of these individually but for something at the back of them all, some living spirit and divine courage that existed in ancient times and of which Taputapuatea was a mute symbol. It was something we Polynesians have lost and cannot find, something we yearn for and cannot re-create.

"Hold it! You can't drive in there!" A Tahitian policeman halted us just as we were about to drive out onto the peninsula on which Taputapuatea is built. After we explained our mission, the policeman waved us past. Then we saw it: Taputapuatea standing out majestically above the flat tongue of land jutting into the lagoon. But it was all different. The long-deserted temple was alive with people, probably for the first time since the old gods were abandoned a century and a half ago. What is more, the courtyard and the great stone altar were completely cleared of vegetation and restored to their original condition.

Soon the twin sails were visible on the horizon. The excited crowd packed the shore to watch *Hokule'a* sail in. Kealanahele was standing on the beach in front of the crowd. He was naked but for eight ti leaves, four in front and four in back, hanging from a sennit cord tied around his waist. Even that was a compromise. The day before he had explained how the gods should be

---

* Peter H. Buck, *Vikings of the Sunrise*, J. B. Lippincott, Philadelphia, 1938, pp. 81–82.

approached naked, and warned that should he receive the call during the forthcoming ceremony, all the rest of us from *Hokule‘a* would have to strip also. That would cause a stir, I had protested, explaining that while Tahitian maidens may think nothing of going bare breasted, Tahitians of both sexes abhor the idea of anyone seeing their genitals. Kealanahele had evidently partially heeded my plea to respect Tahitian modesty (not to mention mine!). His wearing of the ti leaf skirt, Kealanahele said before disrobing and then donning it in front of the startled onlookers lining the beach, would suffice for all of us.

Hokule‘a moved slowly toward the shore and was anchored 100 yards off the beach. A dozen husky young Tahitians, each carrying a long staff tipped with bunches of ti leaves to indicate their ritual purpose, escorted our crew to a spot in the shallows where specially selected pieces of white coral had been cached. Each crewman was directed to pick up a chunk of coral, carry it ashore, then walk through an archway made of palm fronds and deposit it next to the walls of an ancient stone structure. There a tall, spare Tahitian *kahuna* and his helpers arranged the coral into a rectangle, making a miniature temple enclosure. This ground, he gravely informed us, was to be the land of *Hokule‘a* forever after.

Then the guides, carrying their ritual staves before them, led us inland to Taputapuatea, where the bulk of the crowd awaited us. Kawika and the crew were directed to the courtyard in front of the altar. I was asked to translate the welcoming speeches of the Raiatean dignitaries standing on a low stone platform at the base of the altar.

The first speech, given by a Raiatean religious leader well versed in Polynesian lore, was one to remember.

This is a magnificent day for us because of the research you have undertaken at sea, research into the way of life of our Polynesian ancestors from distant antiquity. We celebrate your voyage to our island in your canoe, a voyage that has made today a great occasion for recalling the past of our homeland. This is our homeland—Raiatea, which long ago was called Havaii. It is from here that your ancestors left to sail over the great ocean. They settled on the islands they discovered, and now you have returned. The people of Polynesia have been overjoyed to hear of your voyage. You are our brothers.

That said it all, summed up the whole project. Neither the speaker nor the multitude of other Tahitians who had feted us during the previous three weeks were burdened with the notion that research into the past and cultural revival could not mix. Our research into ancient Polynesian voyaging had indeed made this day a great one for the hundreds of Polynesians gathered at Taputapuatea to celebrate *Hokule'a's* pilgrimage to Raiatea, an island that once bore the same name (save for the use of the *v* instead of the *w* sound) as our home islands, and was the starting point for many a legendary voyage.

After more speeches and a round of traditional chants, it was Hawaii's turn. Kealanahele took over. Garbed more modestly now in a boldly patterned Tahitian *pareu* (pah-ray-oo) cloth wrapped around his hips, he assumed authority and brusquely shooed all the kids and photographers from their sacrilegious perch atop the altar. Then he ordered the spectators cleared from the courtyard immediately in front of the altar, after which he turned to his assistant, Sam Ka'ai, the sculptor who had fallen ill after sending us off from Maui. Sam—now fully recovered and looking his old self with his full black beard, whale's-tooth necklace and traditional rain cape made of long, stiff leaves—listened to Kealanahele's instructions, then turned and led our Tahitian escorts around the clearing, stationing each one at intervals to make a semicircle focused upon the altar. Their job was to keep the pressing crowd back with their long, ti-leaf-tipped staves.

The astonished Tahitians accepted this with surprisingly little grumbling. They were mystified and not a little impressed. "The Hawaiians are indeed strict!" exclaimed one spectator.

To signal the start of the ritual, Sam Ka'ai, looking more than a little like a two-legged porcupine in his bristly rain cape, marched around the perimeter of the clearing, stopping four times

to blow his conch. Then Kealanahele took his two rounded rocks
and began to strike them together, producing a patterned series
of loud taps that penetrated the hot, still air.

Kealanahele had enjoyed an unusual religious education on
his home island of Hawaii. Friday through Sunday he was guided
by his grandfather, a Christian minister. Monday through Thurs-

day he had received instruction in the ancient religion from his
great-grandfather, the last hereditary keeper of Kamehameha the
Great's war temple. Now, following the teachings of his great-
grandfather, our *kahuna* was using rocks rather than words to
speak to the spirits. First he asked permission for the male crew
members to be in the semicircle. Then he asked that the two

female crew members, whom he had stationed outside the space, be allowed to come forward and join the men. According to his religious training, women were not ordinarily allowed to be at a temple during an important ceremony. Once Kealanahele received a message from the spirits that permission had been granted, he had Ka'ai fetch the women.

Then he struck a series of taps, each one meant to stand for a primeval god of Hawaii, after which he and Ka'ai placed plant offerings before the altar and had the *tikis* from the canoe brought forward and set down at the base of the altar. The *tikis* were carefully propped up so that they faced forward to gaze upon the return crew and the crowd behind them. Then our *kahuna* and his assistant prostrated themselves before the two blankly staring figures.

Save for the tapping of the rocks, all this was done in impressive silence. Kealanahele and his assistant were studies in ritual solemnity. The crowd was abnormally quiet, partly out of awe but probably more out of their intense curiosity to see what the Hawaiians would do next.

The silence was broken for the final rite, the recitation of the names of all who had sailed *Hokule'a* to Tahiti, and all who would sail her back. Billy Richards, who had followed the canoe to Raiatea with Kimo and another ex-crewman, was now within our circle at Kealanahele's request. A strange bond existed between the two. Our *kahuna* was his own man, and full of surprises at that. Before the voyage, Kealanahele had named Billy as his "spiritual double." Then when he flew down to Tahiti, Kealanahele explained to incredulous Tahitian reporters how mental signals unconsciously transmitted back to Hawaii by Billy had allowed him to plot the canoe's progress to Tahiti. Kealanahele now maintained that Billy's participation was crucial. His job was to recite the names of each person who had sailed to Tahiti, saying each name twice—once to register it with the spirits of Taputapuatea, and again to spread it all over Polynesia.

Billy began his recital listlessly. Limply standing before the altar, he pronounced the names of Kawika, Lyman, myself and several others not of his gang in a low, flat monotone. Then his body straightened as his voice rose when he came to the names of his fellow protesters. With arms raised to the sky, fists clenched and head thrown back, Billy screamed their names out over the temple grounds and the crowd of stunned Raiateans gathered there.

Following Billy's histrionics, a last dramatization of the gang's hankering for glory, the solemn tone of the ceremony was reestablished when the young Hawaiian physician who would accompany the return crew to Hawaii recited their names in calm, measured tones. Then our ti-leaf leis were collected and placed before the altar. A chorus of "Hawaii Aloha," the anthem we had sung with such hope upon our departure from Honolulu, closed the ceremony.

The crowd began to disperse, although many Raiateans stayed around, debating earnestly the meaning of what they had just witnessed. They were plainly perplexed as to what the Hawaiians had been up to with all the rock-tapping, prostrating before wooden images and then Billy's screaming. "Who was that crazy man?" asked one puzzled onlooker. Another, more impressed by the mystery of it all, exclaimed, "The Hawaiians are really heathens!" Yet their ancestors of many centuries past would have found our ceremony mild. That was when, according to legend, delegates from the many islands in this corner of the South Pacific sailed once a year to Taputapuatea to celebrate their "Friendly Alliance."*

The great double-canoes came in two groups, one sailing in from the islands to leeward, the other from Tahiti and the other islands to windward. After lining up in a double row outside the "Sacred Pass" through the reef, the conches would sound and, to the beat of a great drum, the canoes would be slowly paddled through the pass and toward shore. Once the canoes touched the beach, the human sacrifices carried aboard, plus others provided by the Raiateans, were laid down as rollers over which the canoes were drawn onto the land. Then the

---

* Summarized from Teuira Henry, *Ancient Tahiti*, B. P. Bishop Museum, Honolulu, 1928, pp. 123–127.

chiefs and priests would march inland to the temple for the series of awesome rites that would last for days.

Soon after the end of the ceremony came the welcome invitation from our hosts to come and eat: *"Haere mai tama'a!"* We were directed over to a long shed made of saplings stuck into the ground, bent over and tied together to make a series of arches, then covered with palm fronds. Inside, mountains of roast pig, baked taro and other tempting foods awaited us. This feast was unique among all those we had enjoyed since first touching on Mataiva nearly a month earlier. There were no tables or chairs, no plates, glasses or silverware. Sitting cross-legged on the ground, we ate with our hands from large platters woven of freshly picked leaves. Instead of the usual soft drink or beer, we were handed a newly opened green coconut to quench our thirst. Sam Ka'ai was especially impressed. As a Hawaiian and an artist, the meal to him was an exercise in Polynesian aesthetics.

"Aloha! Aloha! Aloha!"
After Kawika finished his departure speech—said in a mixture of Tahitian and Hawaiian that the crowd readily understood—he and the crew waded out to the canoe, unfurled the sails and were off, headed back to Tahiti for the final loading.

Brisk trades now ruffled the formerly calm lagoon waters. Kawika headed directly for the pass, the sacred pass of legend. But he could not make it out in one tack. The wind and the current were pushing the canoe toward the coral on the lee side of the pass. Nor should he have sailed directly out through the sacred pass, according to an elderly Raiatean woman who kept saying, "That's not the way it was done in ancient times."

Just as it looked like the canoe was going to smash onto the reef, Kawika brought her smartly about and headed down the lagoon on the other tack.

After sailing till well out of sight around the point, Kawika tacked the canoe back toward the pass. As she came into sight again, we could see from shore that the canoe was on target, sailing on a reach with a clear shot at the pass. The Raiatean dowager was now won over. Our canoe, she exclaimed, was tacking back and forth to get out of the pass "just like the canoes in ancient times." Soon *Hokuleʻa* was through the pass, riding over the swells of the fabled "Sea of the Moon" bound for Tahiti and then home.

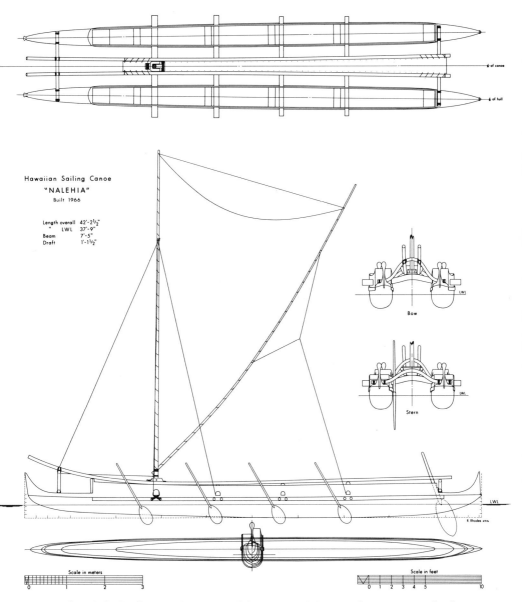

Hawaiian Sailing Canoe
"NALEHIA"
Built 1966

Length overall		42'-2½"
"	LWL	37'-9"
Beam		7'-5"
Draft		1'-1½"

Bow

Stern

LWL

R. Rhodes del.

Scale in meters

Scale in feet

Sail and deck plans, end views and lines of Nalehia. *End views omit third through fifth crosspieces.*

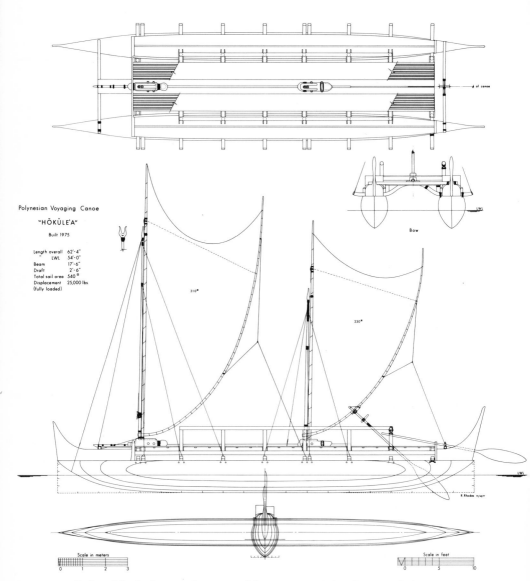

Polynesian Voyaging Canoe

"HŌKŪLE'A"

Built 1975

Length overall	62'-4"
" LWL	54'-0"
Beam	17'-6"
Draft	2'-6"
Total sail area	540 □
Displacement	25,000 lbs
(fully loaded)	

Bow

310"

230"

Scale in meters

Scale in feet

Sail and deck plans, end views and lines of Hokule'a. *Sleeping shelters, animal cages, and stern rails are not shown.*

APPENDIX II

Projected and Actual Course of Hokule'a

Projected course (shown with a dashed line) is from Ben R. Finney, "New Perspectives on Polynesian Voyaging," in G. Highland, et al. (eds.), *Polynesian Culture History*, Bishop Museum Press, Honolulu, 1967. Actual course is based on noon positions (except for May 2, 3, 4 and 14, when dead-reckoning estimates were used) taken by navigator L. Burkhalter on the yacht *Meotai* on the voyage to Tahiti, and taken by navigators L. Puputauki and J. Lyman on board *Hokule'a* for the return voyage to Hawaii.

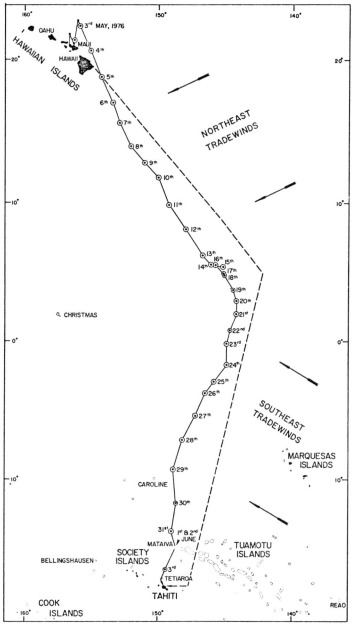

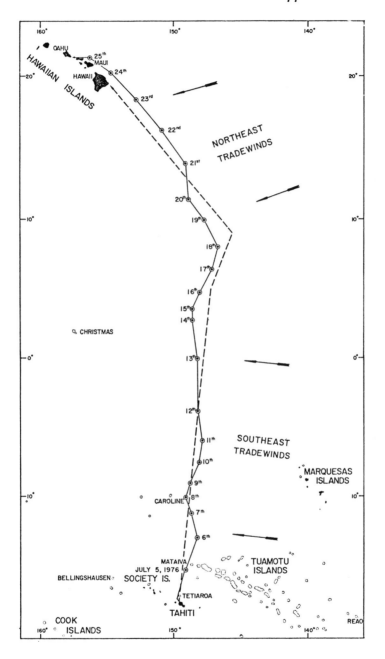

APPENDIX III

"Okay, I accept that Andrew Sharp and his followers greatly under-estimated Polynesian voyaging capabilities. But, what about Thor Heyerdahl and his theory that Polynesia could not have been settled by sailing east from Indonesia against the winds and currents, and that it must have been settled by migrants drifting from the Americas? You say that Heyerdahl has it backwards, but *Hokule'a* sailed over only part of the migration route. I still want to know how early voyagers could have sailed their canoes 7,000 miles across the ocean against the prevailing winds and currents."

The above challenge is not imaginary. During lectures about the voyage I have frequently been asked about Heyerdahl's theory and about how Polynesians could have made their way across the Pacific against the elements. The archaeological and linguistic evidence for the ultimate Southeast Asian origin of the Polynesians has recently been summarized in a pair of scholarly books.* Here I wish to outline in sailing terms how the seemingly impossible task of migrating east-ward against wind and sea was accomplished.

Stated in most general terms, Heyerdahl's basic thesis is that in ancient times the oceans were avenues not barriers to human migra-tion. The irony is that this man who has done so much through his dramatic voyages to make the public conscious of the possibilities of early oceanic voyaging should choose to downplay to the point of

---

* Peter Bellwood, *Man's Conquest of the Pacific*. Oxford University Press, New York, 1979; Jesse Jennings (ed.), *The Prehistory of Polynesia*, Harvard University Press, Cambridge, Mass., 1979.

292

denying the maritime achievements of those preeminent voyagers of the ancient world: the Polynesians.

That is because, as noted in Chapter 2, Heyerdahl believes that early voyagers were essentially drifters, moving with the prevailing winds and ocean currents across the sea. To him it is absurd to think canoes could have traveled from Indonesia to Polynesia because of the difficulty of sailing against the elements. Thus he claims that the first migrants came the easy way, drifting from the Americas. Heyerdahl identifies two American homelands: the Peruvian coast from which balsa raft voyagers drifted to Easter Island or to other islands in the Tuamotus and the Marquesas groups positioned to catch rafts carried from South America by the South Equatorial Current and the southeast trade winds; the Northwest Coast of North America from where dugout canoes drifted via the North Equatorial Current and the northeast trade winds to Hawaii and from there to other Polynesian islands where their passengers presumably met and amalgamated with descendants of earlier arrivals from South America.

When forced to admit that his theory runs counter to the linguistic evidence which ties Polynesia firmly to Indonesia and other islands of Southeast Asia, Heyerdahl ingeniously invokes the winds and currents once more. Canoe voyagers from the Indonesia-Philippines area who spoke a language ancestral to Polynesian tongues were caught, he theorizes, by a succession of currents and winds that swept them first north past Japan and then east across the Pacific to the Northwest Coast from whence they or their descendants were swept to Polynesia to implant their language and culture.

That South Americans could have drifted to Polynesia seems plausible. The balsa raft, as the Kon-Tiki expedition demonstrated, is a most seaworthy craft. Moreover, acceptance of the hypothesis that one or more such rafts actually reached Polynesia in prehistoric times helps solve the puzzle of how the Polynesians obtained the sweet potato, the only plant of South American origin among the plants they cultivated. While some anthropologists have hypothesized that the Polynesians sailed their canoes to South America and back to fetch the sweet potato, I find it easier to assume that these valuable tubers arrived on a one-way raft voyage, perhaps somewhere in the Marquesas Islands, and that Polynesians subsequently spread the plant, by canoe, around the islands. That Indians from the Northwest Coast might also have drifted to Polynesia is possible, but more doubtful. More likely is the possibility that disabled fishing craft from Japan or other North Asian regions could have drifted across the Pacific and then out to Hawaii or other Oceanic islands. This actually occurred in the last century; such drift voyages in prehistoric times could explain the resemblances of certain fishhook types and other items of Polynesian fishing technology to artifacts of North Asian derivation.

My point remains, however, that any such drifters from the east would have found the islands already inhabited—by Polynesians who had sailed there from the west. This original, Polynesian, settlement of the islands was but a final chapter in the island by island spread of the Austronesian speaking peoples over two oceans from a homeland thought to be in or around the Indonesian Archipelago.

Austronesia (literally, "Southern Islands") is primarily a linguistic term used for the family of related languages found on islands spanning the Indian and Pacific Oceans. From a center in Southeast Asia these voyaging people settled islands as far west as Madagascar and as far east as Easter Island. That the oceangoing canoe, either in its outrigger or double-canoe form, was the vehicle for this extraordinary oceanic migration is apparent from the chart opposite which shows the distribution of Austronesian languages and of outrigger and double-canoes. The two distributions coincide except in areas like Ceylon and East Africa where outrigger canoes seem to have outdistanced Austronesian languages.

The eastward expansion of the Austronesians probably began some 5,000 years ago. But they were not the first people to enter the Pacific. Upon moving eastward these sea people found New Guinea and adjacent islands to be already inhabited by the more land-oriented, darker-skinned Melanesian people who had apparently migrated there some 40,000 or more years earlier during the last Ice Age. At that time the huge amounts of water locked up in the glaciers had drastically lowered the sea level thereby narrowing the channels between Indonesia (then a peninsula of Asia) and New Guinea (then joined with adjacent islands and Australia into a large continent) so that rafts or other rudimentary craft could be used to make the relatively short crossings. Some Austronesians settled down on the coast of New Guinea and adjacent islands. Other more adventurous ones kept moving to the east and soon reached islands never before occupied by man.

Some of these sea rovers then headed north into Micronesia where they met other Austronesian groups that had sailed there directly from the Philippines. Others identifiable as the immediate ancestors

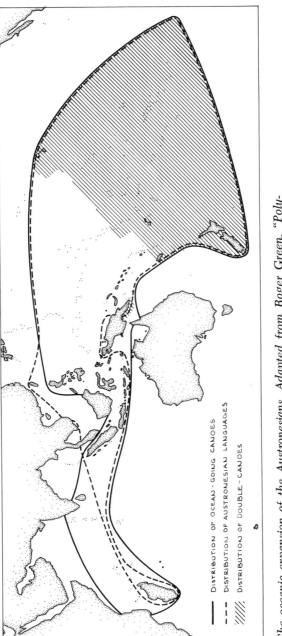

The oceanic expansion of the Austronesians. Adapted from Roger Green, "Poly-nesian Ancestors," in James Siers, Taratai, Milwood Press, Wellington, 1977; Edwin Doran, Jr., Nao, Junk and Vaka: Boats and Culture History, Texas A&M University, College Station, 1973; and A.C. Haddon and James Hornell, Canoes of Oceania, Vol. III, B.P. Bishop Museum, Honolulu, 1938

DISTRIBUTION OF OCEAN-GOING CANOES

DISTRIBUTION OF AUSTRONESIAN LANGUAGES

DISTRIBUTION OF DOUBLE-CANOES

of the Polynesians kept pushing eastward to reach the large archipelagoes of Fiji, Samoa and Tonga on the western fringe of Polynesia proper. This thrust into the central Pacific was made possible, theorizes Roger Green who has done the basic archaeology in the region, by the development of the double-canoe as a stable, heavy-capacity, voyaging craft. Once these islands—which are thought to be the cradle where Polynesian culture took on its final form and hence to be the immediate homeland of the Polynesians—were fully colonized, the movement eastward resumed. Canoes reached the Marquesas and Tahiti, and from there moved north, southeast and southwest so that by 750 A.D. all the main archipelagoes of Polynesia had been settled.

This spread across the Pacific was therefore not a swift and concerted migration. There was no *Kon-Tiki*-like voyage in reverse. The movement was a slow process of generation after generation of voyagers finding new lands, colonizing them, and then moving on again—either because of population pressure, war, famine or the very Polynesian desire to explore and see what lay over the horizon. Once we absolve the early voyagers of the task of sailing thousands upon thousands of miles to the east in one great leap, the feat of settling Polynesia begins to look more possible. To appreciate fully how that movement was accomplished, we now have to look closely at the nature of the so-called prevailing winds and currents.

A chart showing the prevailing winds and ocean currents by series of arrows marching across the oceans is a misleading guide for assessing the possibilities of early voyaging. "Prevailing" does not mean 100 percent of the time. Winds and currents are not invariable. They shift direction and wax and wane in strength. In some areas of the tropical Pacific, for days and sometimes weeks on end, the easterly trade winds are replaced by westerly winds, and the ocean currents flow less vigorously and less directly westward.

Contrary to the impression Heyerdahl wishes to impart to his readers, when Austronesian voyagers began their move into the Pacific they could have taken advantage of extremely favorable winds to move east. At the western end of the South Pacific, from Indonesia to New Guinea and sometimes beyond, a monsoon pattern exists. Whereas the southeast trade winds predominate during the Southern Hemisphere winter months of June, July and August, during the summer months of December, January and February, northwest winds, ideal for sailing to the east, predominate.

While such seasonal wind shifts do not show up on charts illustrat-

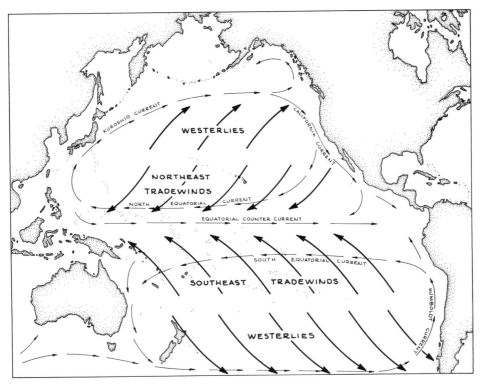

Prevailing directions of winds and ocean currents

ing global patterns of air circulation with a simplified pattern of arrows, they are clearly depicted on the pilot charts upon which sailors depend for their information of the likely wind patterns they will encounter at any particular time of the year. On pilot charts, which are issued on monthly or tri-monthly periods, these wind patterns are depicted for each five-degree square of latitude and longitude by a diagram called a *wind-rose*. Each wind-rose summarizes wind observations made by merchant ships and naval vessels since the last century in terms of wind frequency and strength for eight points of the compass. The arrows at each point fly with the wind toward the center of the rose. The length of the arrow when compared to the accompanying scale gives the percent of total observations in which the wind was blowing from or near the given direction. The number in the center of the circle gives the percentage of calms, light airs and variable winds. The number of feathers indicates the average force according to the Beaufort scale.

Below are a pair of wind-roses, taken from pilot charts published by the U.S. Navy Hydrographic Office, which illustrate the seasonal wind shifts in the waters around the Bismarck Archipelago, an area north of the eastern end of New Guinea through which Austronesian voyagers passed. During the trade wind season of June, July and August winds unfavorable for voyaging to the east (winds blowing from the northeast, east and southeast) occur 67 percent of the time. During the opposite time of the year when the wind flow reverses, winds most favorable for voyaging to the east (winds blowing from the northwest, west and southwest) occur 72 percent of the time. Thus any sailor wishing to move east would wait for the season of westerly winds.

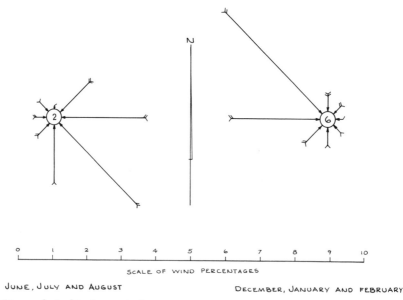

SCALE OF WIND PERCENTAGES

JUNE, JULY AND AUGUST   DECEMBER, JANUARY AND FEBRUARY

Bismarck Archipelago wind-roses

This pattern of marked seasonal wind shifts weakens the farther east you travel from New Guinea but does not wholly die out until you are past Tahiti. During the summer, trade winds in this area are periodically replaced by winds blowing from the west and northwest, and other directions favorable for sailing to the east. A pair of wind-roses from the waters just north of Samoa illustrates this. In December, January and February the winds blow from south, southwest, west, northwest and north, all directions that allow easy sailing to the east, 37 percent of the time.

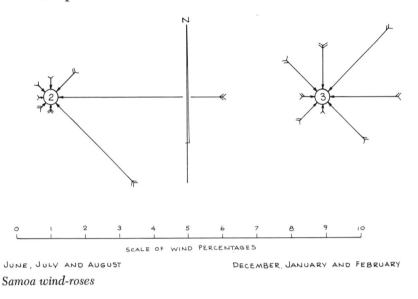

SCALE OF WIND PERCENTAGES

JUNE, JULY AND AUGUST   DECEMBER, JANUARY AND FEBRUARY

Samoa wind-roses

These favorable winds do not, however, occur randomly one day out of three. Typically they come in spells lasting anywhere from a few days to a week or sometimes more. This happens when a low pressure zone extends eastward into the Pacific from the Southeast Asian-Australian monsoon region, overwhelms the trade winds and sets up a counter flow of westerly winds that in weather map after weather map consulted frequently covers all or part of the Polynesian migration trail as far east as Tahiti. This pattern is illustrated in the chart on p. 300 in which surface wind flow for January 16, 1979 is shown with streamlines drawn by University of Hawaii meteorologist James Sadler from a U.S. Weather Service map for that date based on information gathered from shore stations, ships and satellite photographs. The westerly winds, which were blowing in the 20- to 30-knot range between Samoa and Tahiti, had already been prevailing in this region for several days and were to continue for another week before they died down and the easterly trade winds resumed.

Weather-wise Polynesians knew these wind shifts well. According to Captain Cook and other admiring visitors, they could even predict

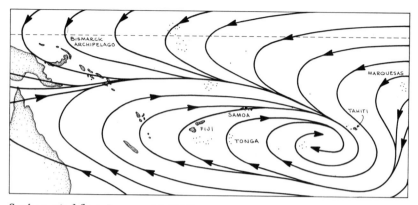

Surface wind flow, January 16, 1979

their coming several days in advance. Waiting for the onset of westerly winds was a common sailing strategy for making eastward crossings. That is what the Tahitians did when they wanted to sail east to the Tuamotus, and what the Rarotongans did when they wanted to sail east to make a pilgrimage to Tahiti or Raiatea. That they might have to wait a year for the right season to roll around again was an accepted part of the rhythm of voyaging life. Better to wait a year for the west wind than try to tack dead into the southeast trades. Applied to the entire west to east length of the migration trail, waiting for the west wind was a strategy that would have allowed the early voyagers to sail, slowly and from island to island, far out into the Pacific, accomplishing the seemingly impossible task of moving directly against the prevailing winds and currents.

Yet, they would not have waited for those westerly winds, or used them to make increasingly long voyages into the unknown, unless their canoes had some windward ability. To brave the open ocean, and fully exploit shifting wind patterns, these early voyagers would have needed canoes capable, like *Hokuleʻa*, of sailing swiftly across the wind and of pointing moderately well to windward. The capability to reach across the wind and beat to windward would have been particularly useful once the early voyagers left the zone of alternating monsoon winds and entered the open Pacific with its less-predictable and shorter-lived spells of westerly winds.

Suppose, for example, voyagers left Tonga or Samoa to explore to the east with a strong westerly wind behind them. It is unlikely that any one low pressure system would last long enough to carry them all the way to the Marquesas or some other eastern Polynesian landfall. More than likely, they had to play the winds, tacking to windward once the westerly winds died and the trade winds resumed, then taking advantage of another spell of westerly winds, then tacking once more into the trades, and so on until land was finally reached. Thus it must have been a combination of windward ability and the strategy of waiting for the west wind that enabled Polynesians to explore and settle their island domain.

But why did the Polynesians sail so far out into the Pacific? Why did they keep pushing to the east? Population pressure, war and famine, and an adventurous voyaging spirit only partially explain this movement. There was also a logic that compelled the early voyagers to keep moving east.

We live on a water planet, unique in the solar system. Seen from space, the earth is a shining blue sphere, partly covered with clouds of condensed water vapor with only shadowy hints of solid land here and there. Yet those born and bred on continents, the vast majority of humankind, tend to forget the oceanic character of our globe's surface—that over 70 percent is covered by water. Because of their millenia-long experience of sailing the sea the Polynesian world view was more oceanic, and more accurate. They had learned that the ocean extended in all directions; that everywhere they sailed islands broke the surface of the sea; and that if they sailed east the islands they reached would be uninhabited and thus ideal for colonization.

To explore east also made good sailing sense, particularly once the voyagers were out in the open Pacific where easterly winds were more dominant. In this situation to sail downwind with the trades is a risky exploring strategy for should you want to turn back for home you would have to beat back into the trades, or wait for a wind shift on some strange island probably already inhabited by people who would not necessarily be hospitable to strangers. To sail to the east, using a westerly wind shift, would be the safer option. Should the explorers, after failing to find land, wish to head back home, they could wait for the wind to shift back and run home before the trades.

However, we should not exaggerate the ease with which this long migration was accomplished. It must have been a costly, as well as slow, movement. Many a canoe must have been overwhelmed in heavy seas leaving those still alive to drift with the wreckage until exhaustion or sharks finished them. Still other voyagers must have succumbed when their food and water was exhausted after they had failed to find land. Violent storms must also have taken their toll, particularly when low pressure systems generating westerly winds intensified into full-fledged storms or even hurricanes. Even if canoes might have survived the fury of wind and sea, they would have stood a good chance of being smashed upon reefs or islands lying in their wind-driven path. That latter possibility was one reason why we waited until the end of the Southern Hemisphere summer to leave Hawaii. We could have planned to leave several months earlier than we did in order to reach the South Pacific during the tail end of that season in hope of catching some westerly winds to gain any extra easting that might be needed to reach the meridian of Tahiti. However, we did not even consider that as an option because of the chance that westerly winds might drive us into the labyrinth of Tuamotu atolls.

How many expeditions came to grief when canoes broke apart or foundered, or when they were smashed upon reefs, or when voyagers died of thirst, hunger and exposure without sighting land, will never be known. However, some simple arithmetic is sobering. Suppose 10 canoes with 25 persons aboard each were lost every year of the last 2,000 years of Polynesian voyaging. Multiply these together and you get a product of a half-million voyagers lost in the expanse of the Pacific.

Nor should we romanticize this migration to the point of assuming that every canoe departed fully equipped and stocked for a long sea voyage, or that even well-prepared expeditions were necessarily free of strife. We know from oral traditions that groups fleeing war or famine sometimes took to sea in overloaded and ill-found vessels that had little chance of seeing them to new lands. Similarly, the traditions also tell us that even expeditions commanded by strong chiefs and crewed by kinsmen and other subjects were not always free from factionalism at sea, or once land was reached. The troubles surrounding *Hokuleʻa* may have been unique in their modern content, but they were not without traditional precedent. A Fijian commenting on our voyage pointed this out in a timely article following the return of *Hokuleʻa* in which he recounted how, according to legend, after the arrival of the first canoe to reach Fiji quarrels broke out among brothers splitting the group into factions which then set out separately to occupy and populate the other islands of Fiji.*

---

* Lasarusa Vusoniwailala, "Hokuleʻa, the canoe, taught modern man an old lesson." *Pacific Islands Monthly*. May, 1977, pp. 37–38.

Acknowledgments

Laulima is Hawaiian for "many hands," or, figuratively, a group of people working cooperatively together. Both meanings apply to the hundreds of individuals and organizations who helped make the voyage to Tahiti possible. Only a few could be mentioned in the narrative, and any attempt to list all the rest would result in a book-length supplement. The list below of helping persons and groups is, therefore, only partial. I hope that those whose names could not be included will accept my sincere apologies.

Paddles Award Contributors

After the voyage major contributors were recognized by the presentation of a regular paddle, a steering paddle or a steering sweep. Paddles: American Factors, Astech Marine, Bank of Hawaii, Blue Dolphin Room, Castle and Cooke, Coco Palms Resort, Dillingham Shipyard, Hawaii Newspaper Agency, Hawaiian Airlines, Hawaiian Telephone, Holiday Mart, Honolulu Advertiser, Kekaulike Kawananakoa, Lanai Sportswear, Lewers and Cooke, McWayne Marine Supply, Maui Land and Pineapple, Trade Publishing, and Tradewinds Tours. Steering paddles: Alexander and Baldwin, Mr. and Mrs. George R. Carter, Dillingham Corporation, Penelope Gerbode-Hopper, and Western Airlines. Steering sweeps: Penelope Gerbode-Hopper and Po'omai Kawananakoa.

Crossbeams Contributors

Other major contributors were recognized by crossbeams which, since they could not be physically presented, bear names given them by the donors: *Malanai* (Tradewind Tours), *Mamale* (J. F. Deane), *Mo Ka Pawa* (Leonard Mason and family), *Pipiri Ma* (two crossbeams, Committee for the Preservation and Study of Hawaiian Language, Art and Culture), *Tahiti-nui Mare'are'a* (Kenneth Emory and family), *Tiare Apetahi* (Edward Dodd), *Tumoana* (Leon and Melba Finney), plus two crossbeams chris-

303

tened by Abraham Piianaia and Malia Solomon with family names which must be kept confidential.

Nalehia

Among my colleagues at the University of California, Steven Horvath, Jacob Lindbergh-Hansen and Loring Brace were especially encouraging to my unorthodox research plans. Master boatbuilder Harry Davis was my patient mentor in building *Nalehia*. Bill Sellers, Mr. and Mrs. Tom Johnson, Ambrose and Betsy Cramer, plus Pat Pacheco, Mike Martin, George Hunt and several other students were instrumental in making *Nalehia* a reality. Sailing and paddling trials were supported by the University of California, Santa Barbara, the National Science Foundation (Grant No. GS-1244), and the B. P. Bishop Museum, with an assist from the University of Hawaii. Many sailors and paddlers helped in the experiments. Here I would like to recognize those Waikiki Surf Club members who took *Nalehia* out on a 60-mile paddle: Tom Schroeder, Joseph "Nappy" Napoleon, Jr., Rabbit Kekai, Douglas Kekoa, Andy Miller, Mika Laupola, Richard Henning, Nick Beck, Bob Beck, Baldwin "Blue" Makua, Jr., Reginald Malabey and Randy Chun.

Hokule'a

The key parts played by Herb Kane, Rudy Choy and Warren Seamens in designing and building *Hokule'a* have been mentioned. Additional help came from Wright Bowman, Curtis Ashford, Calvin Coito, Tommy Heen, Kimbal Thompson, Bob Lavarre, Lindsey Holz, Lehua Conrad, Dillingham Shipyards, Lewers and Cooke, Hardwood Lumber Company, Slim's Power Tools, McWayne Marine Supply, Fiberglass Hawaii, Eaves and Meredith, Western Airlines and many other workers and firms.

Polynesian Voyaging Society

Directors of the Society through to the completion of the voyage were: Paige Kawelo Barber, Larry Burkhalter, Fred Cachola, Rudy Choy, Kenneth Emory, Charles Thomas Holmes, James Hugho, Herb Kawainui Kane, Kawika Kapahulehua, David Lewis, Cecilia Lindo, Carl Lindquist, David Lyman, Frank Tabrah, Frank Wandell, Les Warren, August Yee and Ben Young. One of the most difficult and least heralded jobs held by a director was that of keeping the books, which accountant Les Warren did with great skill and forebearance.

Advisors to the Board of Directors included Bruce Benson, Ron Delacruz, Vic Fagerroos, Wallace and Moku Froiseth, Homer Hayes, Moe Keale, Kala Kukea, Nancy Lewis, Tay Perry, Colin Perry, Donald Scelsa, Kim

Thompson, Louis Valier, Robert Van Dorpe and Doug Yen. In all cases they helped out with much more than advice.

When it became impossible to continue running the rapidly growing Society from my home, Sandra Maile stepped in to establish our first office. Sandra also had the honor of suggesting that our canoe be named *Hokule'a*. As the Society grew in size and complexity, new personnel were recruited: Sharon Serene to edit a newsletter, Ha'aheo Mansfield and Michele Brown for the office, Nancy Mower and a group of talented writers and artists to compose a series of children's books on voyaging, and Chuck Shipman and other City and County of Honolulu ocean recreation specialists to develop canoe sailing workshops at Kualoa Beach Park where *Hokule'a* was launched.

Launching

Ka'upena Wong officiated, assisted by Keli'i Tau'a, Kalena Silva and chanters from Kamehameha Schools. Rev. David Kaupu of Kamehameha Schools gave the blessing. Paige and Bert Barber led a small army of volunteers to gather and cook the food for our bounteous feast. John Kaha'i Topolinski and the Ka Pa Hula Hawaii dancers, Eddie Kamae and the Sons of Hawaii, and Hoakalei Kamau'u and her hula troupe honored the canoe with chants, songs and dances.

Bicentennial

As part of Hawaii's celebration of the American Bicentennial, we received support from the national and Hawaii Bicentennial Commissions, and welcome encouragement from John Warner, Kent Williams, Thurston Twigg-Smith, Piilani Ramler, John Pincetich and other Bicentennial workers.

Research and Educational Support

The National Endowment for the Arts, the Hawaii Council for Culture and the Arts, the Insular Arts Council of Guam, the Juliette M. Atherton Trust, the McInerny Foundation, the A. N. Wilcox Trust, the F. C. Atherton Trust. The Polynesian Cultural Center and film maker Tip Davis supported various aspects of our effort to make the project educationally significant to the people of Hawaii. The B. P. Bishop Museum opened their facilities to us, and Roland Force, Kenneth Emory, Pat Bacon, Yoshihiko Sinoto, George Bunton, Louis Valier, Willis Moore, Douglas Yen and many other staff members went out of their way to be helpful. The East-West Center, thanks to the vision of Manual Alba, Verner Bickley, Everett Kleinjans, Kenzie Mad, Greg Trifonovitch, Lou Goodman and others, generously supported the participation of sailors from Micronesia, Tahiti, New Zealand and Hawaii. The National Science Foundation (Grant No. SOC 75-13433), the University of Hawaii and the East-West Center supported the pre-voyage study of canoe performance. Donald "Bud" Scelsa was my right hand man for those tests. Edwin Doran, Jr. introduced us to the techniques of precisely measuring canoe performance. Maka'ala Yates, Ralph Sprague, Vince Dodge and others aided in the testing. Naval architect Manley St. Denis took the lines off *Hokule'a*.

Rebuilding

The University of Hawaii, through the efforts of John Craven, Richard Longfield and others, lent us a corner of their Marine Expeditionary Center to work on *Hokule'a* after the swamping. Matson Lines and Seatrain loaned us shipping compartments for storage. Myron Thompson and the Kamehameha Schools cafeteria helped feed those working on the canoe. Art "Sonny" Nelson fabricated the "temporary" sails which took the canoe to Tahiti and back. Members of the Hawaiian entertainment industry who helped us raise funds during the difficult time included: the Aikane Catamaran Group, Bella Richards Hula Troupe, Doug Mossman, Rodney Arias, Keli'i Tau'a and Na Keonimana, Leina'ala Heine, Larry Kimura and Ka Leo Hawaii, Warren Naipo and Son and Louise Kaleiki.

Maui

Along with Sam Ka'ai, those who hosted us on Maui just before departure included: Rev. Abraham Williams, Aimoku Pali and family, Levan Sequiera, John Hanchett, Ned Lindzey, Leon and Joanne Sterling, Manu Kahaialii and Earl Kukahiko. Their hospitality was matched by many more people on Maui and the other islands where *Hokule'a* touched in her travels around Hawaii.

The Voyage

Meotai captain Bob Birk, along with crewmen Bud Sanders and Mike Hope and Ed O'Brien did a magnificent job of shadowing *Hokule'a* over thousands of miles of lonely ocean. Also serving aboard the *Meotai* were two Society board members: Frank Wandell and Larry Burkhalter. In addition to making a photographic record, Frank kept the news of our progress flowing back to Hawaii and ahead to Tahiti. Larry, whose talents as a lawyer in Admiralty had already served the project, drew upon his Merchant Marine and Navy experience to take the daily navigational fixes needed to document the canoe's progress.

The U.S. Coast Guard gave needed safety advice. James Sadler, Klaus Wyrtki, Anders Daniel, Tom Schroeder, Dixon Stroup, Colin Ramage, Rockne Johnson, Martin Vitousek and other meteorologists and oceanographers of the Hawaii Institute of Geophysics of the University of Hawaii counseled us on weather patterns and ocean currents, as did Captain Jean Rondiex of the *Coriolus*. Louis Valier furnished valuable star information. The U.S. Navy provided extra safety gear. The C. J. Hendry Company loaned us a pair of life rafts. The Coleman Company gave us sleeping bags for the cold nights at sea. Edward Houlton and Noel Thompson of the Hawaii Institute of Geophysics helped set up communication procedures. Navy Chief Bill Myerson of the Navy-Marine Corps Military Affiliate Radio System took over the job of making daily contact with the *Meotai*.

Tahiti

Tainui President Alban Ellacott, Vice-President Jacques Drollet, Treasurer Hans Carlson, Secretary Ingrid Cowan, and members Gerard Anapa Cowan, Henri Hiro, Maco Tevane, Raymond Pietri, Louis Lecaill, and Leo Langomazino were our generous hosts in Tahiti. They; various members of the administration of French Polynesia; mayors and chiefs Tu Tefaafano of Mataiva, Georges Pambrun of Papeete, Francis Sanford of Faaa, Gaston Flosse of Pirae, William Coppenrath of Mataiea, Tutaha Salmon of Tautira, Philippe Brotherson of Uturoa, Haurai Tarati of Taputapuatea, Guy Sanquer of Opoa, Tetuanui Temauri of Tumaraa, Tamati Brothers of Tehurui, and Mireta Tinorua of Tahaa; pastors Philippe Tupu of Paofai, Ramon Brothers of Mataiea, Tihoni of Tautira, Philippe Ebb of Uturoa, Ihura Ariirau of Opoa, Homai Tauotaha of Tiva, Mauarii Maiohiti of Haamene, and Toofa Turia and Hotu Teanuanua of Mataiva; plus thousands of other Tahitians, Tuamotuans and Raiateans made our stay in their lovely islands unforgettable.

Hotel Bali Hai on Moorea, Huahine and Raiatea, Hotel Taharaa on Tahiti, Hotel Maeva Beach on Tahiti, and Hotel Travelodge on Tahiti provided accommodations for crew and delegates from Hawaii. Among the members of Tahiti's business community, Warren Ellacott of Fare Ute Shipyards, Jean Karoubi of Vaima, Tom Fearon of Hotel Tahara'a, Hugh Kelly, Jay Carlisle and Muck McCullum of Hotel Bali Hai, Jean-Claude Brouillet of Hotel Safari, and Arthur Deane of Vai Arii were typical in their generosity.

Return Voyage

Serving aboard *Hokule'a* for the return home was a fine group of young sailors: Gordon Piianaia, Kimo Lyman, Leonardo Puputauki (from Tahiti), Abraham Ah Hee, Ben Young, Kainoa Lee, Melvin Kinney, Nainoa Thompson, Keani Reiner, Penny Rawlins, Andy Espirito and Maka'ala Yates.

Zulu Kauhi organized the welcome home, featuring the contributions of Tihati and his dance troupe, Kamalei Lililehua, Ka Pa Hula Hawaii,

Gus Hanneman, Na Keonimana, the Robert Cazimero Dancers, and many more talented musicians and dancers.

Others

In addition, I would like to thank Kawika and Birdie Kapahulehua, Sam Kaʻai, Marie Finney, Tommy Holmes, James Houston, Dave Lyman, Sam Kalalau, Alan Howard, Ralph Love and Rodo Williams for commenting on the manuscript, and Lori Chung, Irene Tanaka and Betty Wolfram for their typing.

Others whose ideas, advice and aid were crucial do not fit easily into any one category: Captain Temarii Teai who introduced me to both the Tuamotus and Polynesian seamanship aboard the *Tamara*; Captain Omer Darr whose knowledge of the seaway between Hawaii and Tahiti gained through scores of voyages was so freely shared; Nedo Salmon, Hans Carlson and their families who were so kind to mine in Tahiti; Mary Kawena Pukui, Hawaii's foremost scholar, who cleared up many problems of Hawaiian cultural interpretation; Morna Simeona whose spiritual counsel was invaluable in a time of need; the late Iolani Luahine whose stirring words and graceful movements greeted *Hokuleʻa* upon arrival at Hawaii Island; Woody Brown whose swift catamaran was such an inspiration to a young anthropologist; Katharine Luomala who introduced me to Polynesian anthropology and imparted her respect for the historical and cultural value of the ancient legends; David Roy and his helpers who spent weeks salting and drying fish for the voyage; Likeke and Kahekili Paglinawan who tried so hard to settle differences before we left; Ruth Johnson who assembled *Hokuleʻa* scrapbooks; Dan Won who sheltered *Nalehia* in his backyard until we could re-launch her; Bentley Barnabas whose encouragements all the way from Kansas were greatly appreciated; Charman Akina whose medical aid in Tahiti was most timely; Mary Louise Kekuewa who made the feather pennants flown by *Hokuleʻa*; and my parents Leon and Melba Finney, my wife Ruth and her mother Berniece Sutherlin, and my sons Sean and Gregory, for their unstinting support over the years.